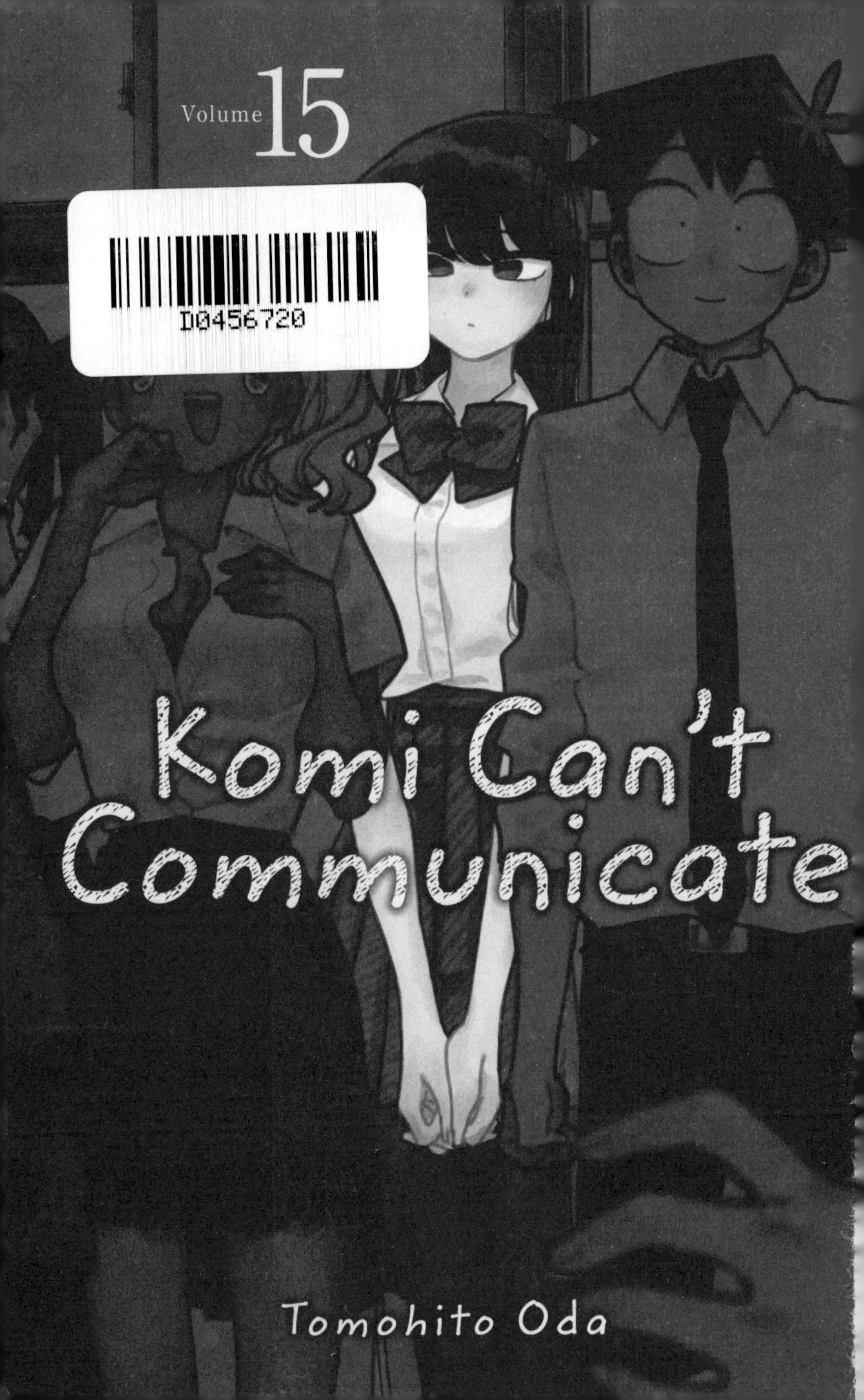
Volume 15
Komi Can't Communicate
Tomohito Oda

# Contents

Communication 196    Clean —————————— 03

Communication 197    Twister —————————— 34

Communication 198    OUT & LAW: The Movie ——— 39

Communication 199    Rock, Paper, Scissors, Hammer, Helmet!————— 57

Communication 200    Student Council ———————77

Communication 201    Smile ——————————— 95

Communication 202    Campaign Rep ——————— 115

Communication 203    Campaign Rep, Part 2———— 133

Communication 204    Height ————————— 151

Communication 205    Height, Part 2 ——————— 156

Communication 206    First Love————————— 159

Communication 207    Dinner Party———————— 169

Bonus ——————————— 188

# Komi Can't Communicate

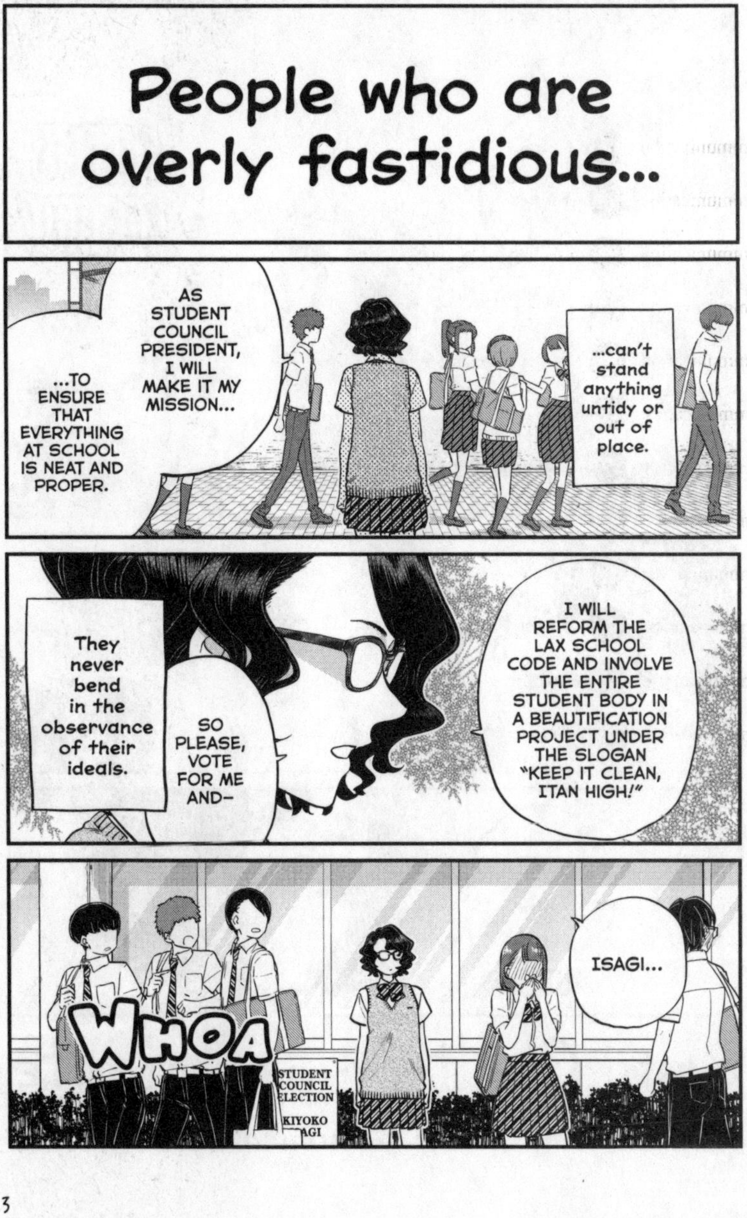
People who are overly fastidious...
...can't stand anything untidy or out of place.
AS STUDENT COUNCIL PRESIDENT, I WILL MAKE IT MY MISSION...
...TO ENSURE THAT EVERYTHING AT SCHOOL IS NEAT AND PROPER.
I WILL REFORM THE LAX SCHOOL CODE AND INVOLVE THE ENTIRE STUDENT BODY IN A BEAUTIFICATION PROJECT UNDER THE SLOGAN "KEEP IT CLEAN, ITAN HIGH!"
SO PLEASE, VOTE FOR ME AND–
They never bend in the observance of their ideals.
ISAGI...
WHOA
STUDENT COUNCIL ELECTION
KIYOKO

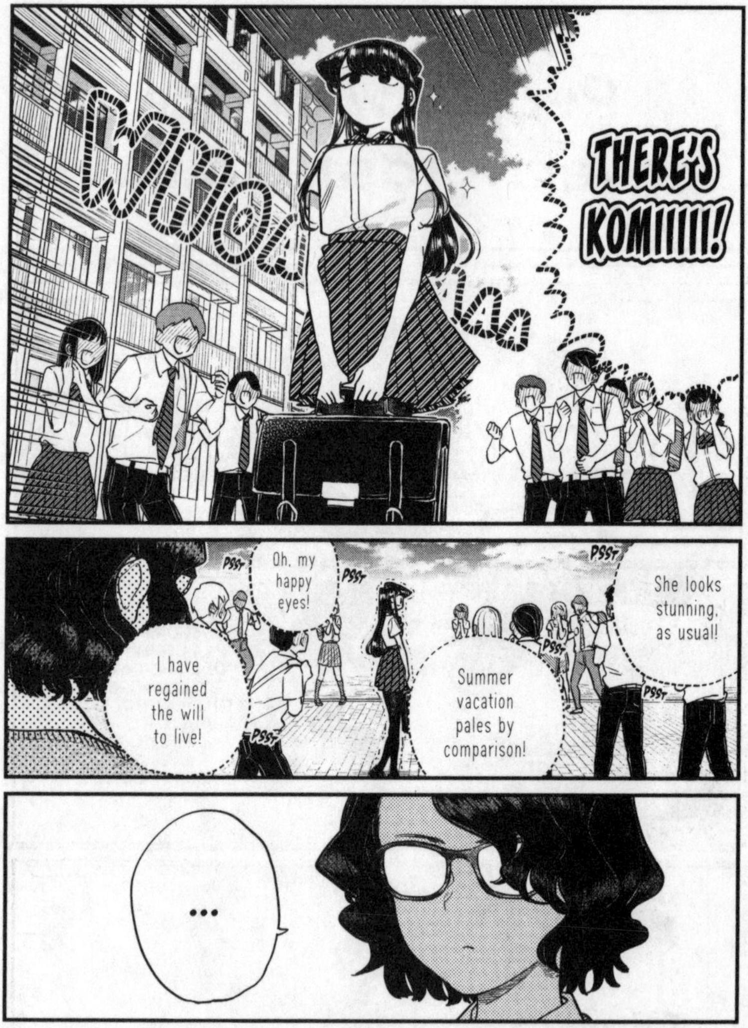
THERE'S KOMIIIIII!
WHOAAAA
PSST
She looks stunning, as usual!
PSST
Summer vacation pales by comparison!
PSST
Oh, my happy eyes!
PSST
I have regained the will to live!
PSST
...

# Komi Can't Communicate

## Communication 196: Clean

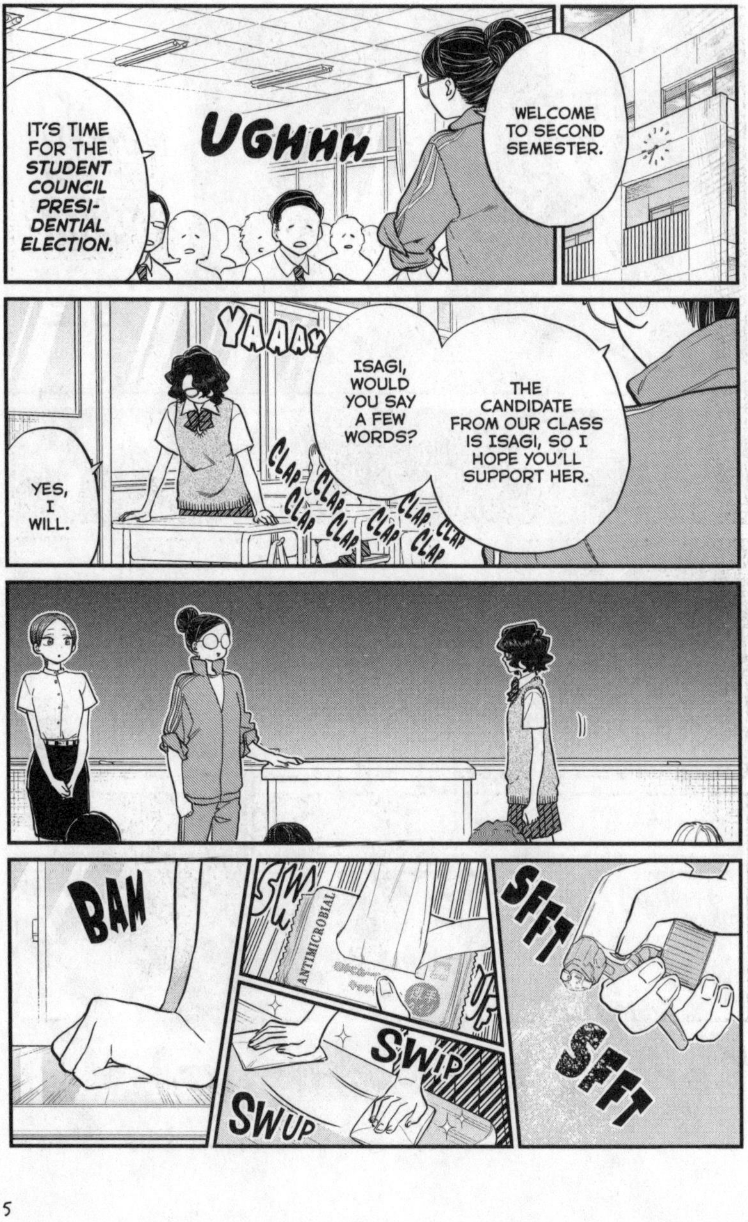
WELCOME TO SECOND SEMESTER.
UGHHH
IT'S TIME FOR THE STUDENT COUNCIL PRESI-DENTIAL ELECTION.
THE CANDIDATE FROM OUR CLASS IS ISAGI, SO I HOPE YOU'LL SUPPORT HER.
ISAGI, WOULD YOU SAY A FEW WORDS?
YAAAY
CLAP CLAP CLAP CLAP CLAP CLAP CLAP CLAP
YES, I WILL.
SFFT
SFFT
ANTIMICROBIAL
SWIP
SWUP
BAM

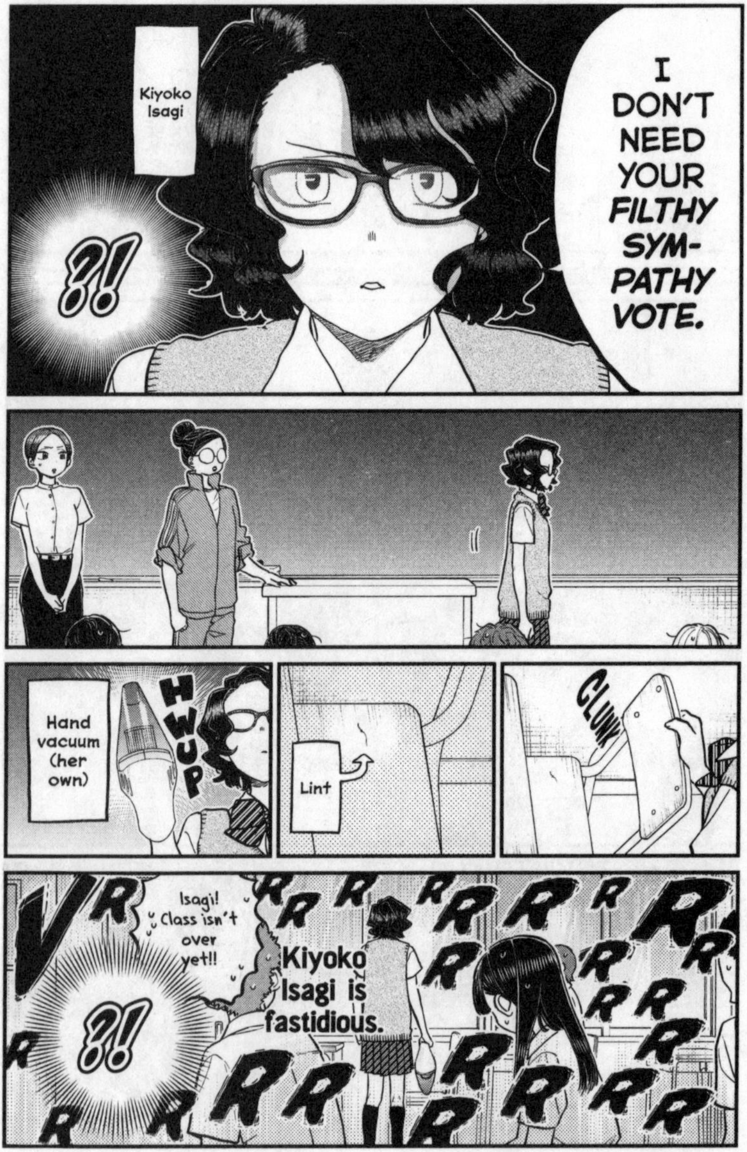
I DON'T NEED YOUR FILTHY SYMPATHY VOTE.
Kiyoko Isagi
?!
CLUNK
Lint
HWUP
Hand vacuum (her own)
VRRRRRRRR
Kiyoko Isagi is fastidious.
Isagi! Class isn't over yet!!
?!

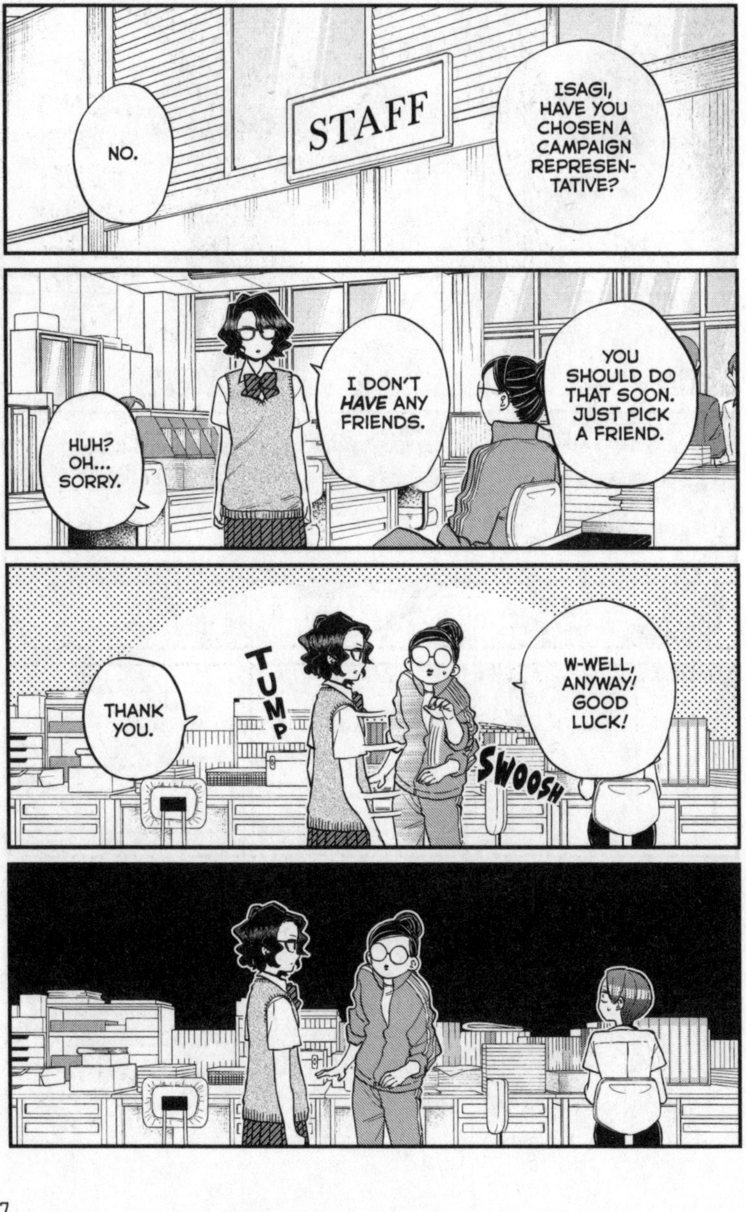
ISAGI, HAVE YOU CHOSEN A CAMPAIGN REPRESEN-TATIVE?
STAFF
NO.
YOU SHOULD DO THAT SOON. JUST PICK A FRIEND.
I DON'T *HAVE* ANY FRIENDS.
HUH? OH... SORRY.
W-WELL, ANYWAY! GOOD LUCK!
SWOOSH
TUMP
THANK YOU.

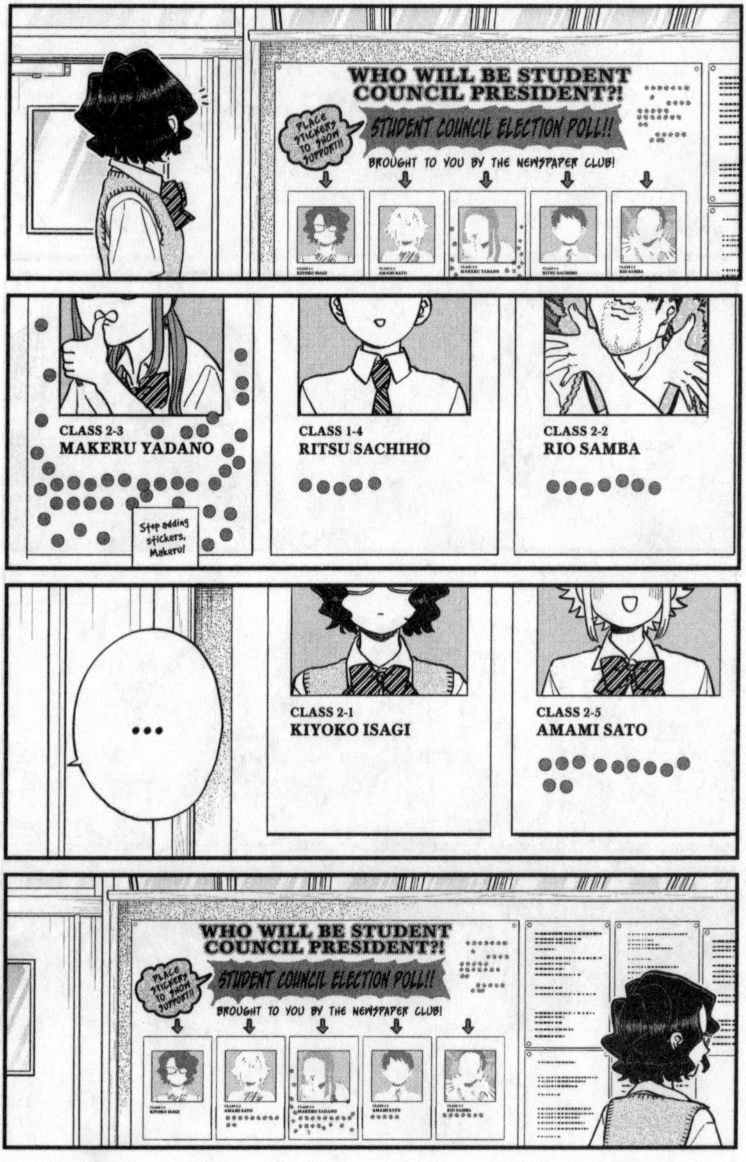
WHO WILL BE STUDENT COUNCIL PRESIDENT?!
PLACE STICKERS TO SHOW SUPPORT!!
STUDENT COUNCIL ELECTION POLL!!
BROUGHT TO YOU BY THE NEWSPAPER CLUB!
CLASS 2-2
RIO SAMBA
CLASS 1-4
RITSU SACHIHO
CLASS 2-3
MAKERU YADANO
Stop adding stickers, Makeru!
CLASS 2-5
AMAMI SATO
CLASS 2-1
KIYOKO ISAGI
...
WHO WILL BE STUDENT COUNCIL PRESIDENT?!
PLACE STICKERS TO SHOW SUPPORT!!
STUDENT COUNCIL ELECTION POLL!!
BROUGHT TO YOU BY THE NEWSPAPER CLUB!

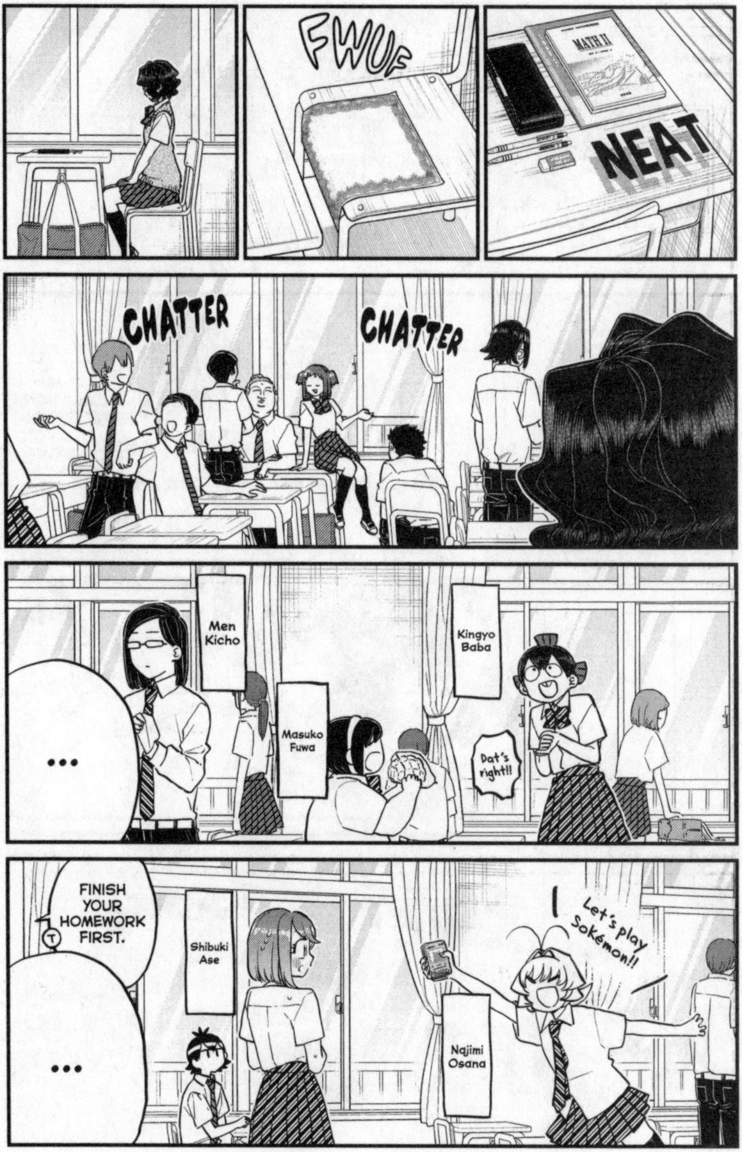
MATH II
NEAT
FWUF
CHATTER
CHATTER
Kingyo Baba
Dat's right!!
Masuko Fuwa
Men Kicho
...
Let's play Sokémon!!
Najimi Osana
Shibuki Ase
FINISH YOUR HOMEWORK FIRST.
...

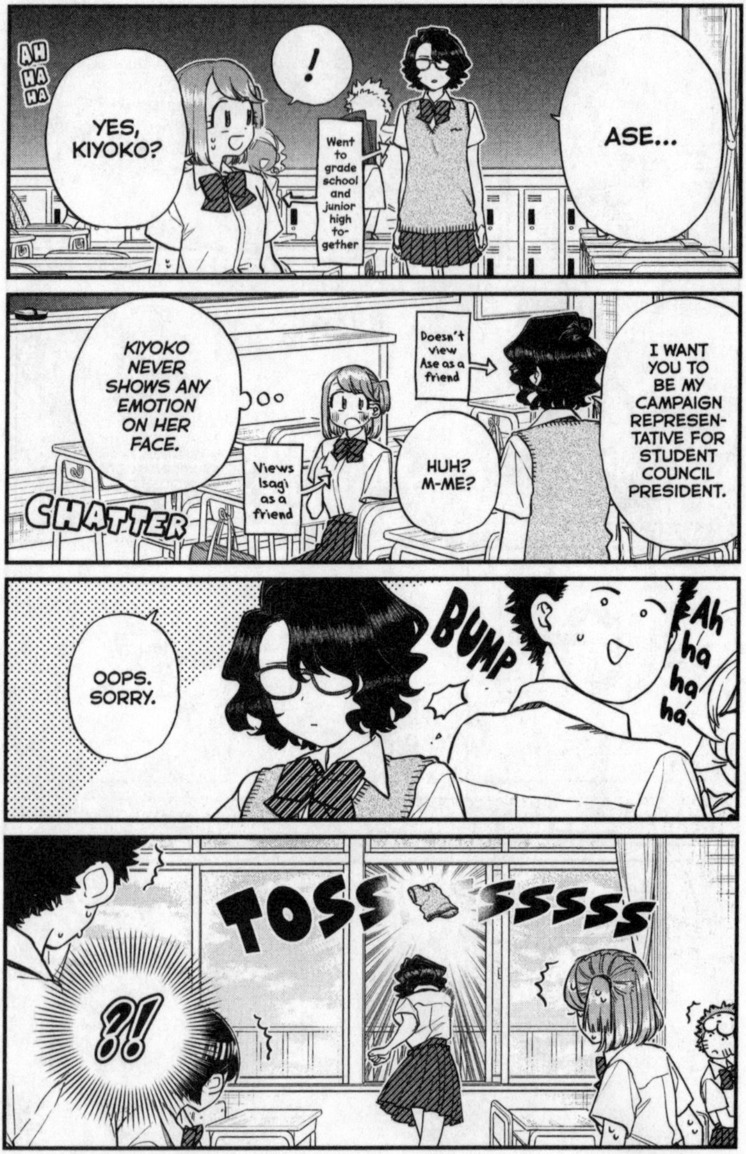
ASE...
!
Went to grade school and junior high together
YES, KIYOKO?
AH HA HA
I WANT YOU TO BE MY CAMPAIGN REPRESENTATIVE FOR STUDENT COUNCIL PRESIDENT.
Doesn't view Ase as a friend
HUH? M-ME?
Views Isagi as a friend
KIYOKO NEVER SHOWS ANY EMOTION ON HER FACE.
CHATTER
Ah ha ha ha
BUMP
OOPS. SORRY.
TOSS
SSSSS
?!

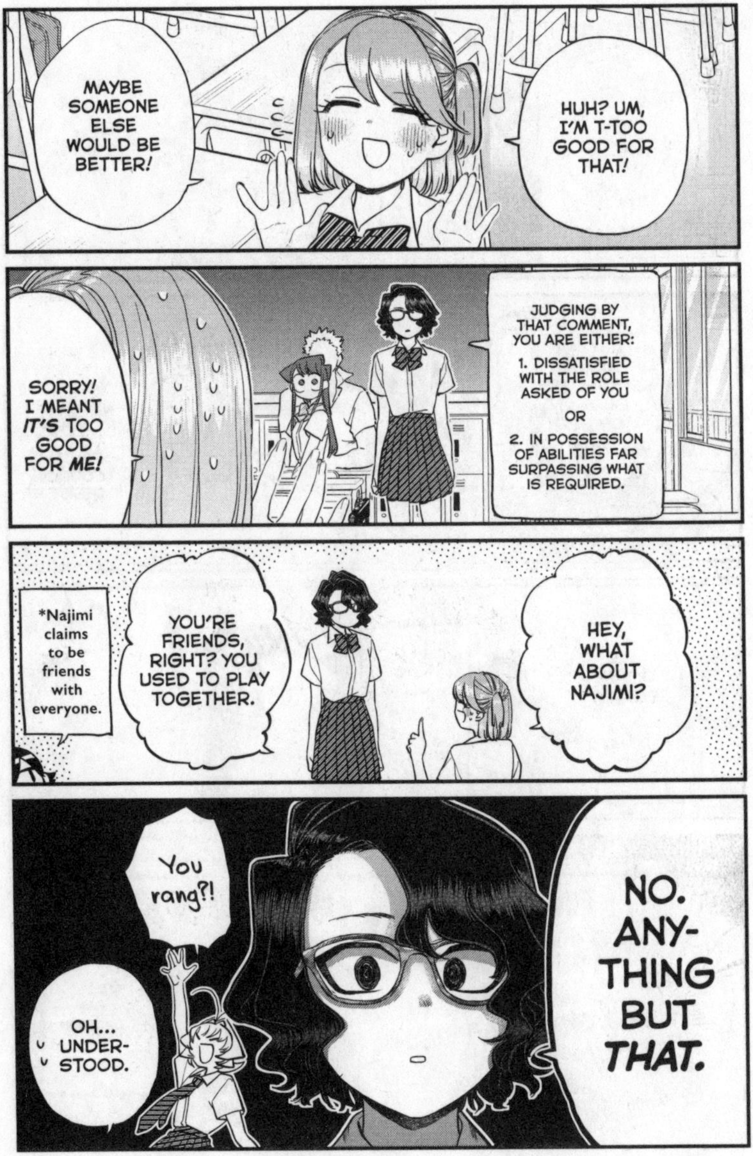
HUH? UM, I'M T-TOO GOOD FOR THAT!
MAYBE SOMEONE ELSE WOULD BE BETTER!
JUDGING BY THAT COMMENT, YOU ARE EITHER: 1. DISSATISFIED WITH THE ROLE ASKED OF YOU OR 2. IN POSSESSION OF ABILITIES FAR SURPASSING WHAT IS REQUIRED.
SORRY! I MEANT *IT'S* TOO GOOD FOR *ME!*
HEY, WHAT ABOUT NAJIMI?
YOU'RE FRIENDS, RIGHT? YOU USED TO PLAY TOGETHER.
*Najimi claims to be friends with everyone.
NO. ANY-THING BUT *THAT.*
You rang?!
OH... UNDER-STOOD.

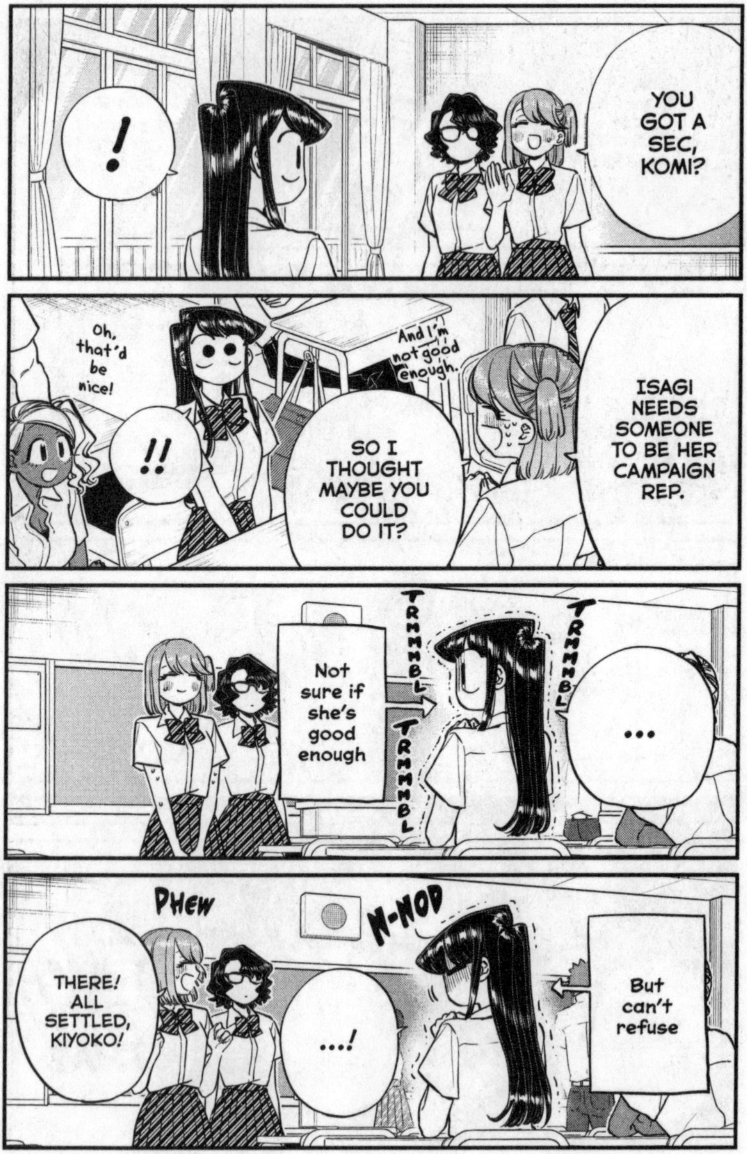
YOU GOT A SEC, KOMI?
!
ISAGI NEEDS SOMEONE TO BE HER CAMPAIGN REP.
And I'm not good enough.
SO I THOUGHT MAYBE YOU COULD DO IT?
!!
Oh, that'd be nice!
...
TRMMMBL
TRMMMBL
TRMMMBL
Not sure if she's good enough
But can't refuse
N-NOD
...!
PHEW
THERE! ALL SETTLED, KIYOKO!

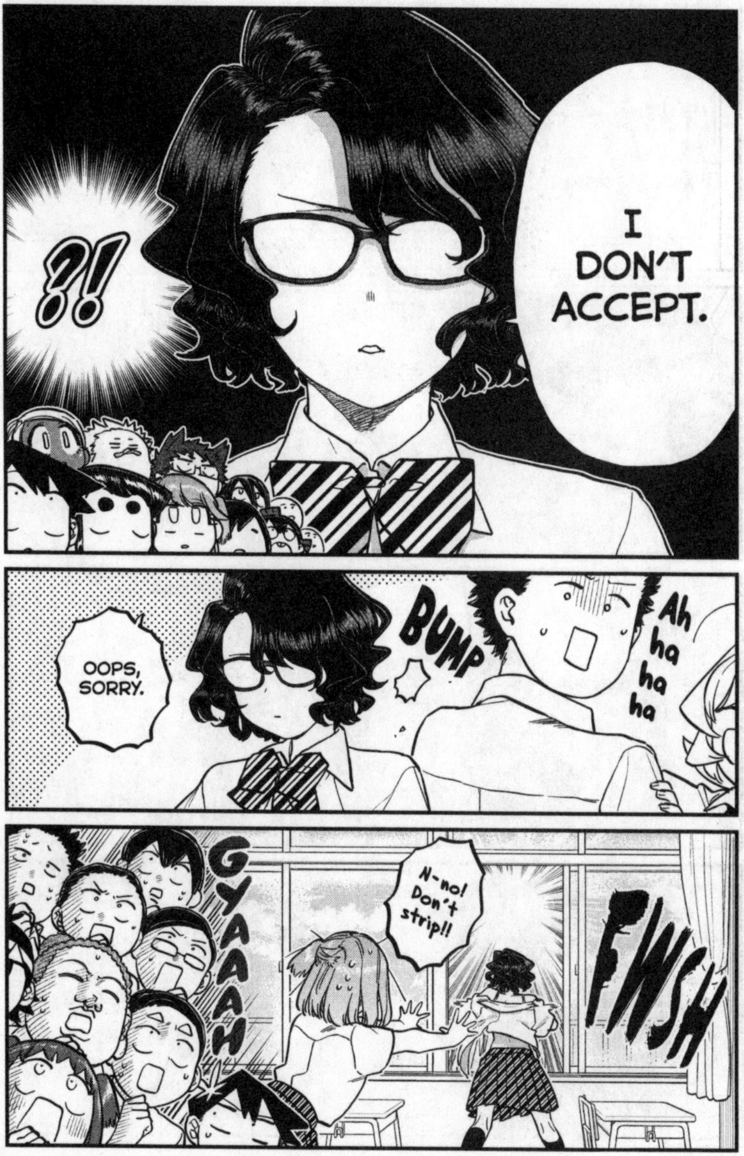
I DON'T ACCEPT.
?!
Ah ha ha ha
BUMP
OOPS, SORRY.
FWSH
N-no! Don't strip!!
GYAAAAH

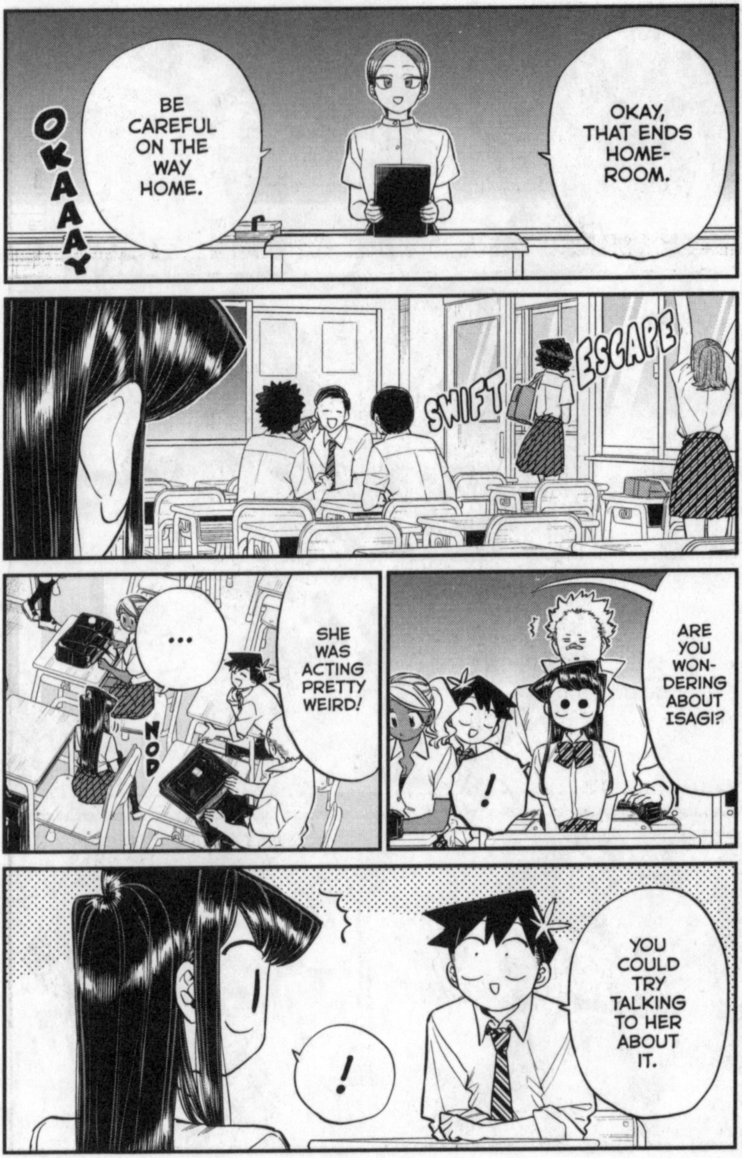
OKAY, THAT ENDS HOME-ROOM.
BE CAREFUL ON THE WAY HOME.
OKAAAY
SWIFT
ESCAPE
ARE YOU WON-DERING ABOUT ISAGI?
!
SHE WAS ACTING PRETTY WEIRD!
...
NOD
YOU COULD TRY TALKING TO HER ABOUT IT.
!

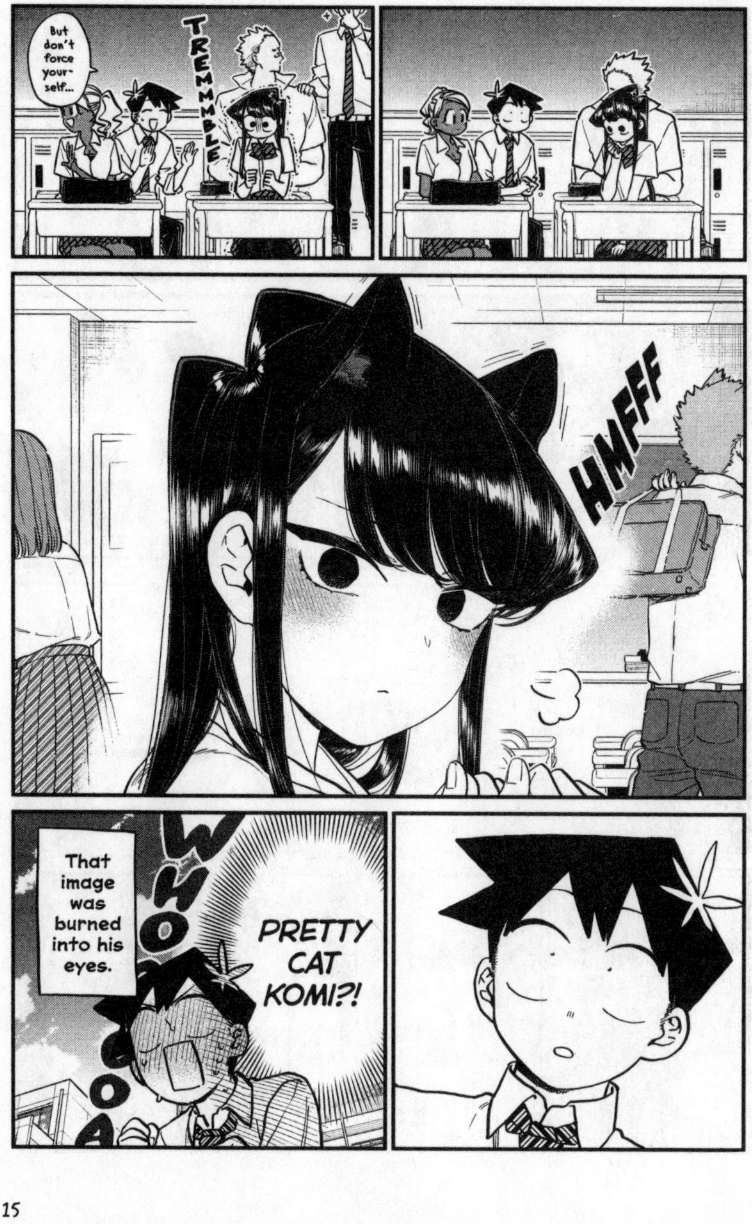
But don't force your-self...
TREMMMBLE
HMFFF
That image was burned into his eyes.
WHOOOOA
PRETTY CAT KOMI?!

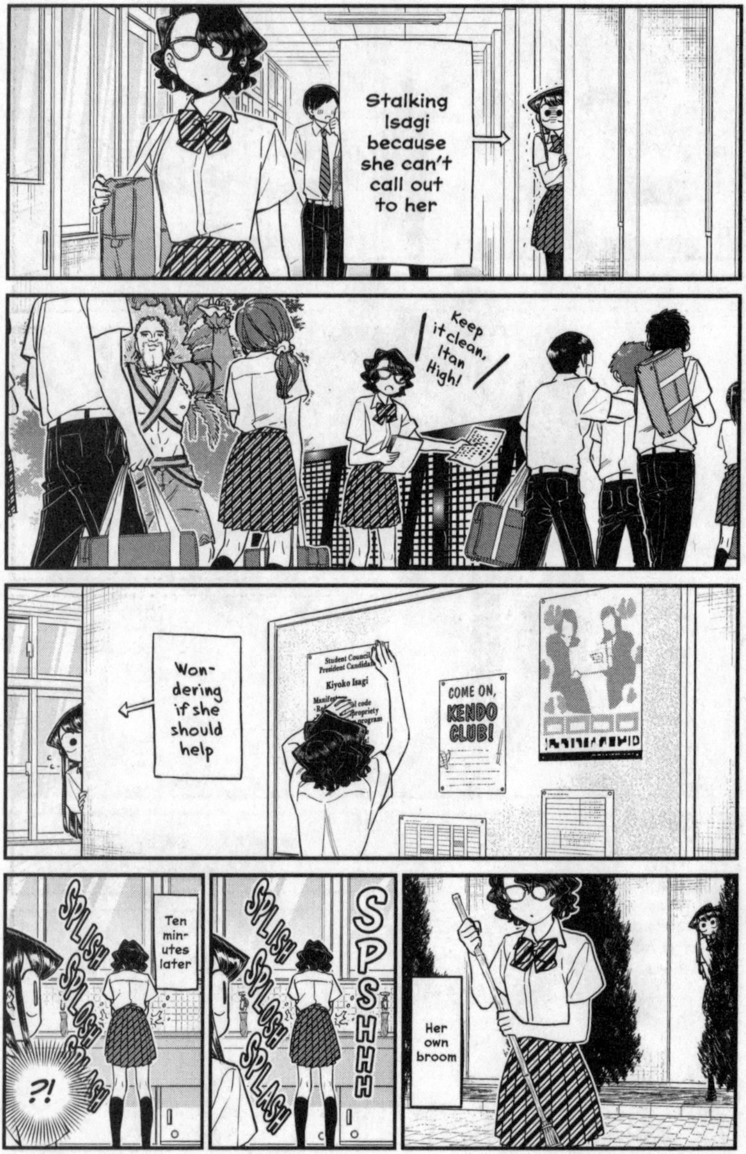
Stalking Isagi because she can't call out to her
Keep it clean, Itan High!
COME ON, KENDO CLUB!
Student Council President Candidate
Kiyoko Isagi
Won-dering if she should help
Her own broom
SPSHHH
SPLISH SPLOSH SPLASH
Ten min-utes later
SPLISH SPLOSH SPLASH
?!

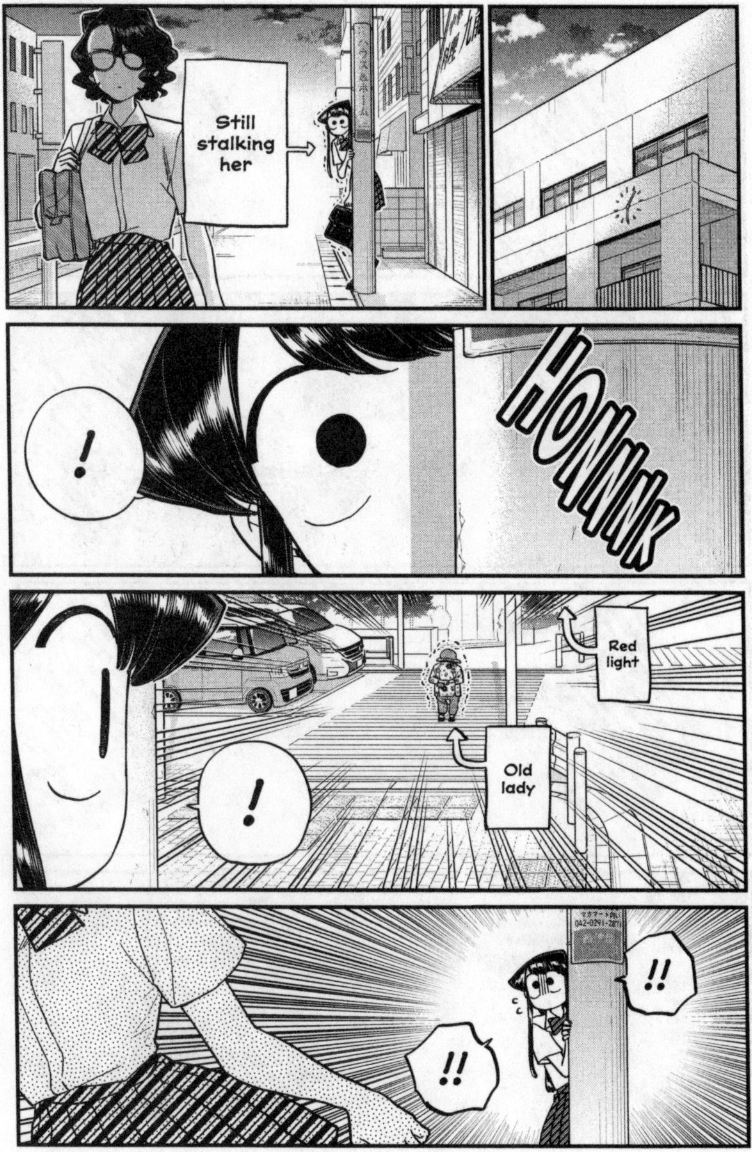
Still stalking her
HONNNK
!
Red light
Old lady
!
!!
!!

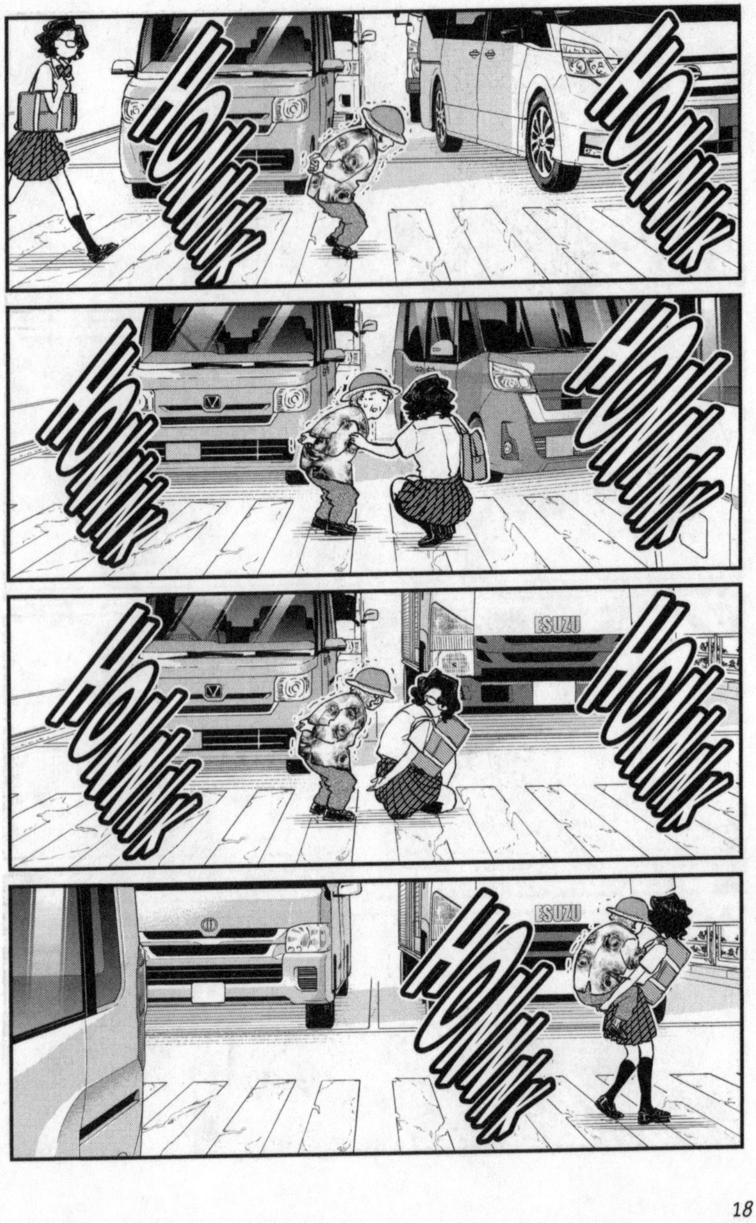
HONNNK
HONNNK
HONNNK
HONNNK
HONNNK
ESUZU
HONNNK
ESUZU
HONNNK

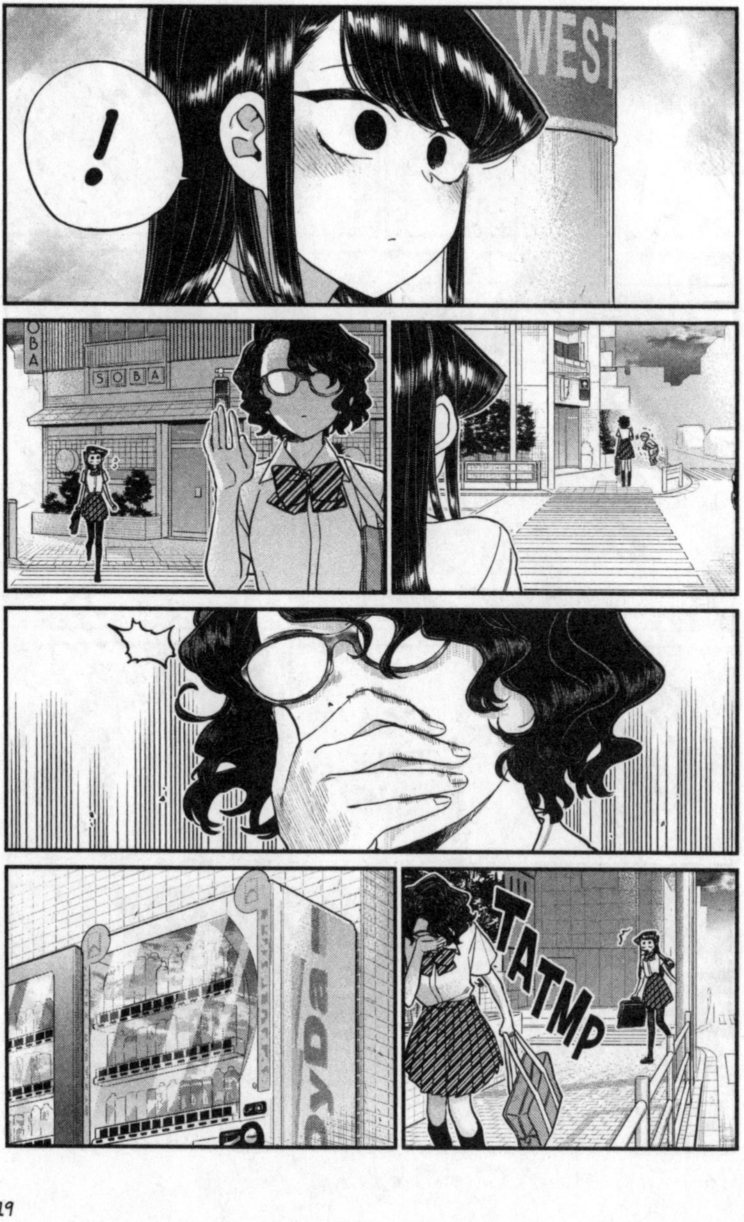
!
WEST
SOBA
TATMP

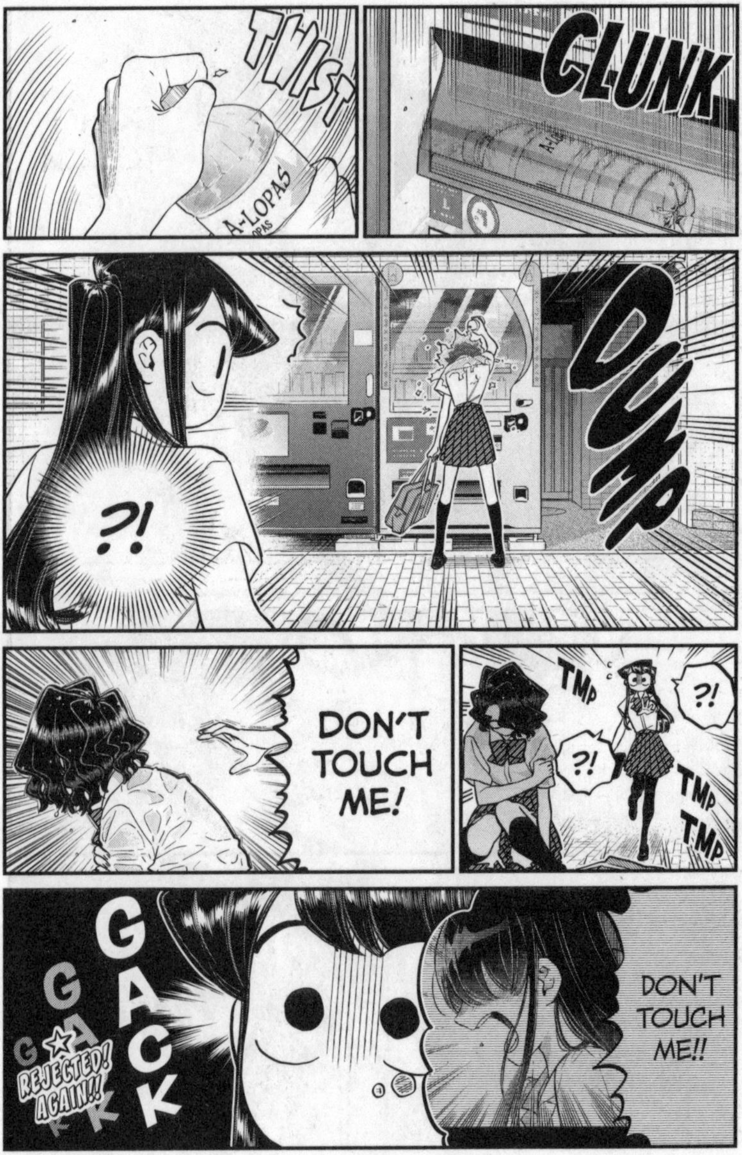
CLUNK
TWIST
A-LOPAS
DUMP
?!
TMP
?!
?!
TMP
TMP
DON'T TOUCH ME!
DON'T TOUCH ME!!
GACK
REJECTED! AGAIN!!

Communication 196 — The End

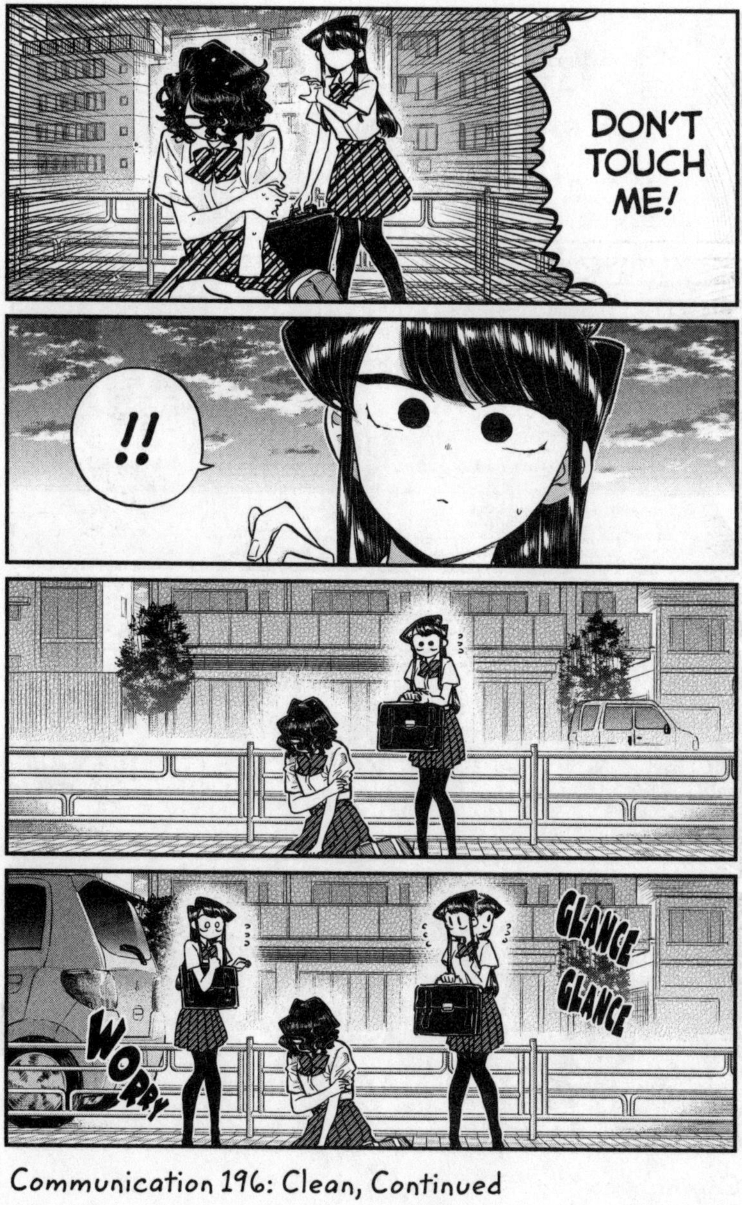
DON'T TOUCH ME!
!!
GLANCE GLANCE
WORRY

Communication 196: Clean, Continued

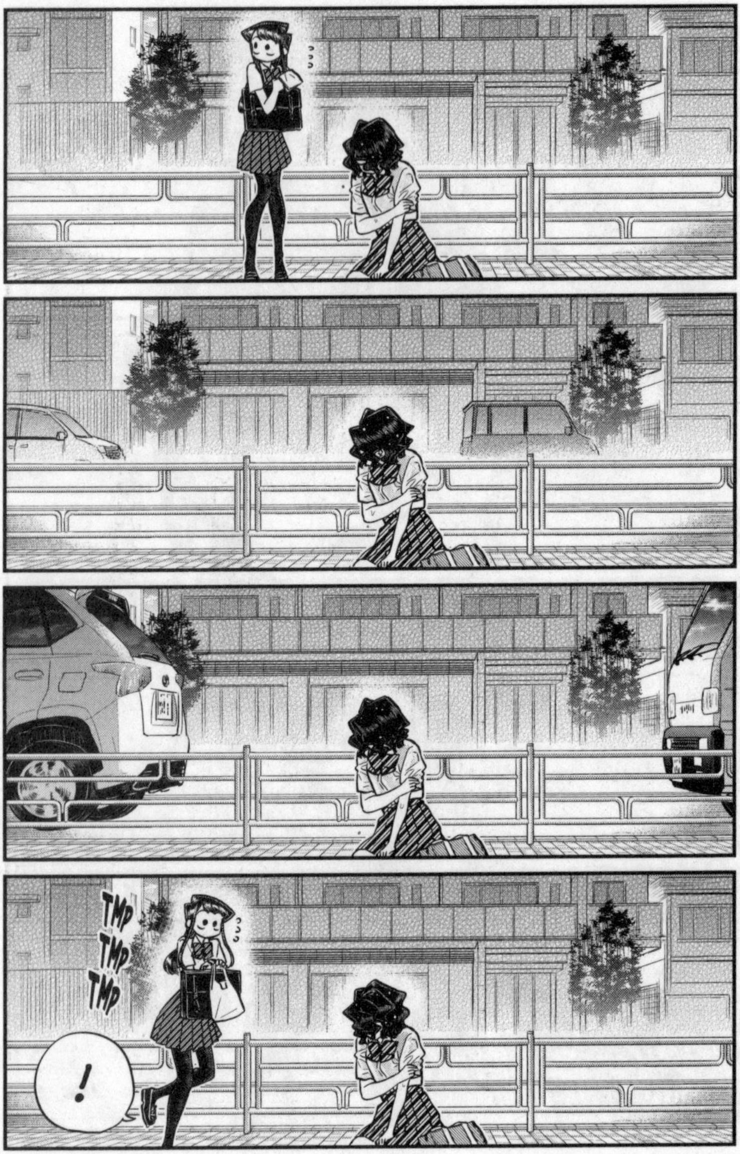
TMP
TMP
TMP
!

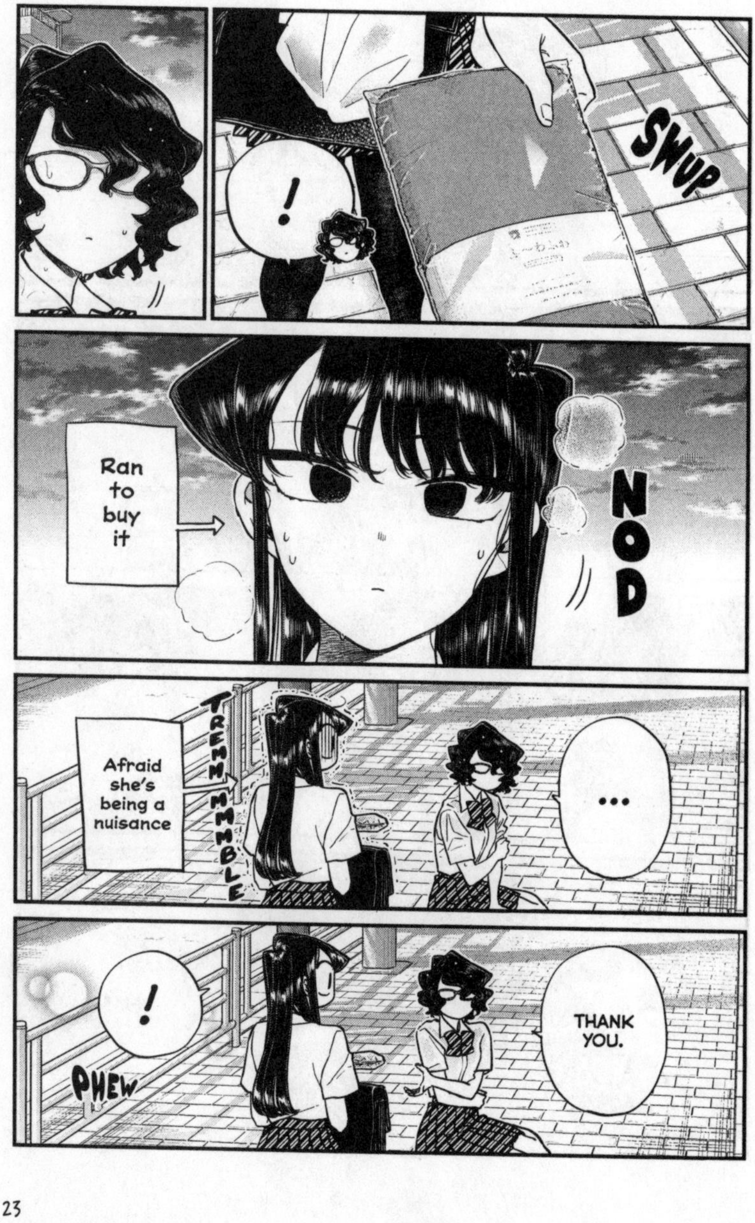
SWUP
!
NOD
Ran to buy it
...
TREMMMMMBLE
Afraid she's being a nuisance
THANK YOU.
!
PHEW

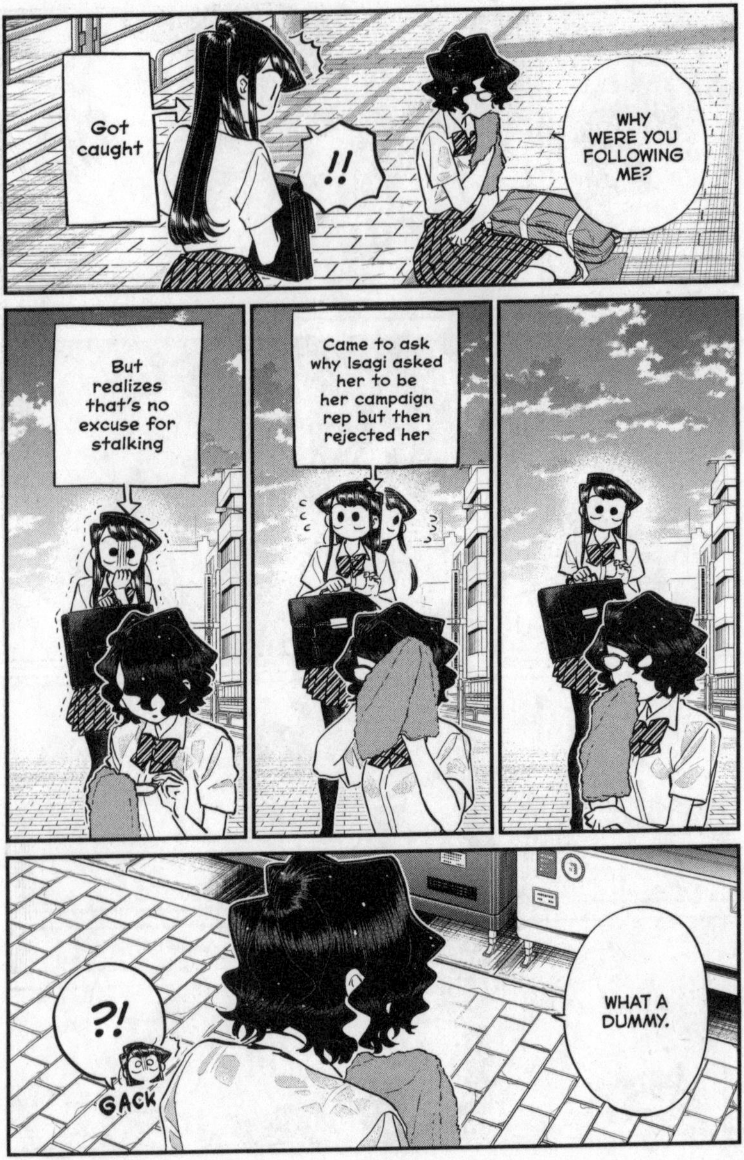
WHY WERE YOU FOLLOWING ME?
!!
Got caught
Came to ask why Isagi asked her to be her campaign rep but then rejected her
But realizes that's no excuse for stalking
WHAT A DUMMY.
?!
GACK

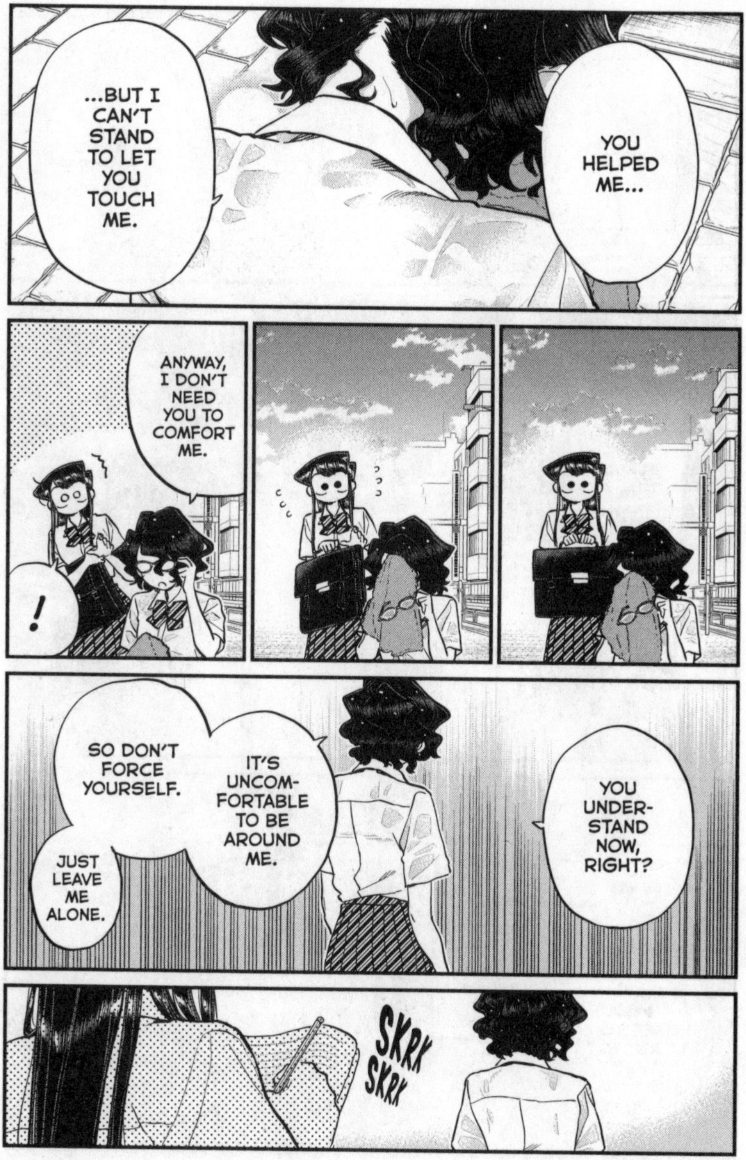
YOU HELPED ME...
...BUT I CAN'T STAND TO LET YOU TOUCH ME.
ANYWAY, I DON'T NEED YOU TO COMFORT ME.
!
YOU UNDER-STAND NOW, RIGHT?
IT'S UNCOM-FORTABLE TO BE AROUND ME.
SO DON'T FORCE YOURSELF.
JUST LEAVE ME ALONE.
SKRK SKRK

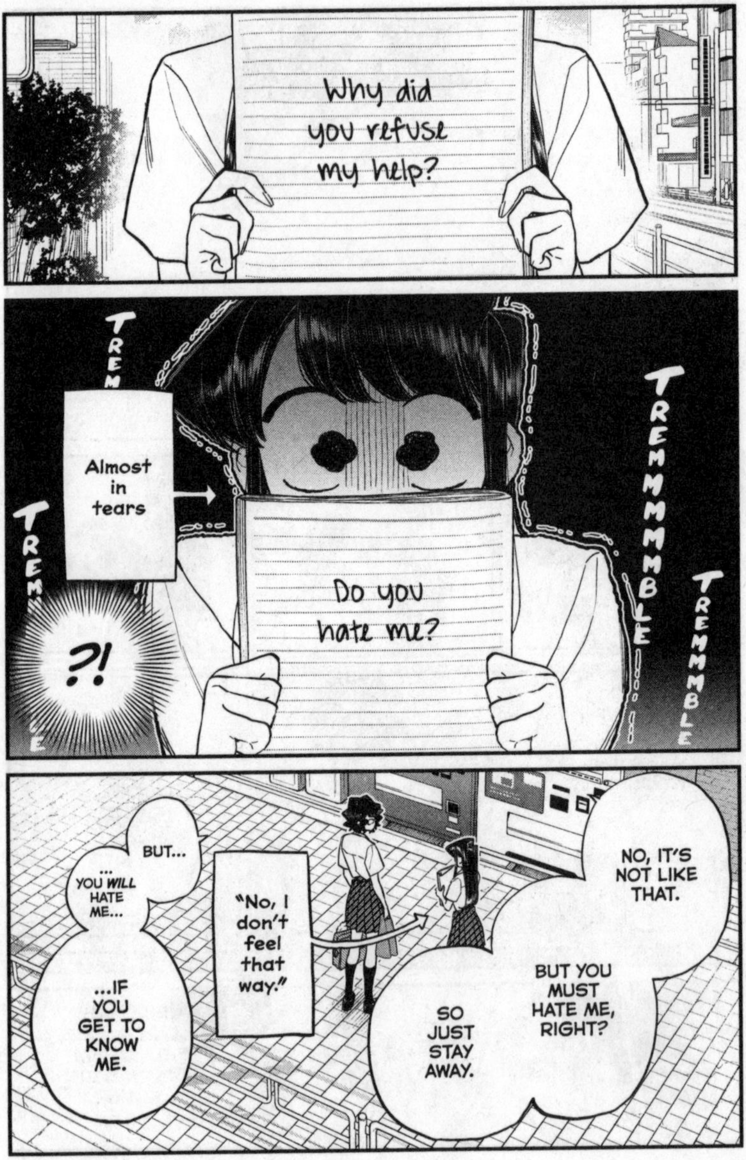

Why did you refuse my help?
TREMMMMBLE
TREMMMBLE
Do you hate me?
Almost in tears
?!
NO, IT'S NOT LIKE THAT.
BUT YOU MUST HATE ME, RIGHT?
SO JUST STAY AWAY.
"No, I don't feel that way."
BUT...
...YOU *WILL* HATE ME...
...IF YOU GET TO KNOW ME.

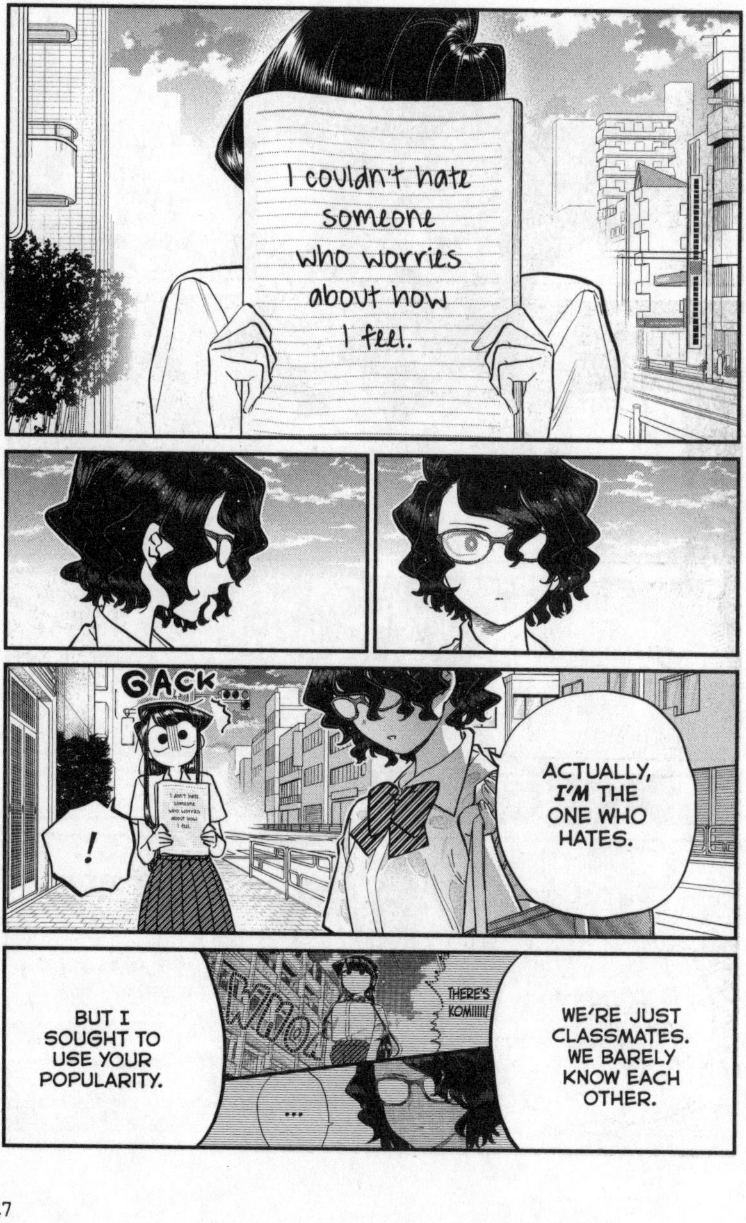
I couldn't hate someone who worries about how I feel.
ACTUALLY, I'M THE ONE WHO HATES.
GACK
!
I don't hate someone who worries about how I feel.
WE'RE JUST CLASSMATES. WE BARELY KNOW EACH OTHER.
THERE'S KOMI!!!!!
...
BUT I SOUGHT TO USE YOUR POPULARITY.

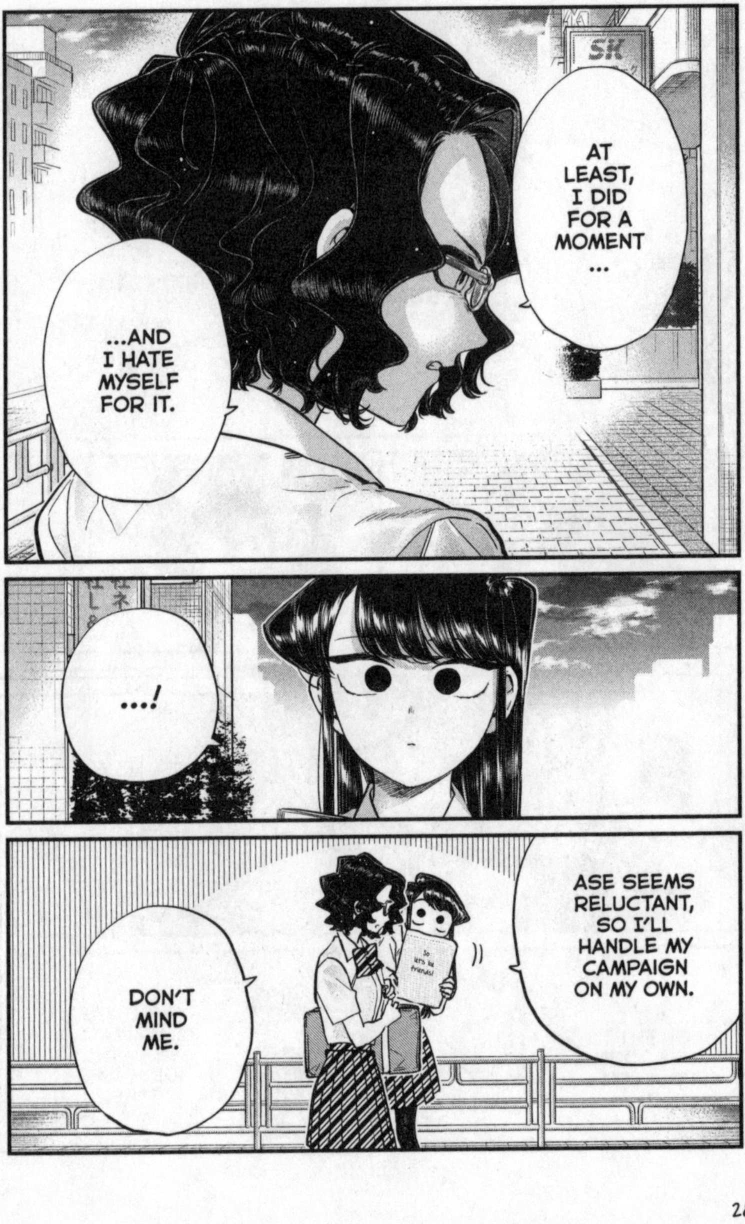
AT LEAST, I DID FOR A MOMENT...
...AND I HATE MYSELF FOR IT.
...!
ASE SEEMS RELUCTANT, SO I'LL HANDLE MY CAMPAIGN ON MY OWN.
DON'T MIND ME.

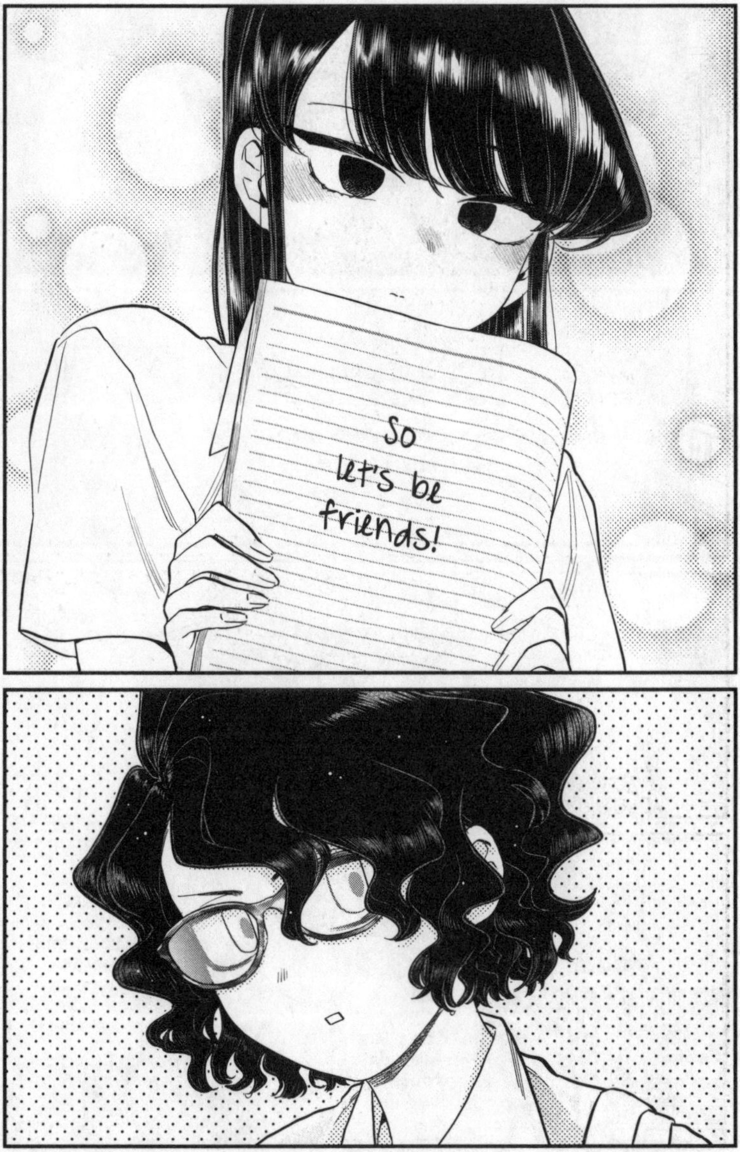
So
let's be
friends!

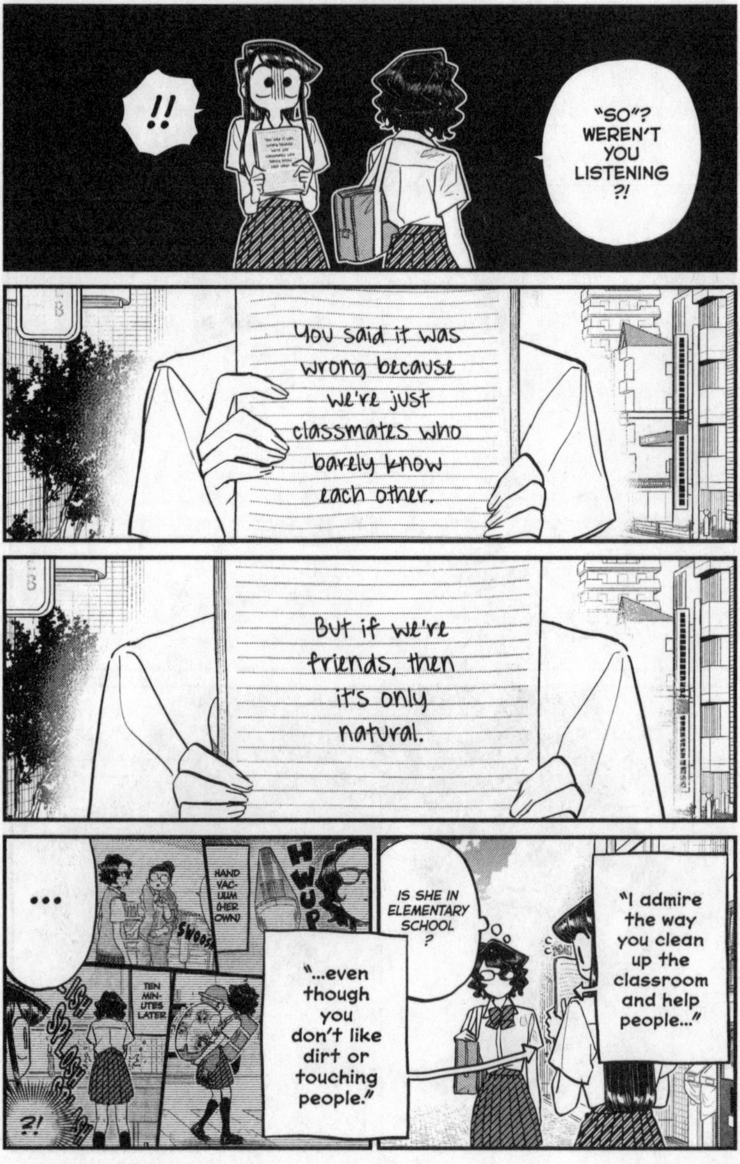
“SO”? WEREN'T YOU LISTENING ?!
!!
You said it was wrong because we're just classmates who barely know each other.
But if we're friends, then it's only natural.
“I admire the way you clean up the classroom and help people...”
IS SHE IN ELEMENTARY SCHOOL ?
“...even though you don't like dirt or touching people.”
...
HWUP
HAND VAC-UUM (HER OWN)
SWOOSH
TEN MIN-UTES LATER
?!

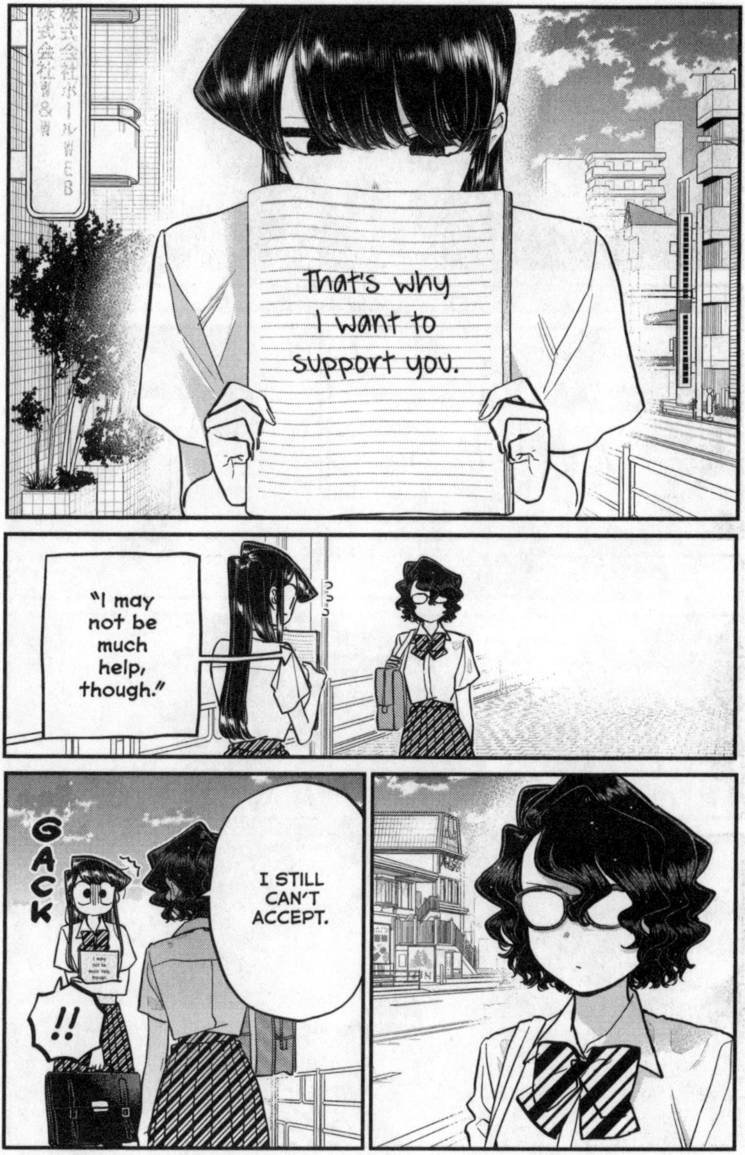
That's why
I want to
support you.
"I may not be much help, though."
I STILL CAN'T ACCEPT.
GACK
!!

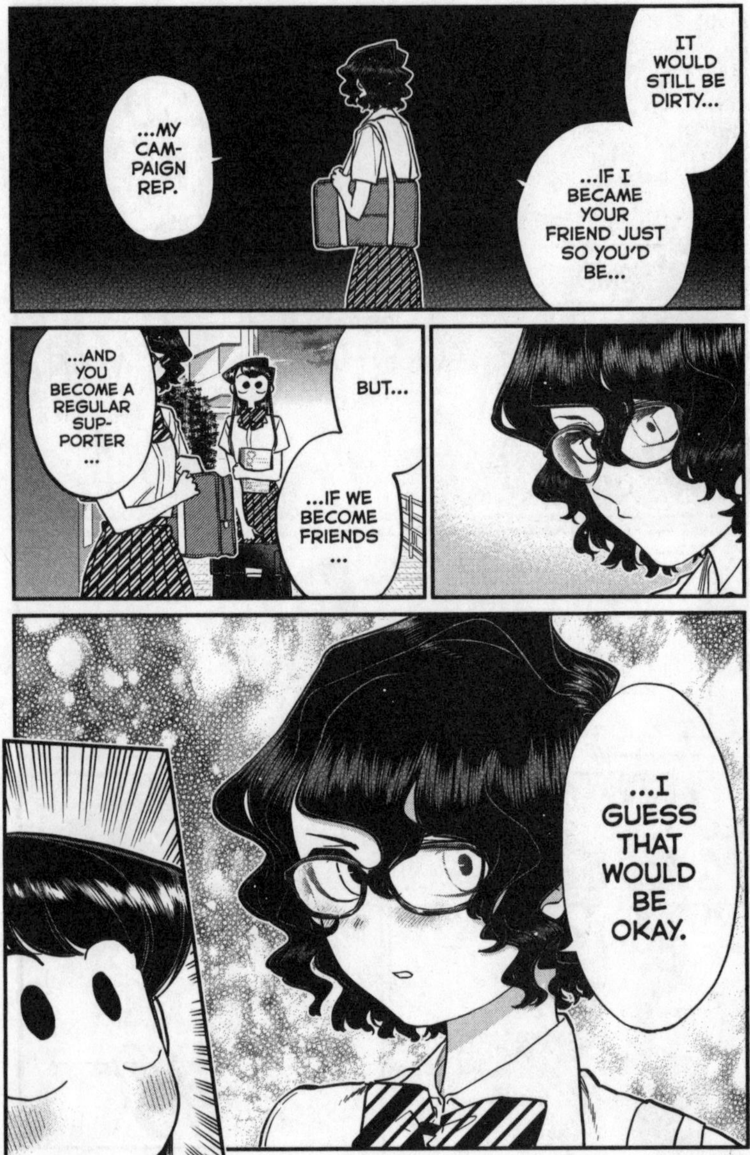
IT WOULD STILL BE DIRTY...
...IF I BECAME YOUR FRIEND JUST SO YOU'D BE...
...MY CAMPAIGN REP.
BUT...
...IF WE BECOME FRIENDS...
...AND YOU BECOME A REGULAR SUPPORTER...
...I GUESS THAT WOULD BE OKAY.

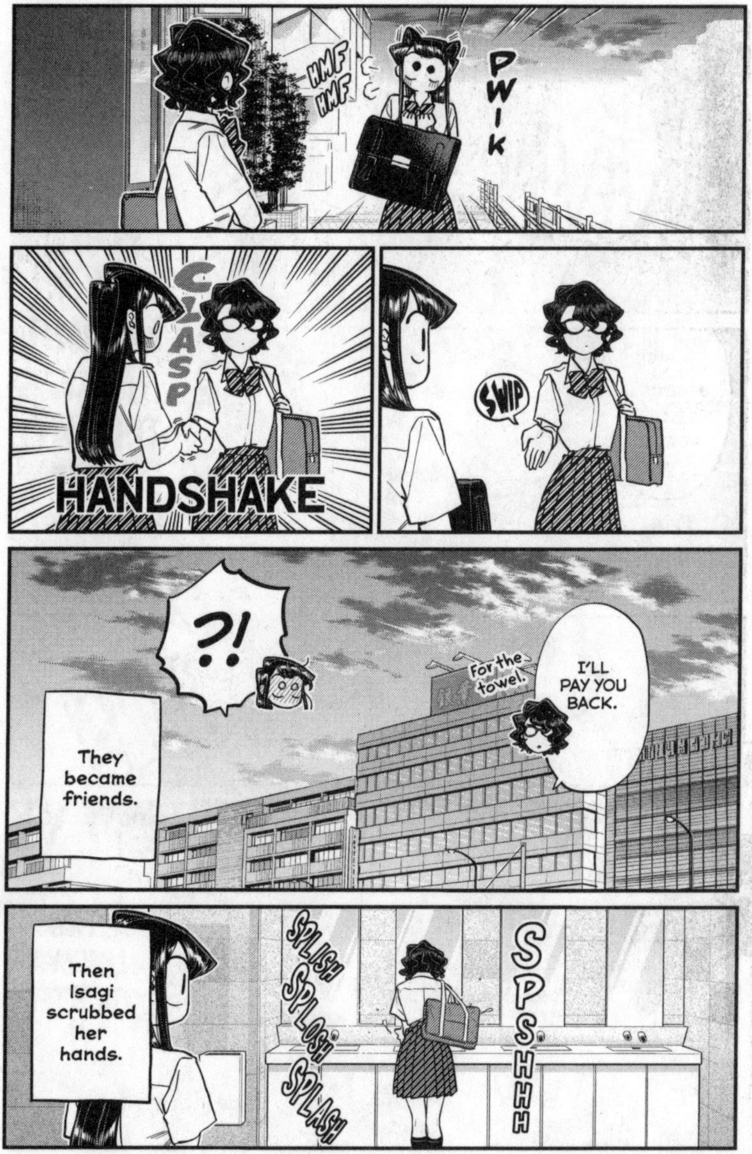
PWIK
HMF HMF
SWIP
CLASP
HANDSHAKE
I'LL PAY YOU BACK.
For the towel.
?!
They became friends.
SPSHHH
SPLISH SPLOSH SPLASH
Then Isagi scrubbed her hands.

Communication 196 — The End

# Komi Can't Communicate

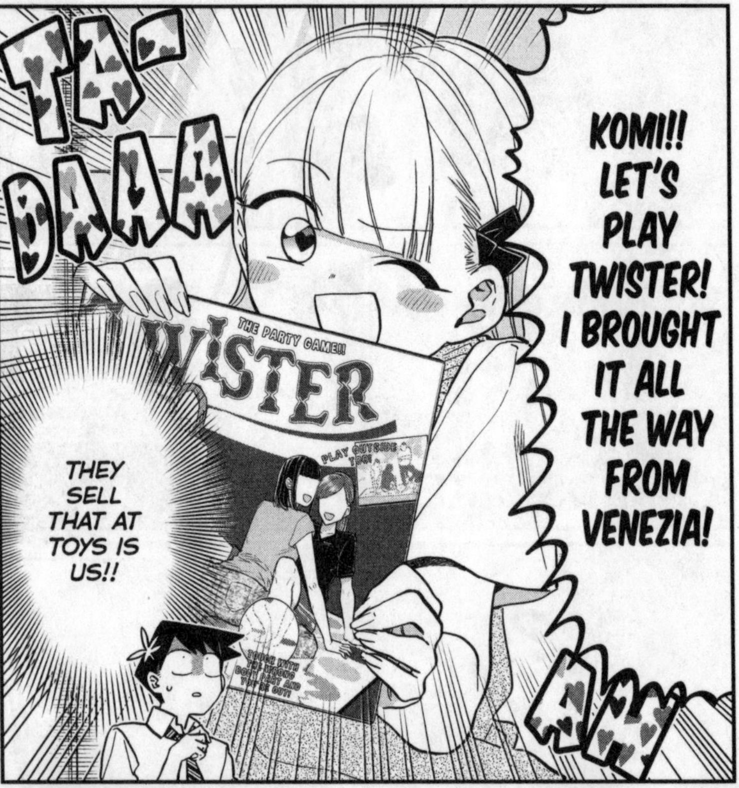
KOMI!! LET'S PLAY TWISTER! I BROUGHT IT ALL THE WAY FROM VENEZIA!
TA-DAAA
THE PARTY GAME!!
TWISTER
PLAY OUTSIDE TOO!
THEY SELL THAT AT TOYS IS US!!
AH

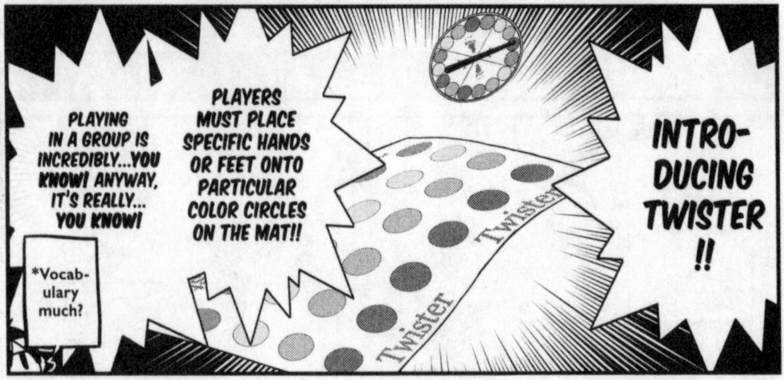
INTRO-DUCING TWISTER!!
PLAYERS MUST PLACE SPECIFIC HANDS OR FEET ONTO PARTICULAR COLOR CIRCLES ON THE MAT!!
PLAYING IN A GROUP IS INCREDIBLY...YOU KNOW! ANYWAY, IT'S REALLY... YOU KNOW!
*Vocab-ulary much?
Twister
Twister

## Communication 197: Twister

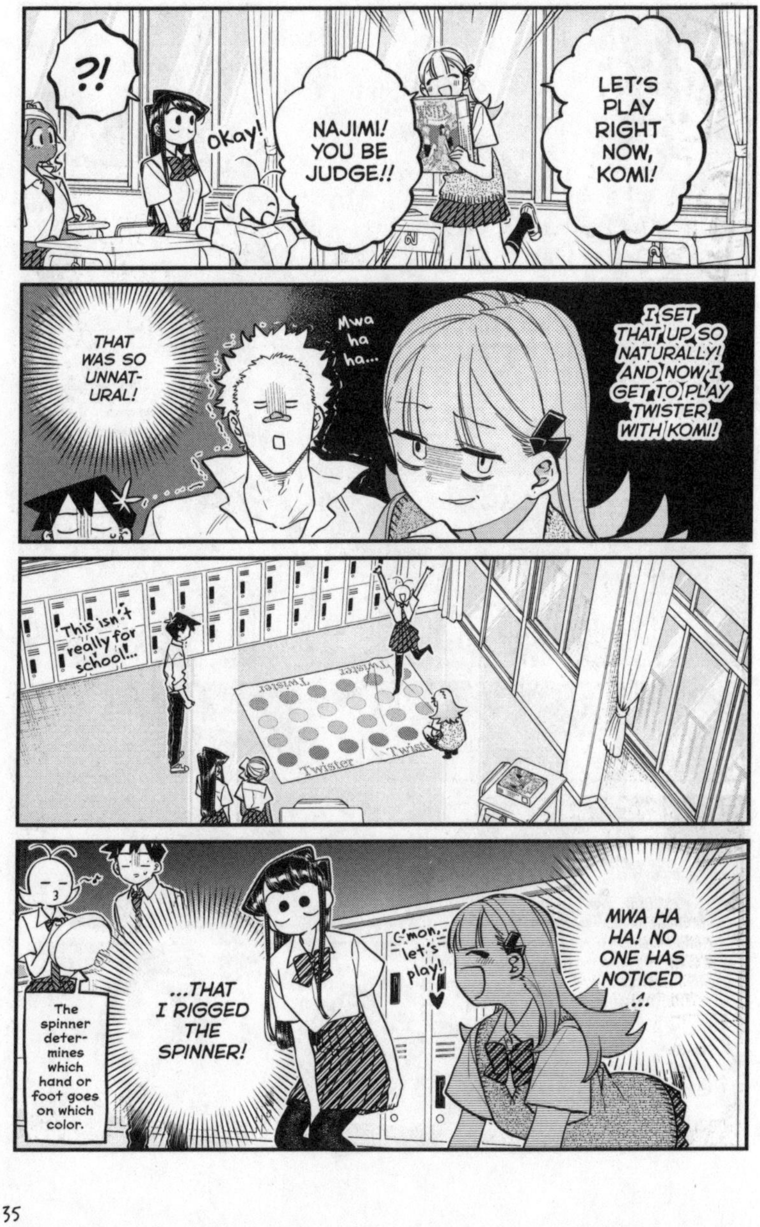
LET'S PLAY RIGHT NOW, KOMI!
NAJIMI! YOU BE JUDGE!!
Okay!
?!
I SET THAT UP SO NATURALLY! AND NOW I GET TO PLAY TWISTER WITH KOMI!
Mwa ha ha...
THAT WAS SO UNNAT-URAL!
Twister
Twister
Twister
Twist
This isn't really for school...
MWA HA HA! NO ONE HAS NOTICED...
C'mon, let's play!
...THAT I RIGGED THE SPINNER!
The spinner deter-mines which hand or foot goes on which color.

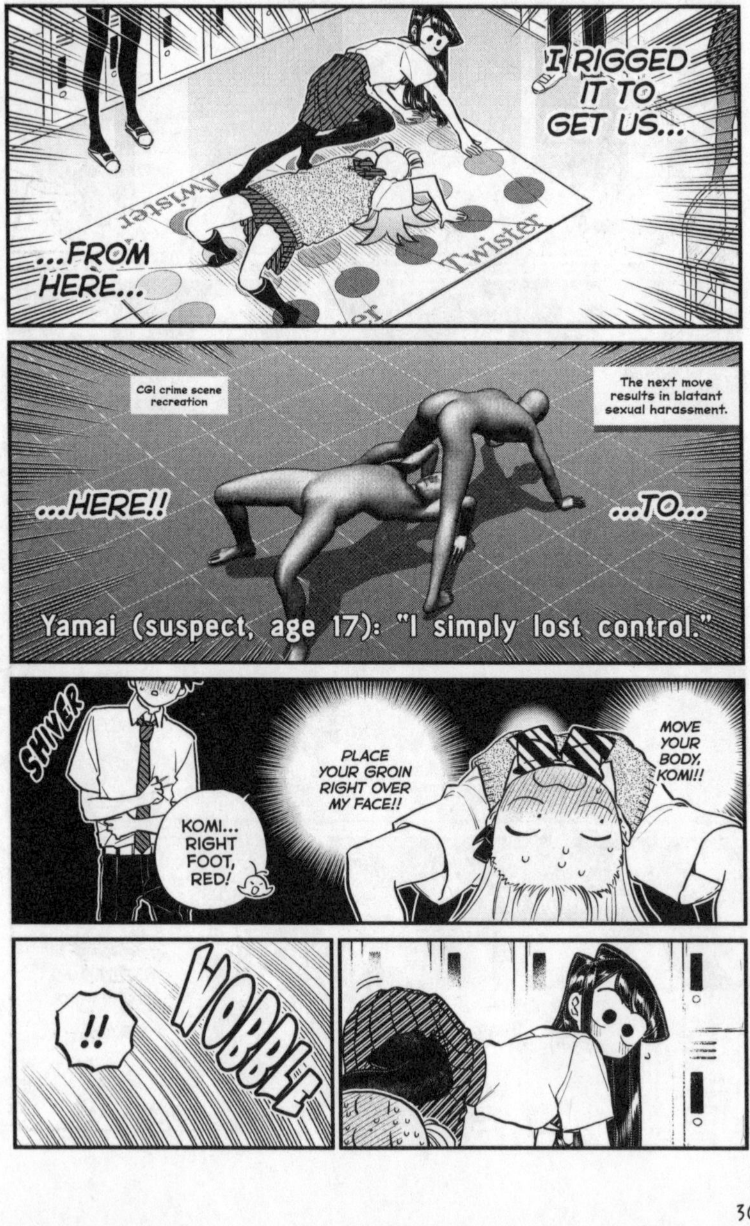
I RIGGED IT TO GET US...
...FROM HERE...
The next move results in blatant sexual harassment.
CGI crime scene recreation
...TO...
...HERE!!
Yamai (suspect, age 17): "I simply lost control."
MOVE YOUR BODY, KOMI!!
PLACE YOUR GROIN RIGHT OVER MY FACE!!
KOMI... RIGHT FOOT, RED!
SHIVER
WOBBLE
!!

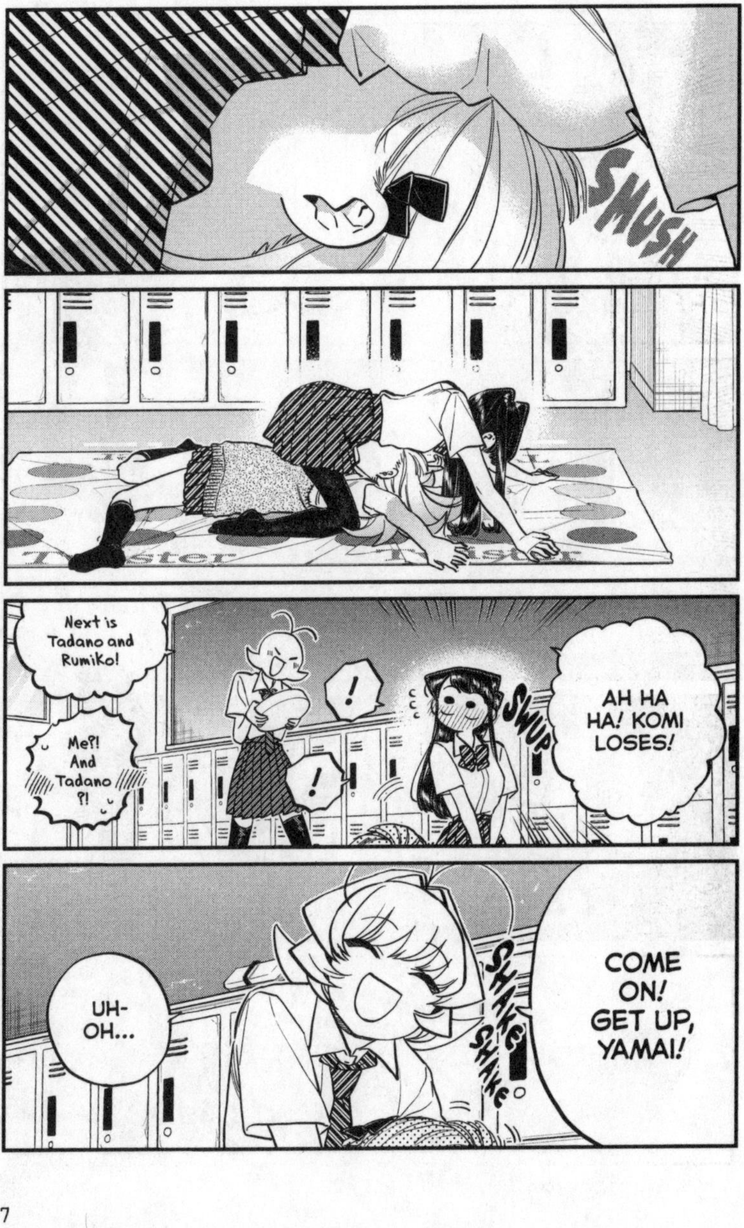
SMUSH
AH HA HA! KOMI LOSES!
SWUP
!
Next is Tadano and Rumiko!
!
Me?! And Tadano?!
COME ON! GET UP, YAMAI!
SHAKE SHAKE
UH-OH...

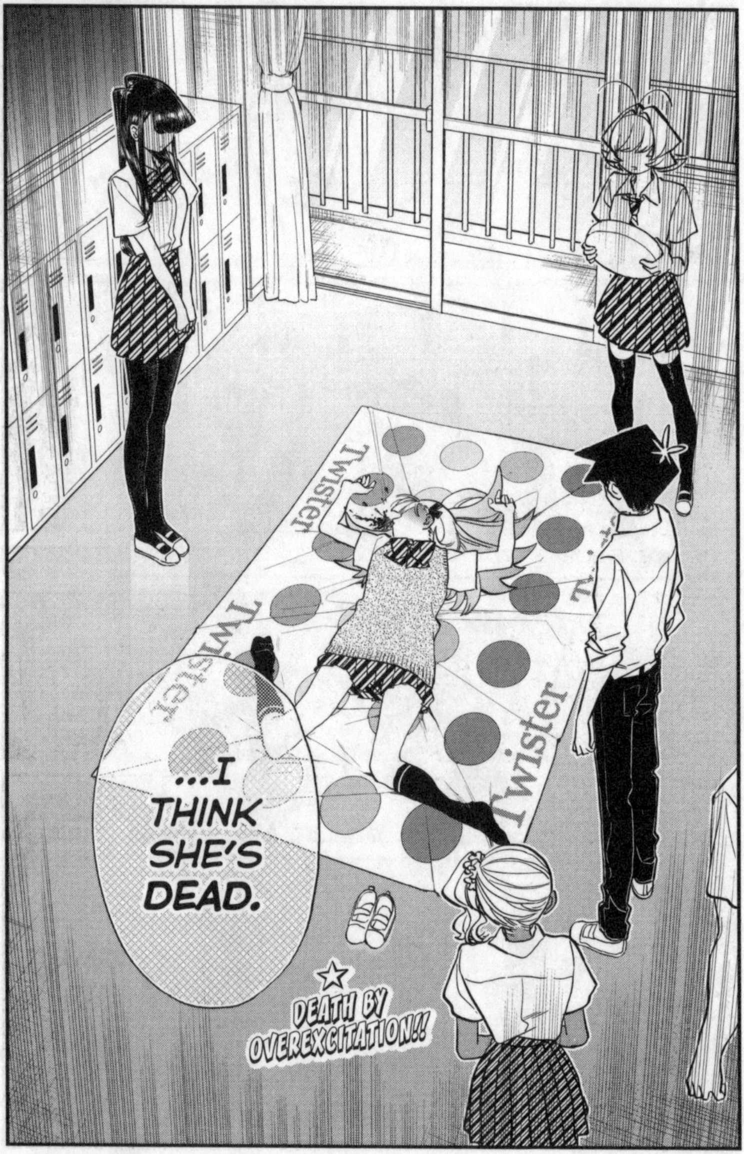
...I THINK SHE'S DEAD.
☆ DEATH BY OVEREXCITATION!!

Communication 197 — The End

Komi Can't Communicate

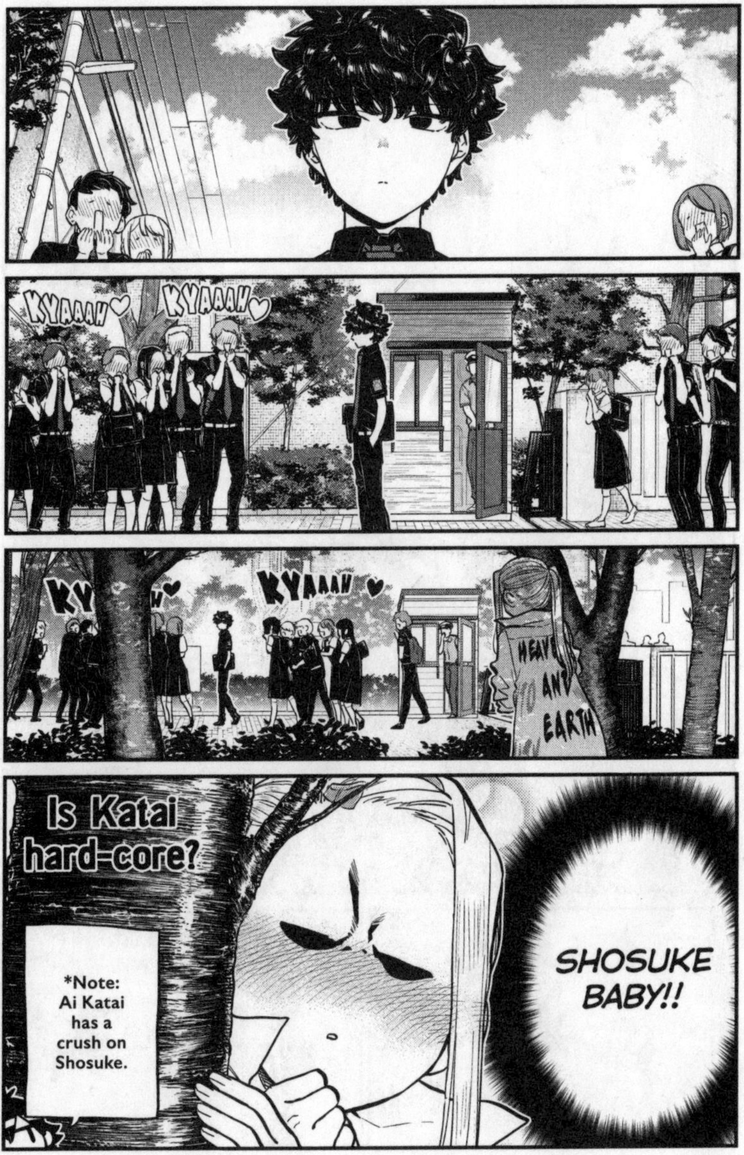
KYAAAH♡
KYAAAH♡
KYAAAH♡
SHOSUKE BABY!!
Is Katai hard-core?
*Note: Ai Katai has a crush on Shosuke.

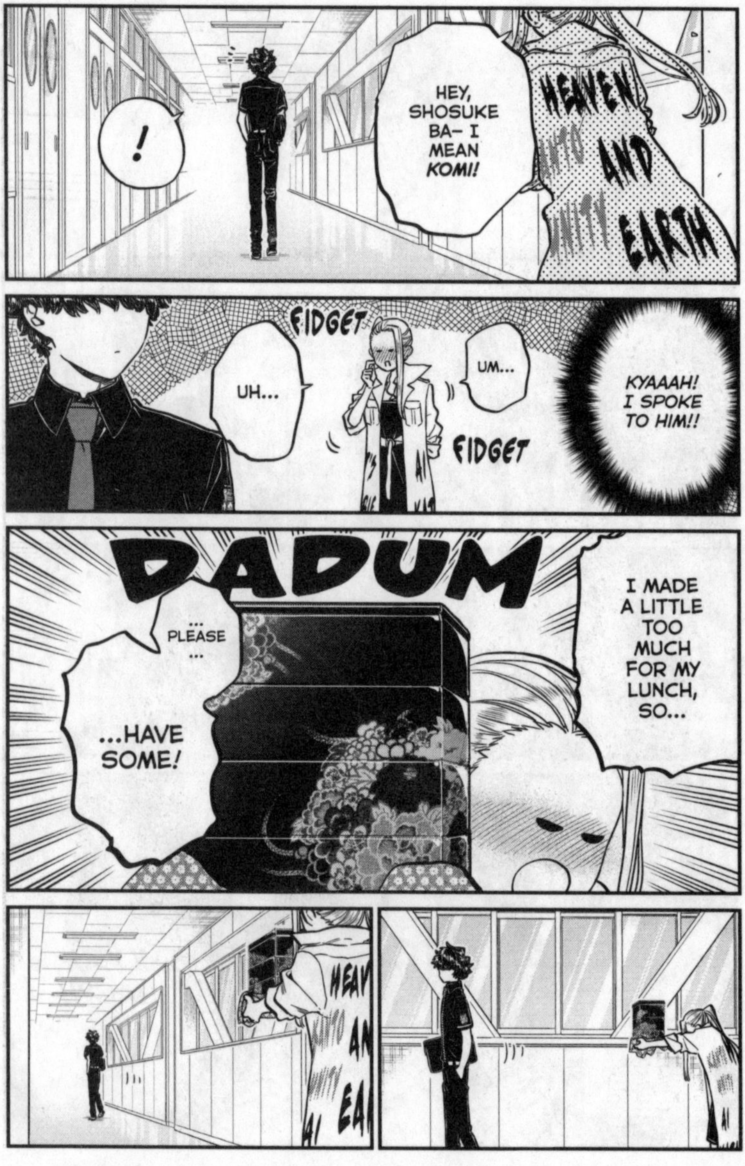
HEY, SHOSUKE BA– I MEAN *KOMI!*
HEAVEN AND EARTH
!
KYAAAH! I SPOKE TO HIM!!
UM...
FIDGET
FIDGET
UH...
I MADE A LITTLE TOO MUCH FOR MY LUNCH, SO...
DADUM
... PLEASE ...
...HAVE SOME!

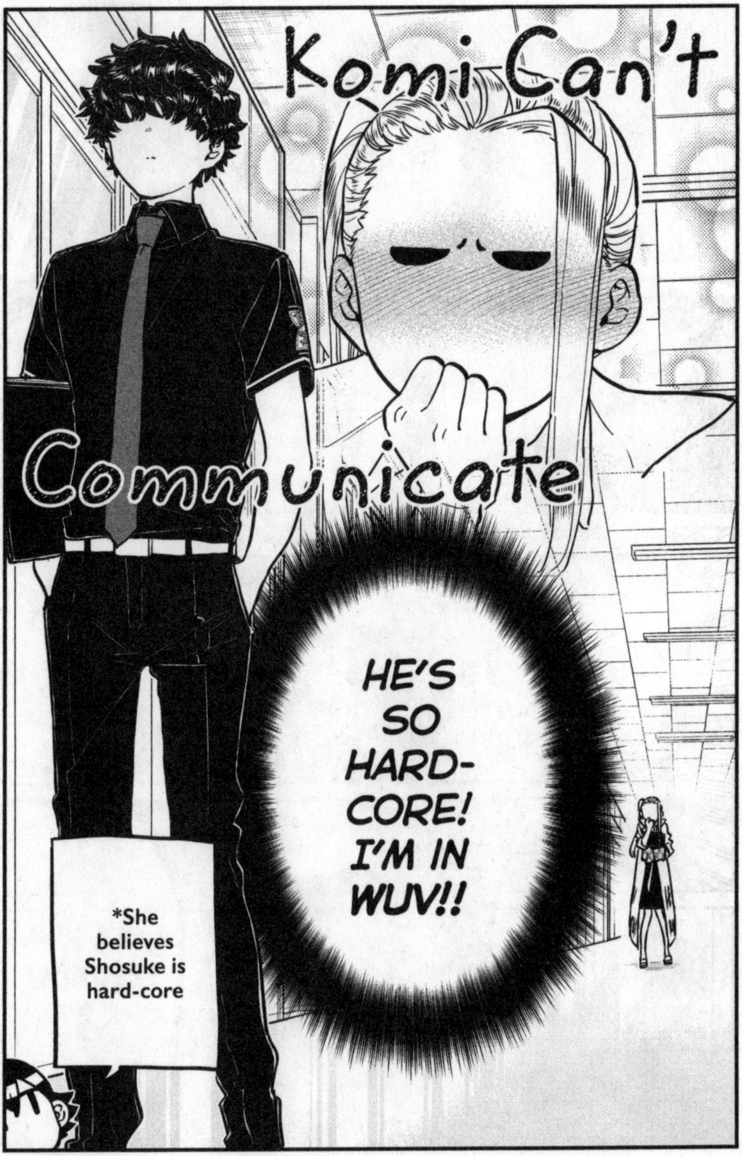
Komi Can't
Communicate
HE'S SO HARD-CORE! I'M IN WUV!!
*She believes Shosuke is hard-core

Communication 198: OUT & LAW: The Movie

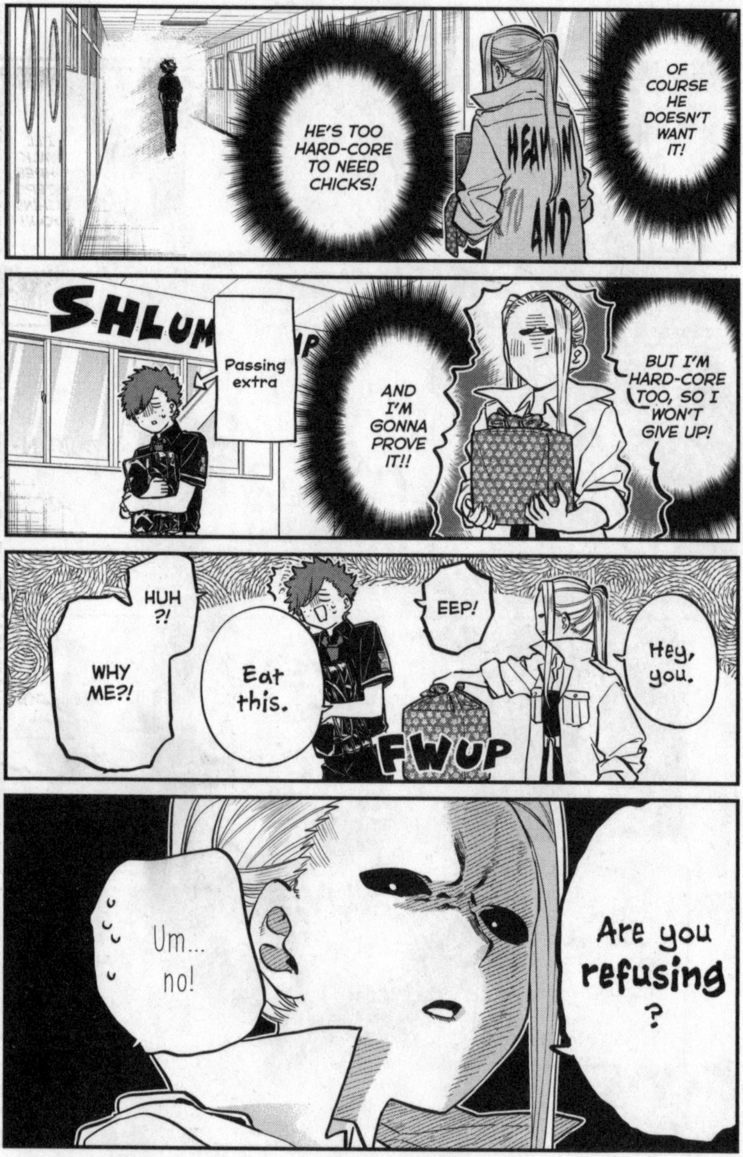
OF COURSE HE DOESN'T WANT IT!
HE'S TOO HARD-CORE TO NEED CHICKS!
BUT I'M HARD-CORE TOO, SO I WON'T GIVE UP!
AND I'M GONNA PROVE IT!!
Passing extra
SHLUM
Hey, you.
EEP!
Eat this.
FWUP
HUH?!
WHY ME?!
Are you refusing?
Um... no!

## Flower of Womanhood...?

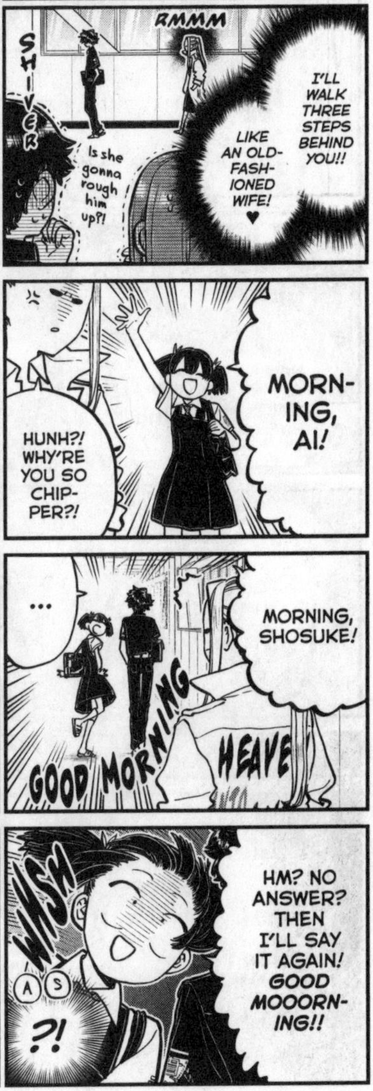
RMMM
I'LL WALK THREE STEPS BEHIND YOU!!
LIKE AN OLD-FASHIONED WIFE! ♥
SHIVER
Is she gonna rough him up?!
MORNING, AI!
HUNH?! WHY'RE YOU SO CHIPPER?!
MORNING, SHOSUKE!
...
HEAVE
GOOD MORNING
HM? NO ANSWER? THEN I'LL SAY IT AGAIN! GOOD MOOORNING!!
WHSH
?!

## Hitomi Gets Through to Shosuke

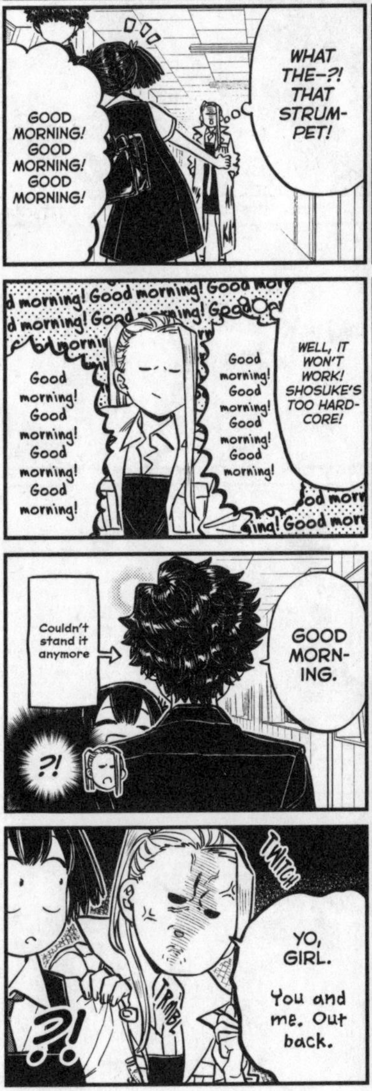
WHAT THE-?! THAT STRUMPET!
GOOD MORNING! GOOD MORNING! GOOD MORNING!
WELL, IT WON'T WORK! SHOSUKE'S TOO HARDCORE!
Good morning! Good morning! Good morning! Good morning!
Good morning! Good morning! Good morning! Good morning!
GOOD MORNING.
Couldn't stand it anymore
?!
TWITCH
YO, GIRL.
You and me. Out back.
THROB
?!

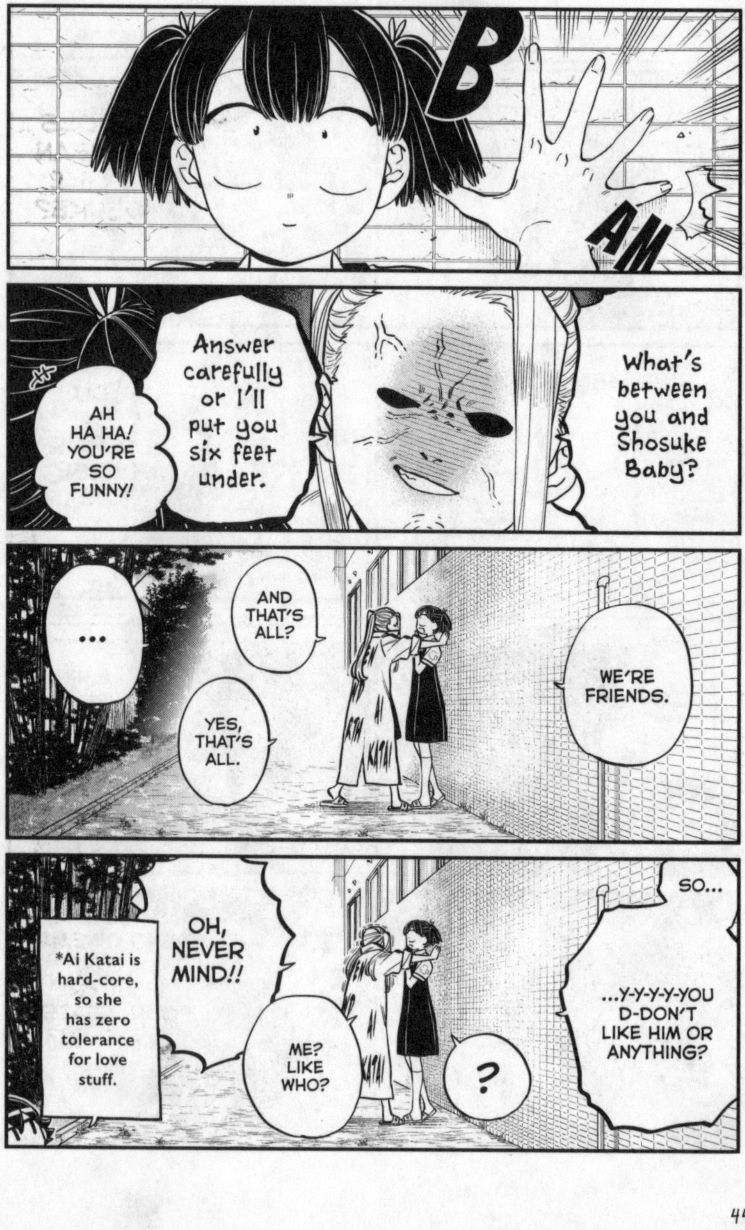
BAM
What's between you and Shosuke Baby?
Answer carefully or I'll put you six feet under.
AH HA HA! YOU'RE SO FUNNY!
WE'RE FRIENDS.
AND THAT'S ALL?
YES, THAT'S ALL.
...
SO...
...Y-Y-Y-Y-YOU D-DON'T LIKE HIM OR ANYTHING?
?
ME? LIKE WHO?
OH, NEVER MIND!!
*Ai Katai is hard-core, so she has zero tolerance for love stuff.

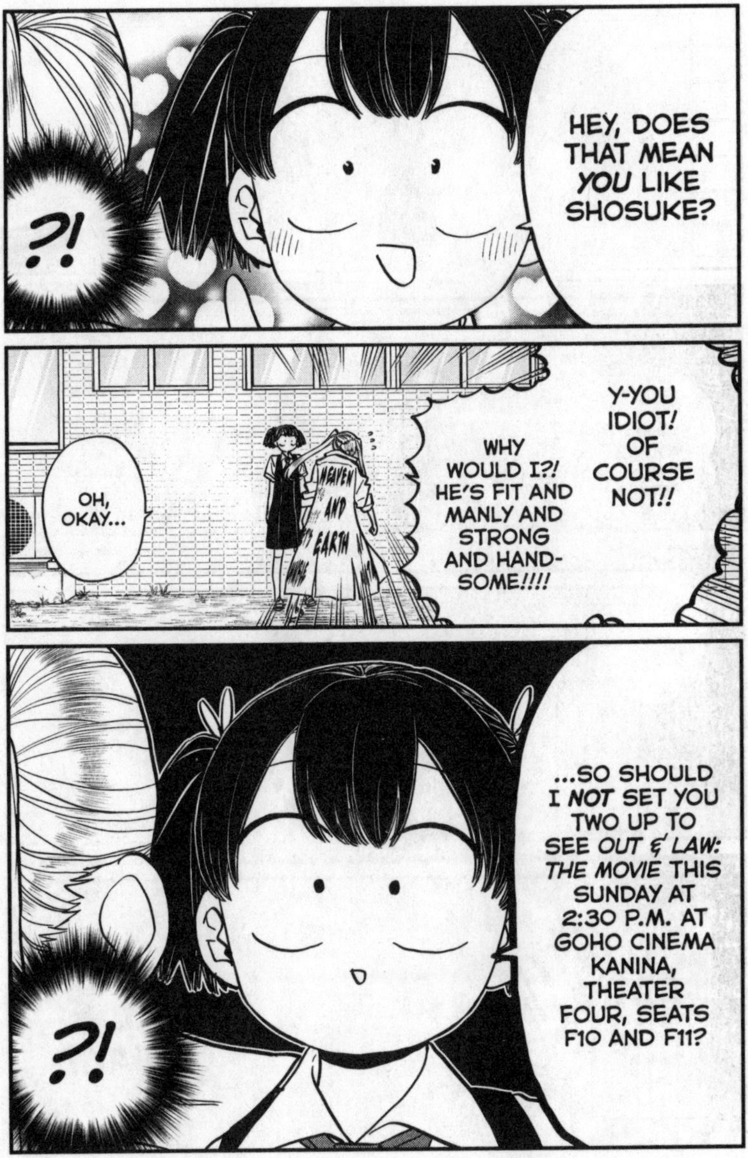
HEY, DOES THAT MEAN *YOU* LIKE SHOSUKE?
?!
Y-YOU IDIOT! OF COURSE NOT!!
WHY WOULD I?! HE'S FIT AND MANLY AND STRONG AND HAND-SOME!!!!
HEAVEN AND EARTH
OH, OKAY...
...SO SHOULD I *NOT* SET YOU TWO UP TO SEE *OUT & LAW: THE MOVIE* THIS SUNDAY AT 2:30 P.M. AT GOHO CINEMA KANINA, THEATER FOUR, SEATS F10 AND F11?
?!

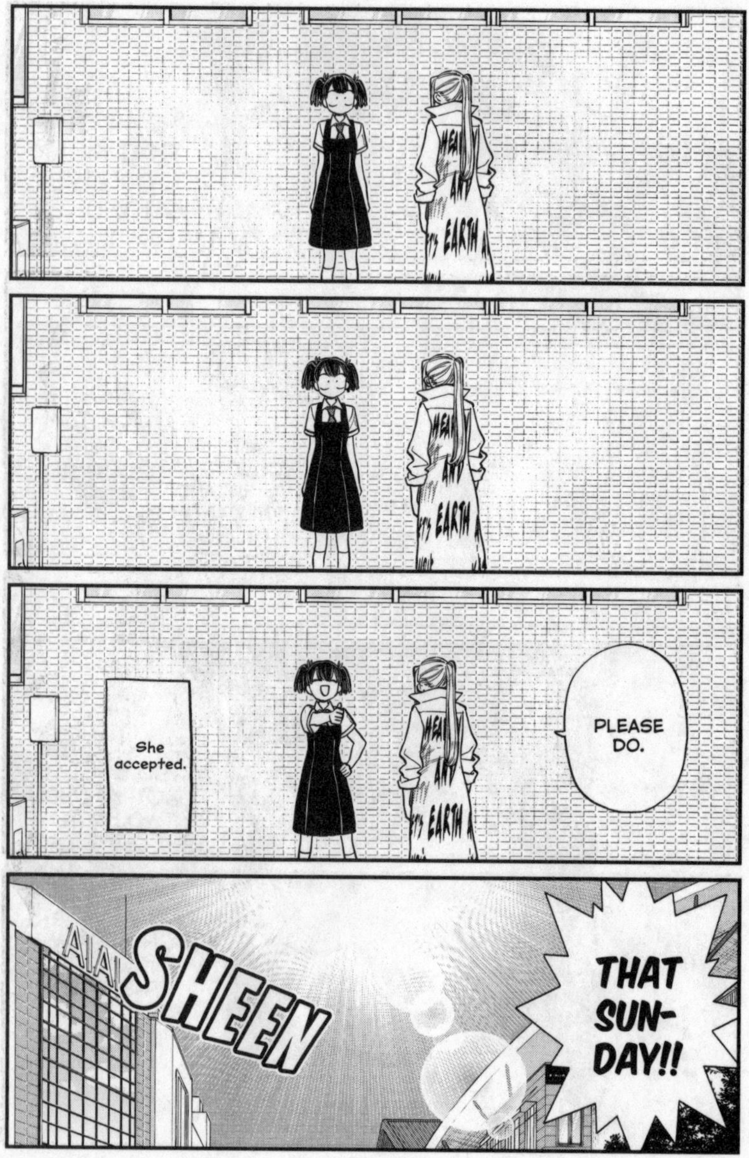
PLEASE DO.
She accepted.
THAT SUN-DAY!!
SHEEN

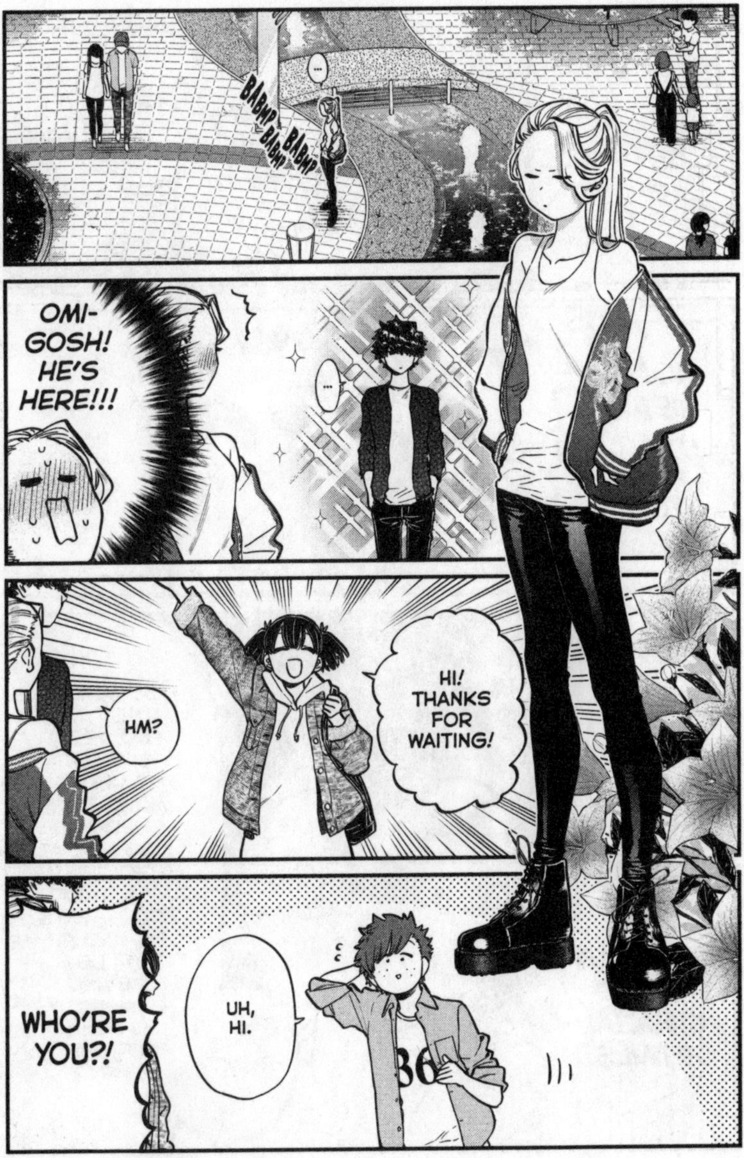
...
BABMP BABMP
BABMP
...
OMI-GOSH! HE'S HERE!!!
HI! THANKS FOR WAITING!
HM?
UH, HI.
WHO'RE YOU?!

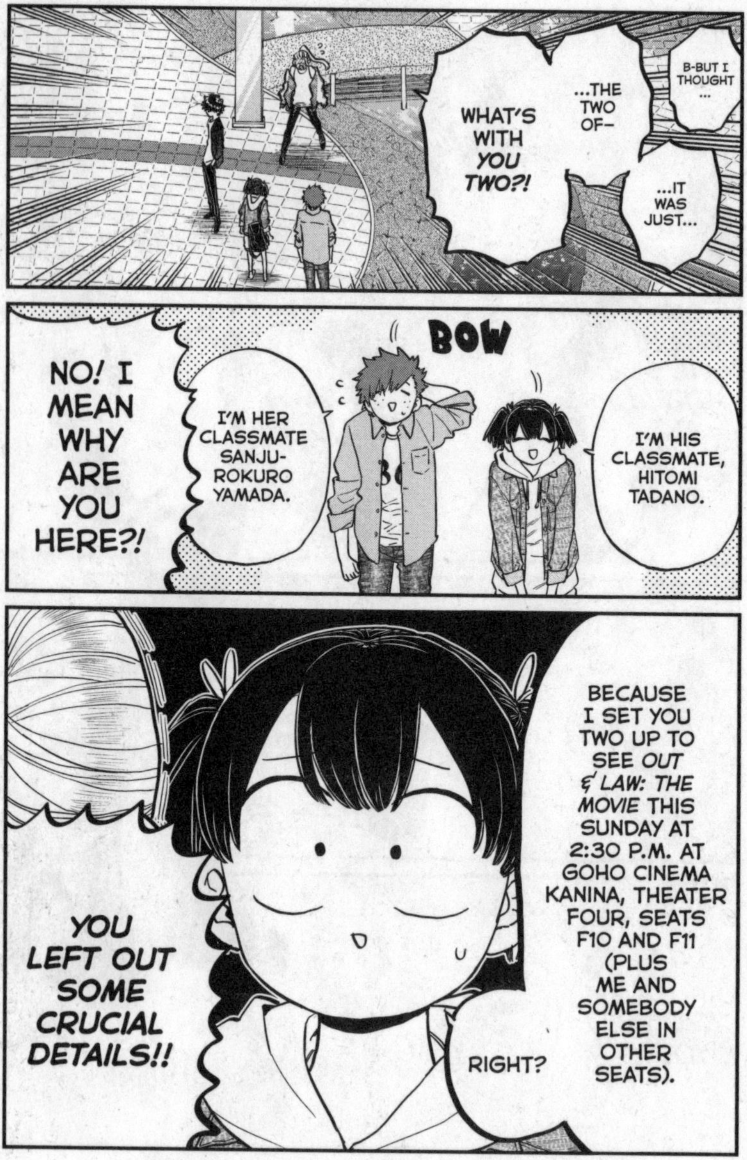
B-BUT I THOUGHT ...
...IT WAS JUST...
...THE TWO OF–
WHAT'S WITH YOU TWO?!
I'M HIS CLASSMATE, HITOMI TADANO.
BOW
I'M HER CLASSMATE SANJU-ROKURO YAMADA.
NO! I MEAN WHY ARE YOU HERE?!
BECAUSE I SET YOU TWO UP TO SEE OUT & LAW: THE MOVIE THIS SUNDAY AT 2:30 P.M. AT GOHO CINEMA KANINA, THEATER FOUR, SEATS F10 AND F11 (PLUS ME AND SOMEBODY ELSE IN OTHER SEATS).
RIGHT?
YOU LEFT OUT SOME CRUCIAL DETAILS!!

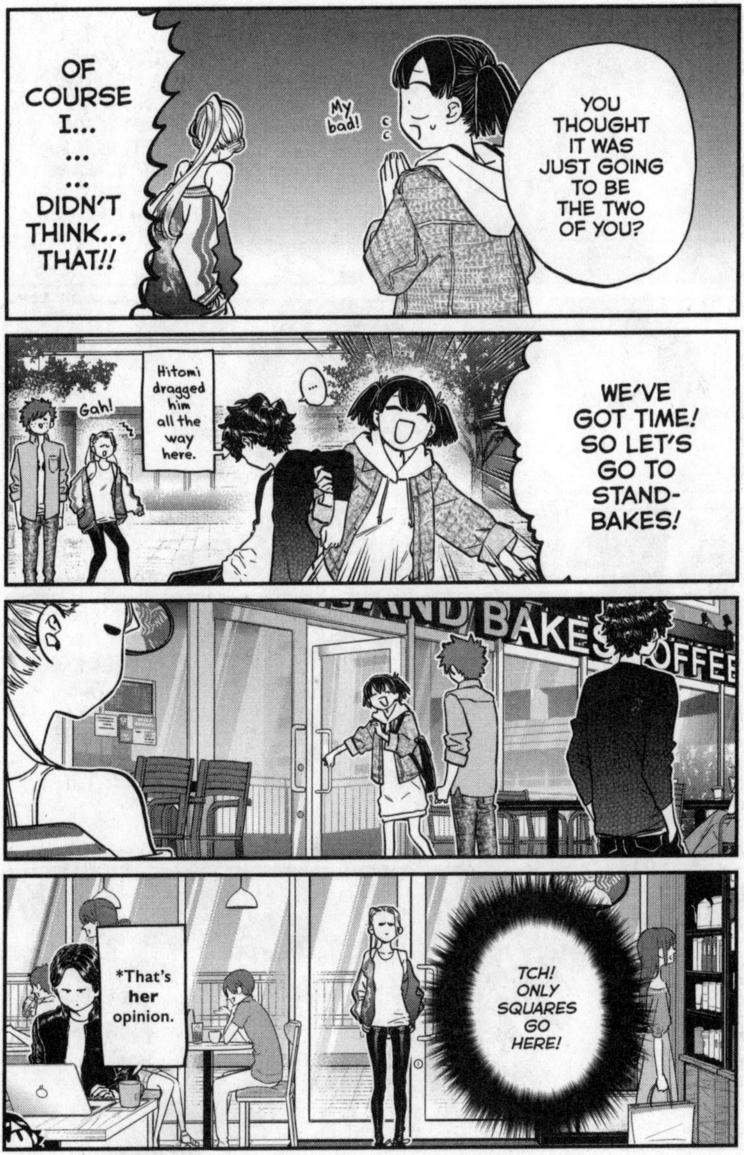
YOU THOUGHT IT WAS JUST GOING TO BE THE TWO OF YOU?
My bad!
OF COURSE I... ... ... DIDN'T THINK... THAT!!
WE'VE GOT TIME! SO LET'S GO TO STAND-BAKES!
...
Hitomi dragged him all the way here.
Gah!
TCH! ONLY SQUARES GO HERE!
*That's **her** opinion.

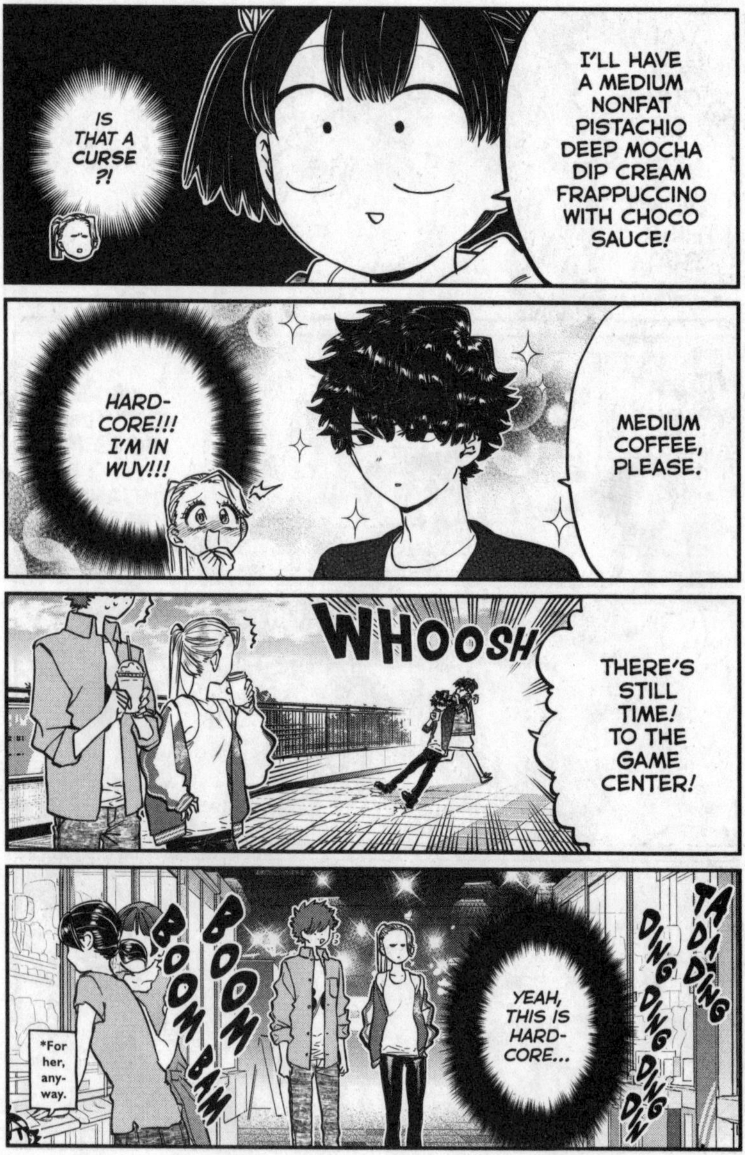
I'LL HAVE A MEDIUM NONFAT PISTACHIO DEEP MOCHA DIP CREAM FRAPPUCCINO WITH CHOCO SAUCE!
IS THAT A CURSE?!
MEDIUM COFFEE, PLEASE.
HARD-CORE!!! I'M IN WUV!!!
THERE'S STILL TIME! TO THE GAME CENTER!
WHOOSH
TA DA DING
DING DING DING DING DIN
YEAH, THIS IS HARD-CORE...
BOOM BOOM BAM
BOOM
*For her, anyway.

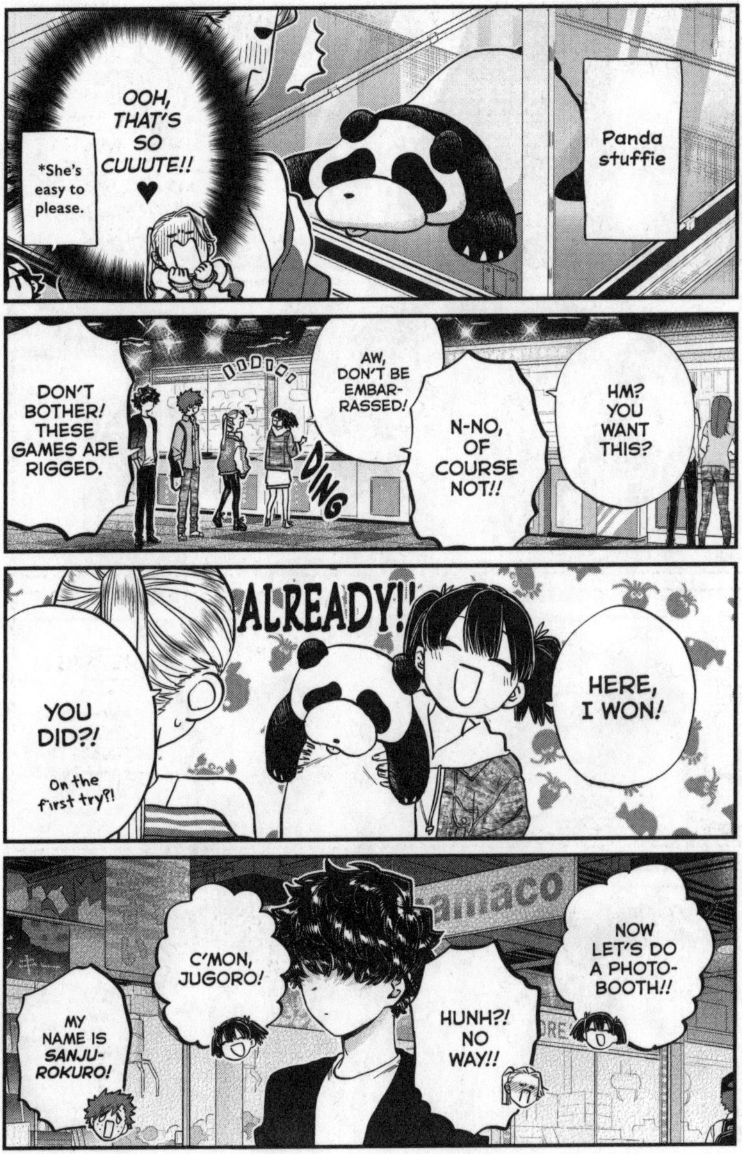
Panda stuffie
OOH, THAT'S SO CUUUTE!! ♥
*She's easy to please.
HM? YOU WANT THIS?
N-NO, OF COURSE NOT!!
AW, DON'T BE EMBARRASSED!
DING
DON'T BOTHER! THESE GAMES ARE RIGGED.
HERE, I WON!
ALREADY!!
YOU DID?!
On the first try?!
NOW LET'S DO A PHOTOBOOTH!!
HUNH?! NO WAY!!
C'MON, JUGORO!
MY NAME IS SANJUROKURO!

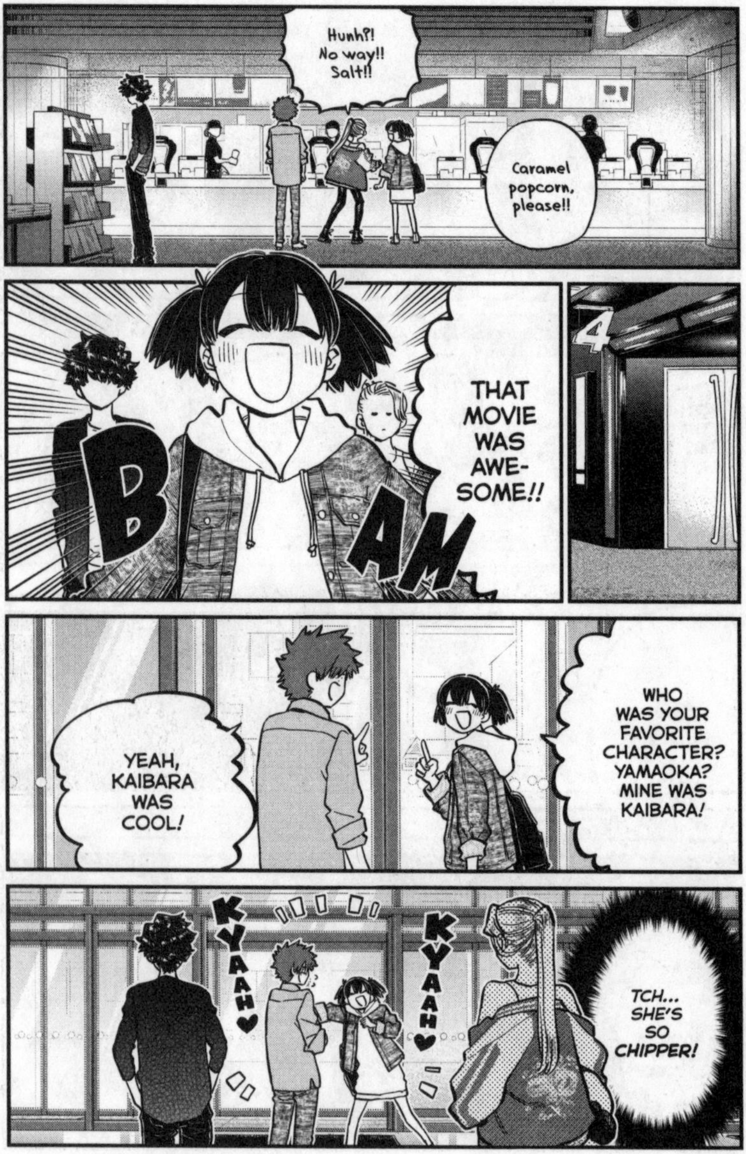
Caramel popcorn, please!!
Hunh?! No way!! Salt!!
THAT MOVIE WAS AWE-SOME!!
BAM
WHO WAS YOUR FAVORITE CHARACTER? YAMAOKA? MINE WAS KAIBARA!
YEAH, KAIBARA WAS COOL!
KYAAH♥
KYAAH♥
TCH... SHE'S SO CHIPPER!

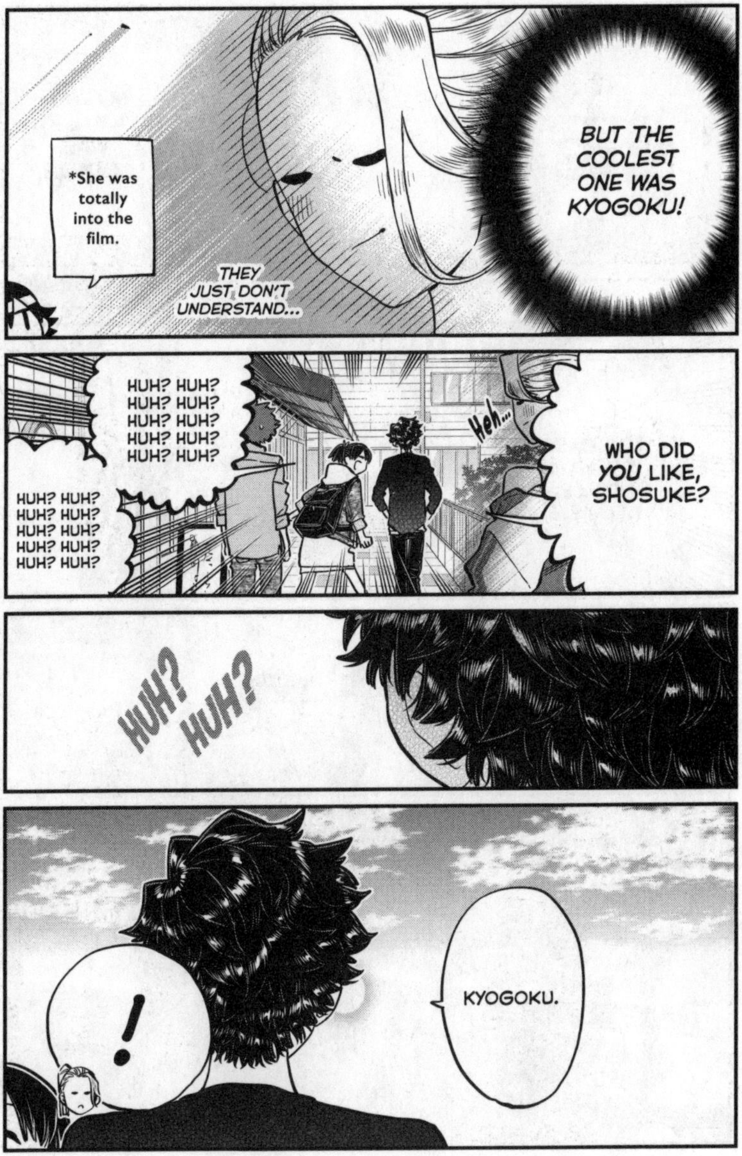
BUT THE COOLEST ONE WAS KYOGOKU!
THEY JUST DON'T UNDERSTAND...
*She was totally into the film.
WHO DID YOU LIKE, SHOSUKE?
Heh...
HUH? HUH? HUH? HUH? HUH? HUH? HUH? HUH? HUH? HUH?
HUH? HUH? HUH? HUH? HUH? HUH? HUH? HUH? HUH? HUH?
HUH? HUH?
KYOGOKU.
!

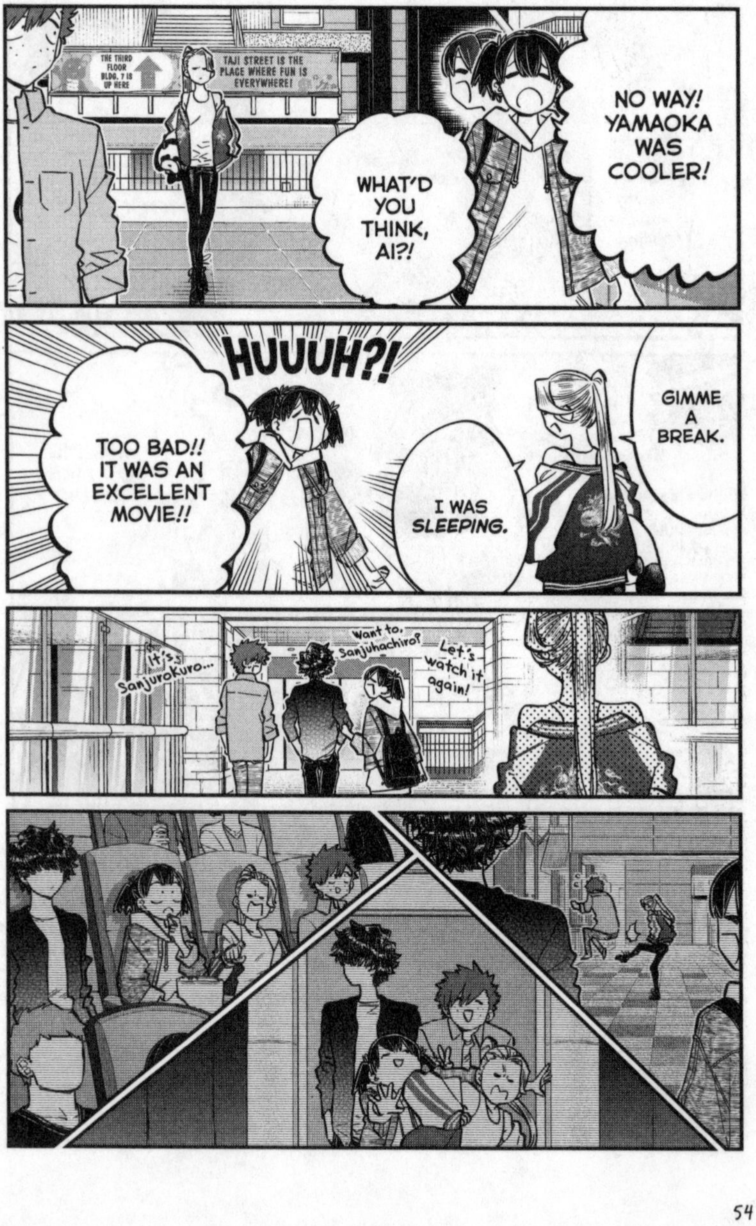
NO WAY! YAMAOKA WAS COOLER!
WHAT'D YOU THINK, AI?!
TAJI STREET IS THE PLACE WHERE FUN IS EVERYWHERE!
THE THIRD FLOOR BLDG. 7 IS UP HERE
GIMME A BREAK.
I WAS SLEEPING.
HUUUH?!
TOO BAD!! IT WAS AN EXCELLENT MOVIE!!
Let's watch it again!
Want to, Sanjuhachiro?
It's Sanjurokuro...

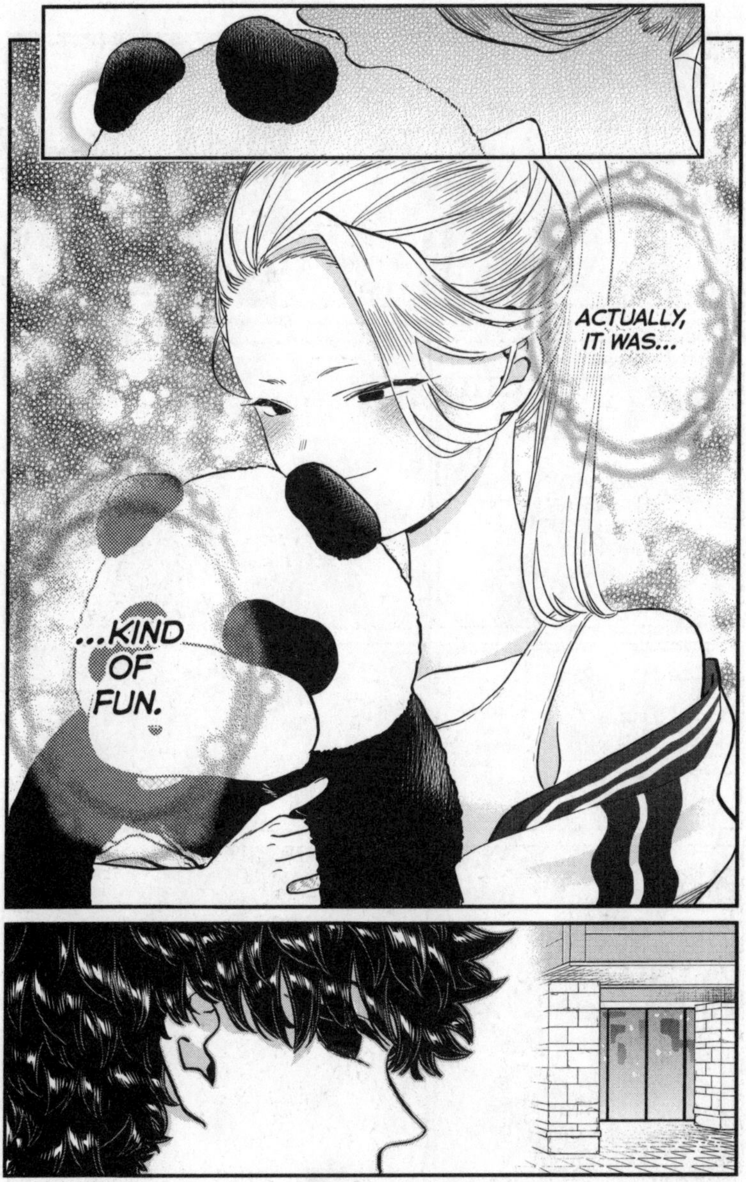
ACTUALLY, IT WAS...
...KIND OF FUN.

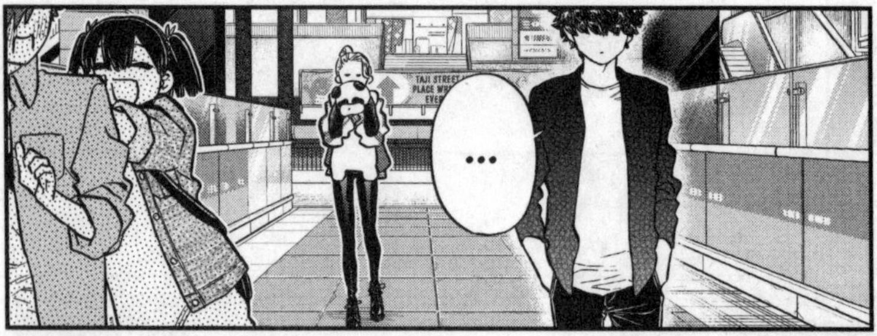
...

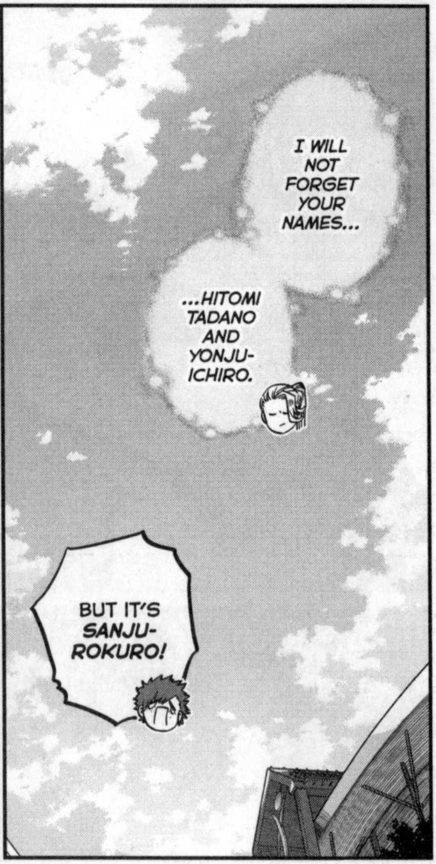
I WILL NOT FORGET YOUR NAMES...
...HITOMI TADANO AND YONJU-ICHIRO.
BUT IT'S SANJU-ROKURO!

Communication 198 — The End

Kyujuro Yamada's Choice

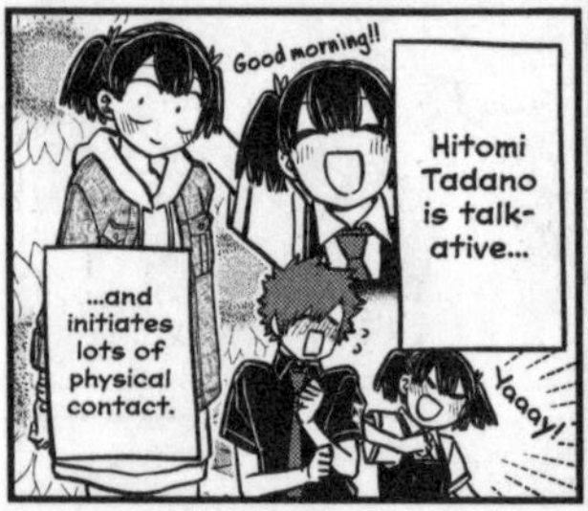
Hitomi Tadano is talk-ative...
Good morning!!
...and initiates lots of physical contact.
Yaaaay!

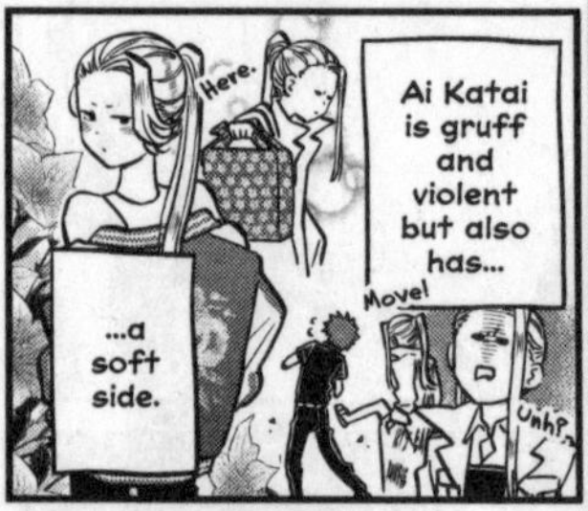
Ai Katai is gruff and violent but also has...
Here.
Move!
Unh?
...a soft side.

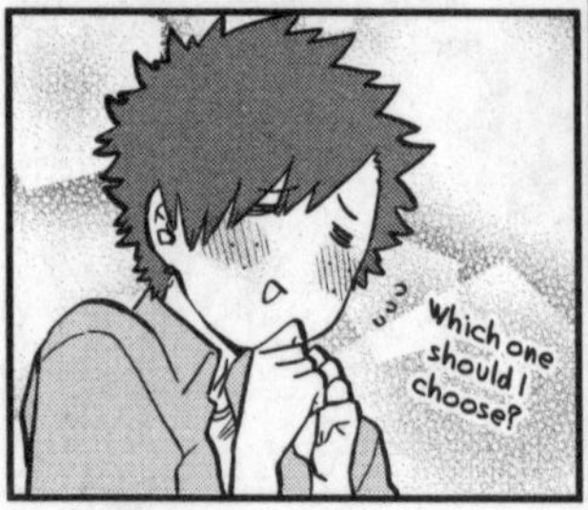
Which one should I choose?

Bonus Communication— The End

# Komi Can't Communicate

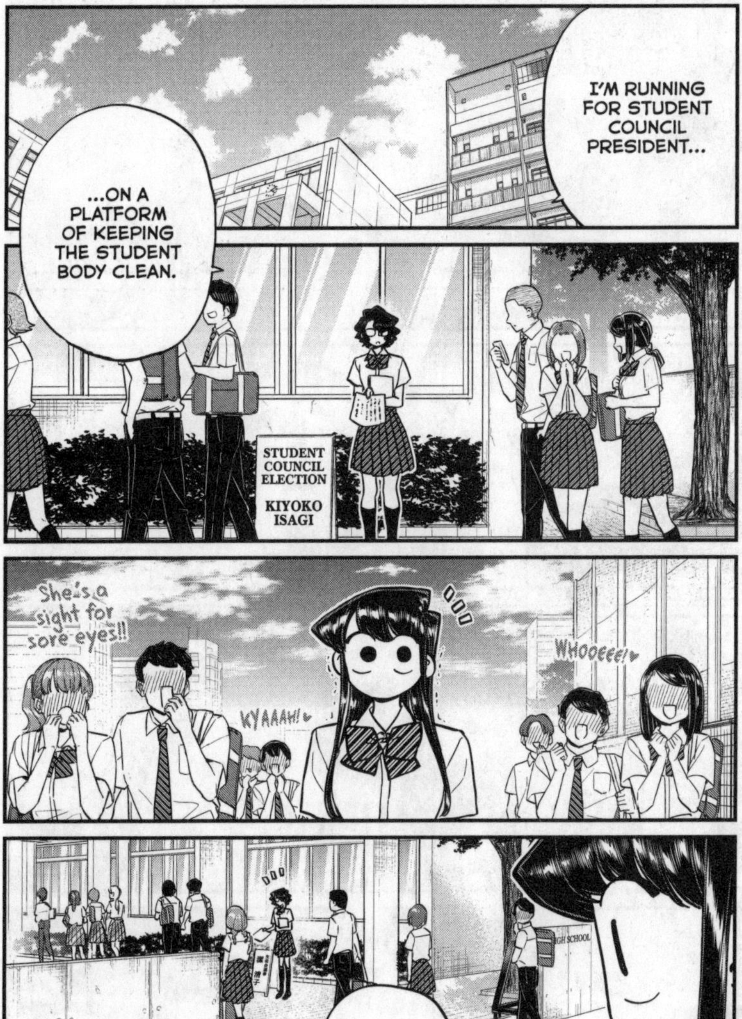
I'M RUNNING FOR STUDENT COUNCIL PRESIDENT...
...ON A PLATFORM OF KEEPING THE STUDENT BODY CLEAN.
STUDENT COUNCIL ELECTION KIYOKO ISAGI
WHOOEEE!♥
KYAAAH!♥
She's a sight for sore eyes!!
!

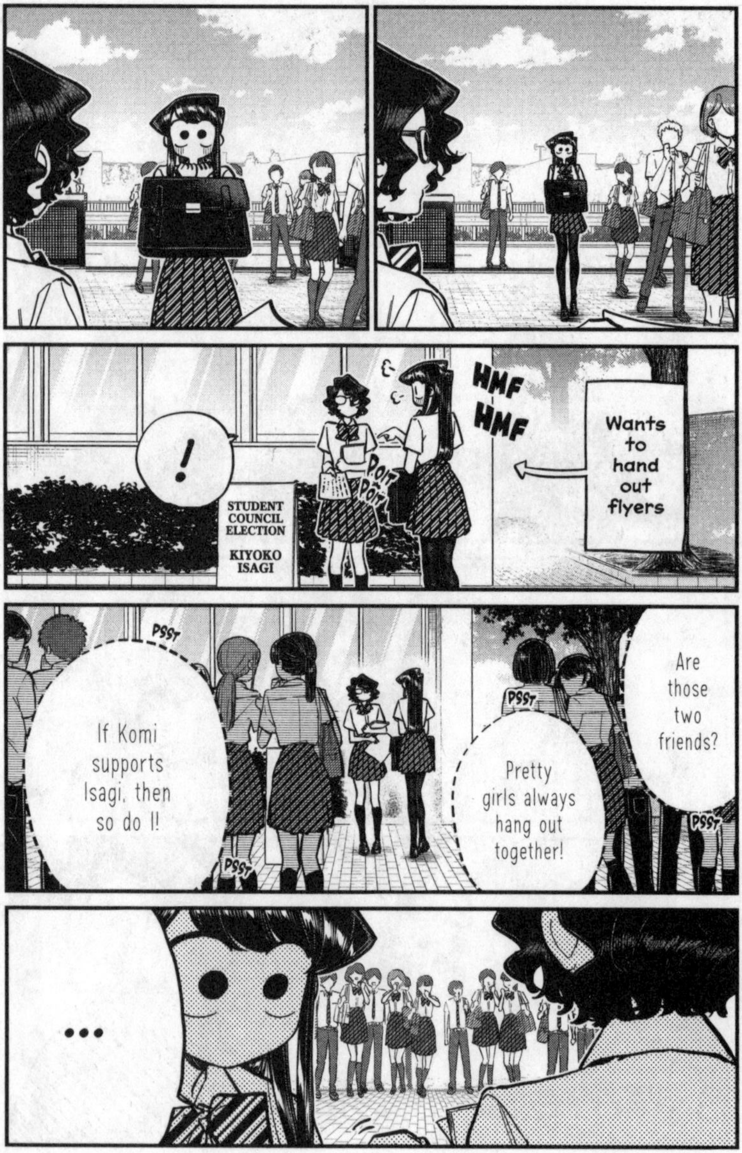
Wants to hand out flyers
HMF HMF
POIT POIT
!
STUDENT COUNCIL ELECTION
KIYOKO ISAGI
Are those two friends?
PSST
PSST
Pretty girls always hang out together!
PSST
If Komi supports Isagi, then so do I!
PSST
...

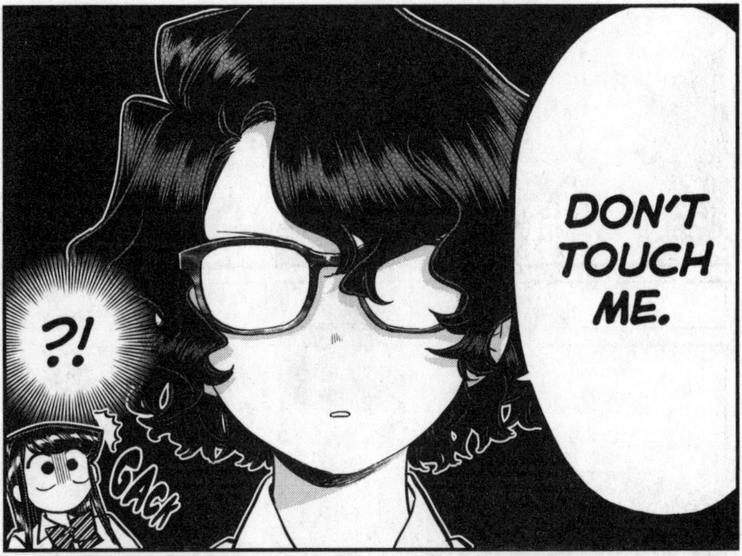
DON'T TOUCH ME.
?!
GACK

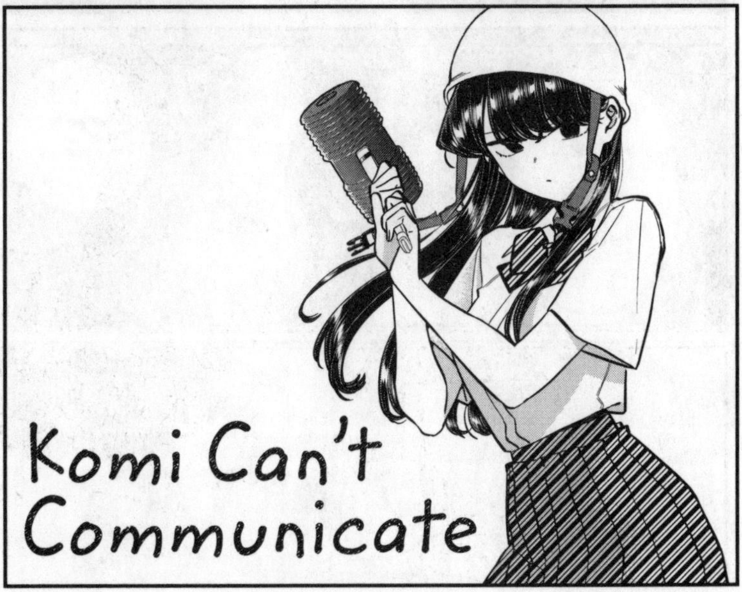
Komi Can't Communicate

Communication 199: Rock, Paper, Scissors, Hammer, Helmet!

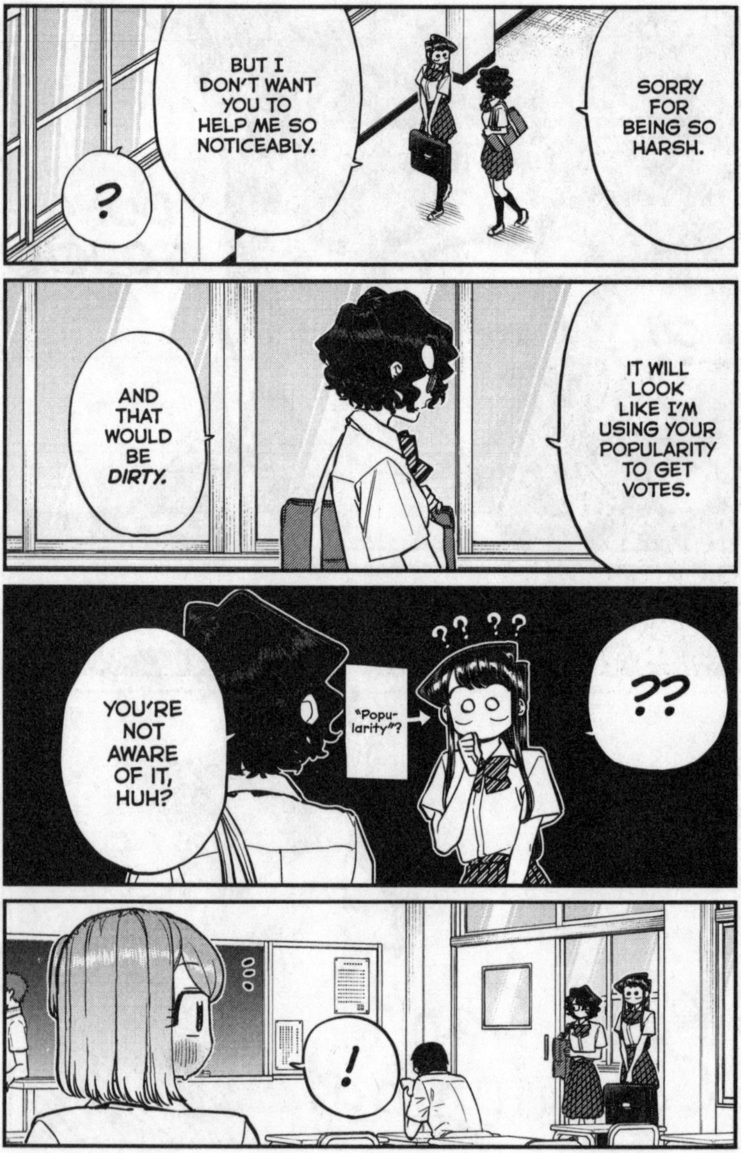
SORRY FOR BEING SO HARSH.
BUT I DON'T WANT YOU TO HELP ME SO NOTICEABLY.
?
IT WILL LOOK LIKE I'M USING YOUR POPULARITY TO GET VOTES.
AND THAT WOULD BE *DIRTY.*
??
"Popu-larity"?
YOU'RE NOT AWARE OF IT, HUH?
!

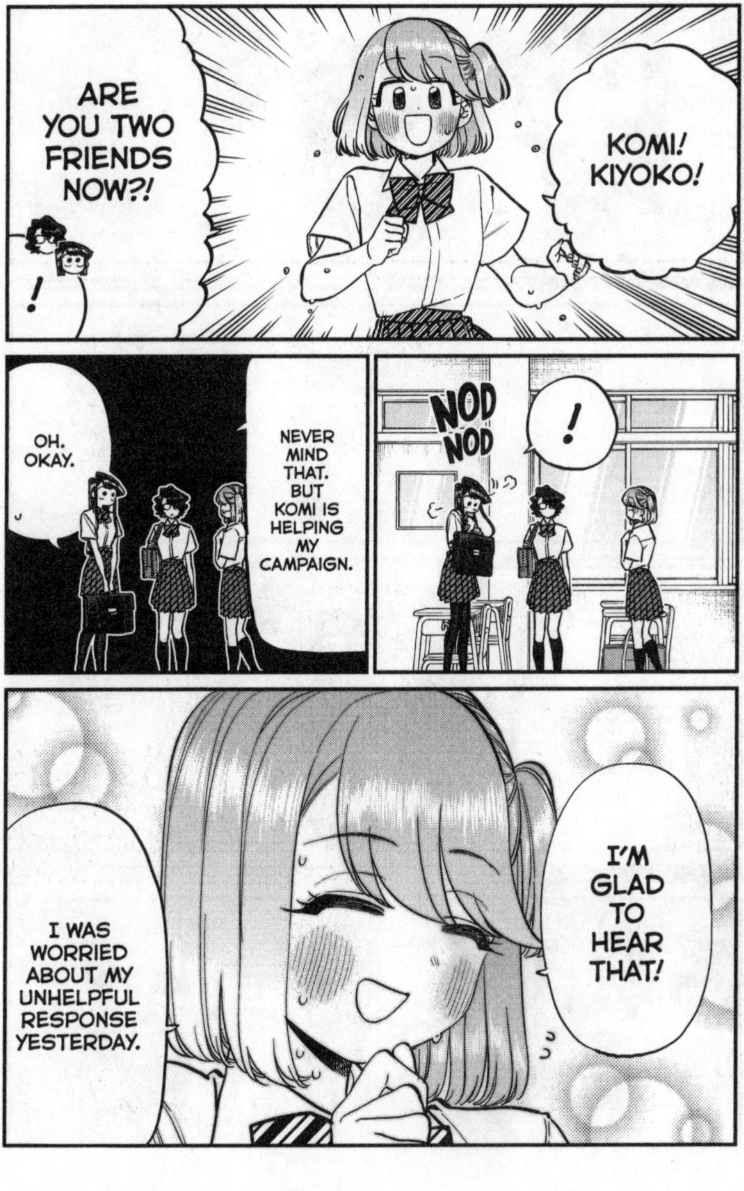
KOMI! KIYOKO!
ARE YOU TWO FRIENDS NOW?!
!
NOD NOD
!
NEVER MIND THAT. BUT KOMI IS HELPING MY CAMPAIGN.
OH. OKAY.
I'M GLAD TO HEAR THAT!
I WAS WORRIED ABOUT MY UNHELPFUL RESPONSE YESTERDAY.

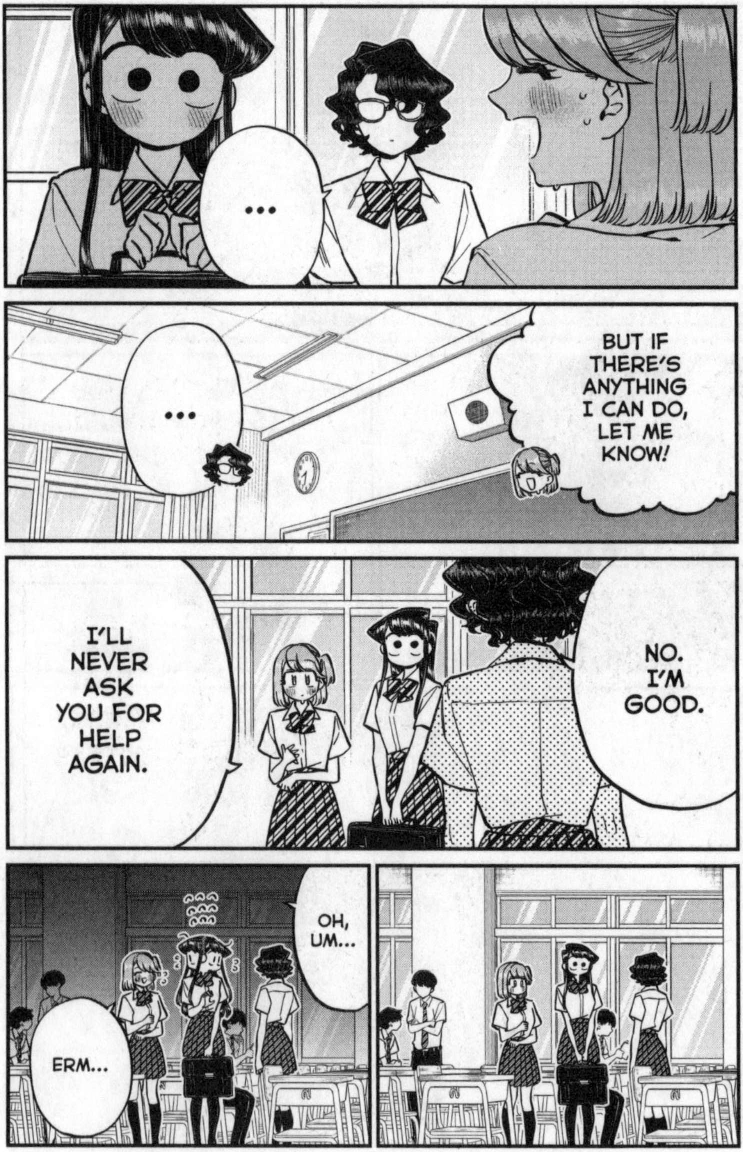
...
BUT IF THERE'S ANYTHING I CAN DO, LET ME KNOW!
...
NO. I'M GOOD.
I'LL NEVER ASK YOU FOR HELP AGAIN.
OH, UM...
ERM...

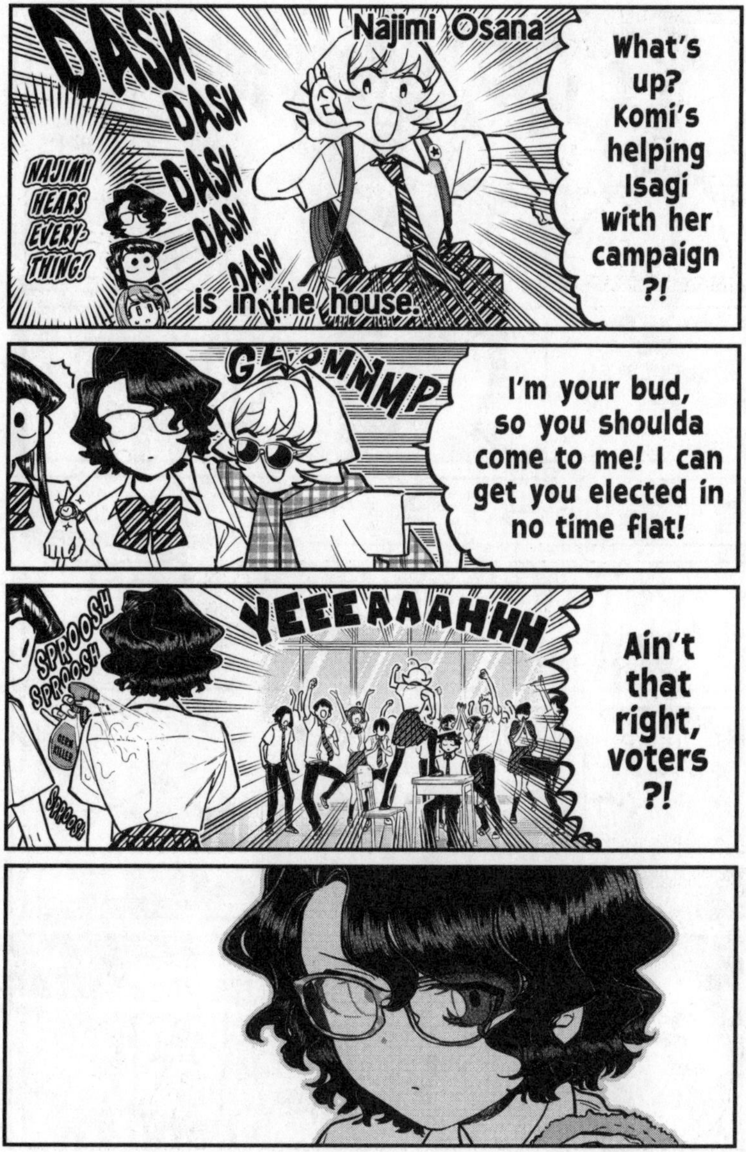
What's up? Komi's helping Isagi with her campaign?!
Najimi Osana
is in the house.
DASH DASH DASH DASH DASH
NAJIMI HEARS EVERYTHING!
I'm your bud, so you shoulda come to me! I can get you elected in no time flat!
GLOMMMP
Ain't that right, voters?!
YEEEAAAHHH
SPROOSH SPROOSH
SPROOSH
GERM KILLER

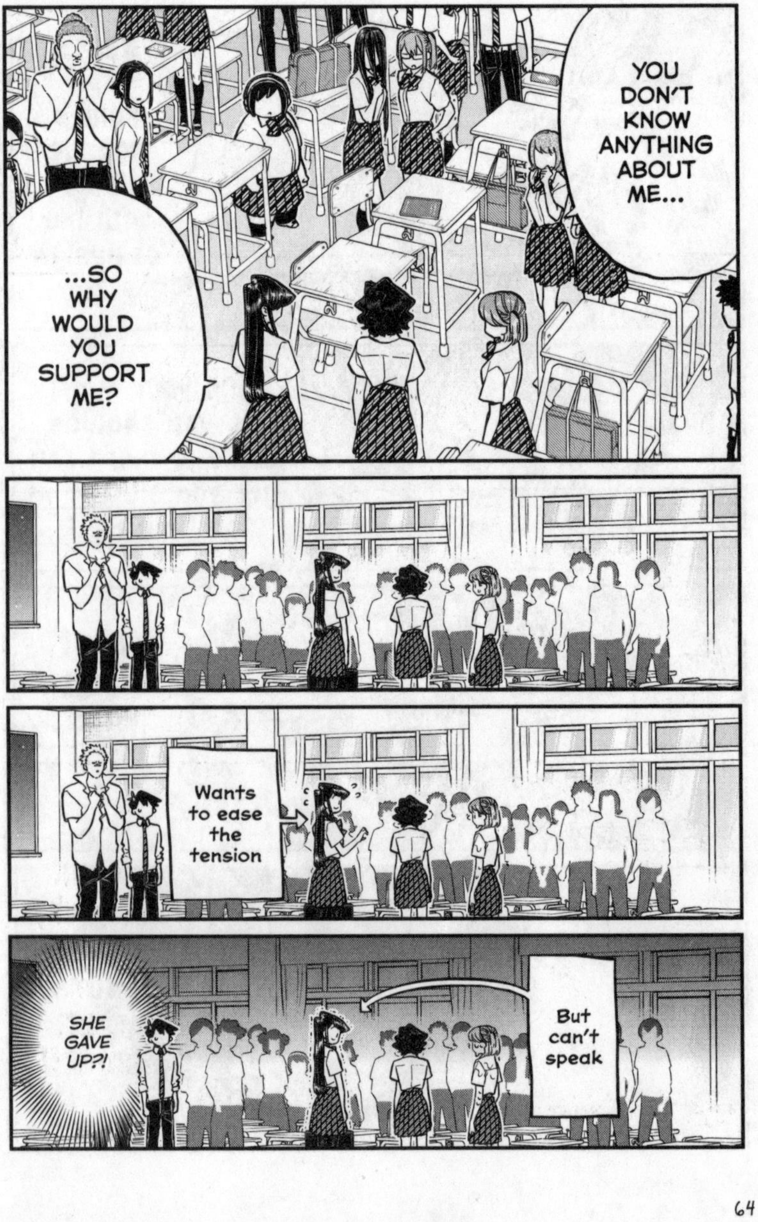
YOU DON'T KNOW ANYTHING ABOUT ME...
...SO WHY WOULD YOU SUPPORT ME?
Wants to ease the tension
But can't speak
SHE GAVE UP?!

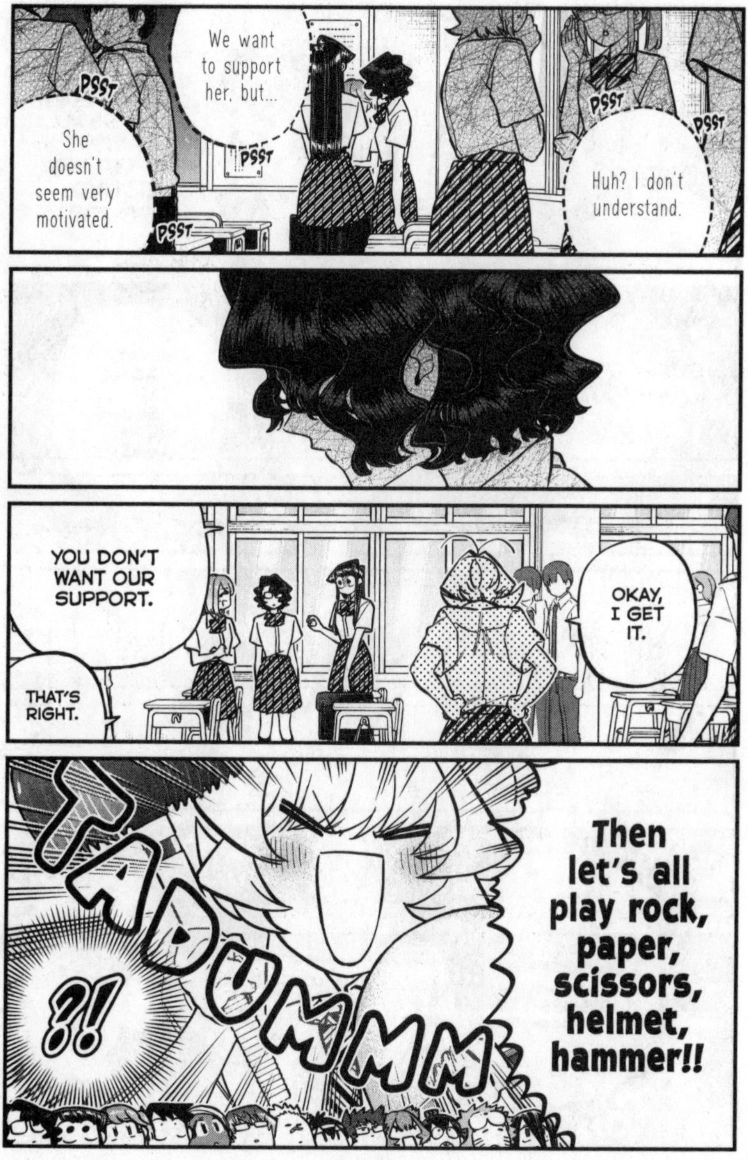
PSST
PSST
Huh? I don't understand.
We want to support her, but...
PSST
PSST
She doesn't seem very motivated.
PSST
OKAY, I GET IT.
YOU DON'T WANT OUR SUPPORT.
THAT'S RIGHT.
Then let's all play rock, paper, scissors, helmet, hammer!!
TADUMMM
?!

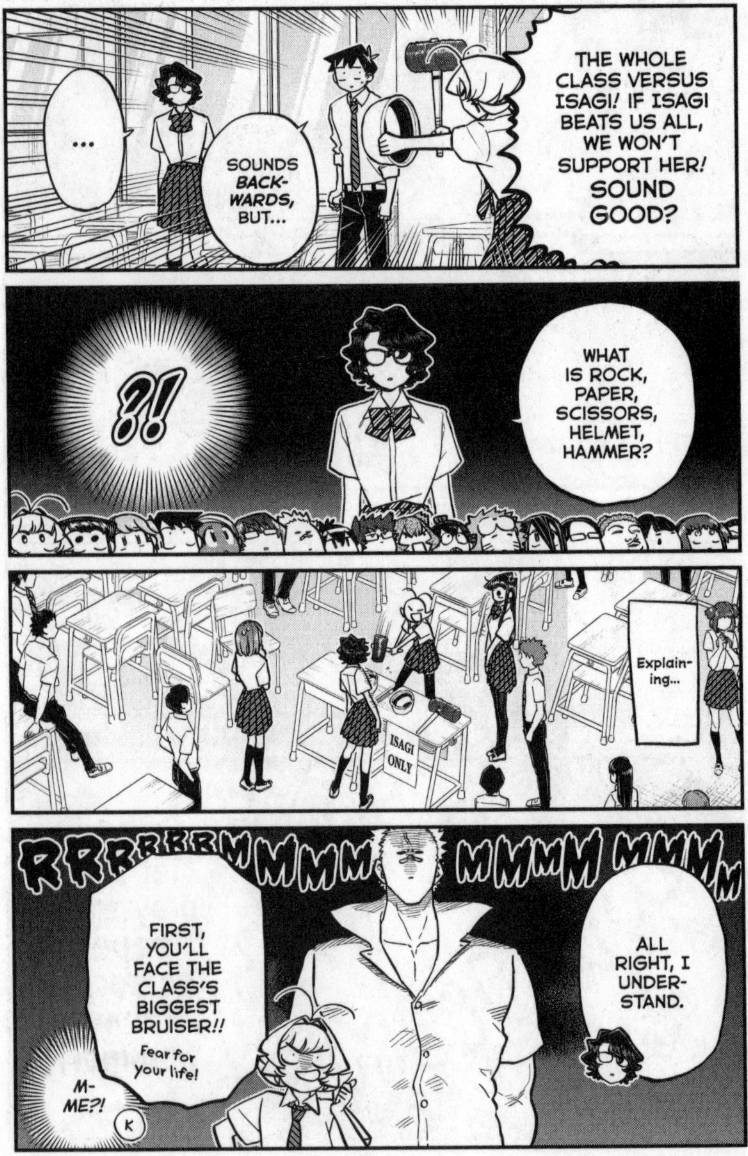
THE WHOLE CLASS VERSUS ISAGI! IF ISAGI BEATS US ALL, WE WON'T SUPPORT HER! SOUND GOOD?
SOUNDS BACKWARDS, BUT...
...
WHAT IS ROCK, PAPER, SCISSORS, HELMET, HAMMER?
?!
Explaining...
ISAGI ONLY
RRRRRMMMMM MMMM MMMMM
ALL RIGHT, I UNDERSTAND.
FIRST, YOU'LL FACE THE CLASS'S BIGGEST BRUISER!!
Fear for your life!
M-ME?!
K

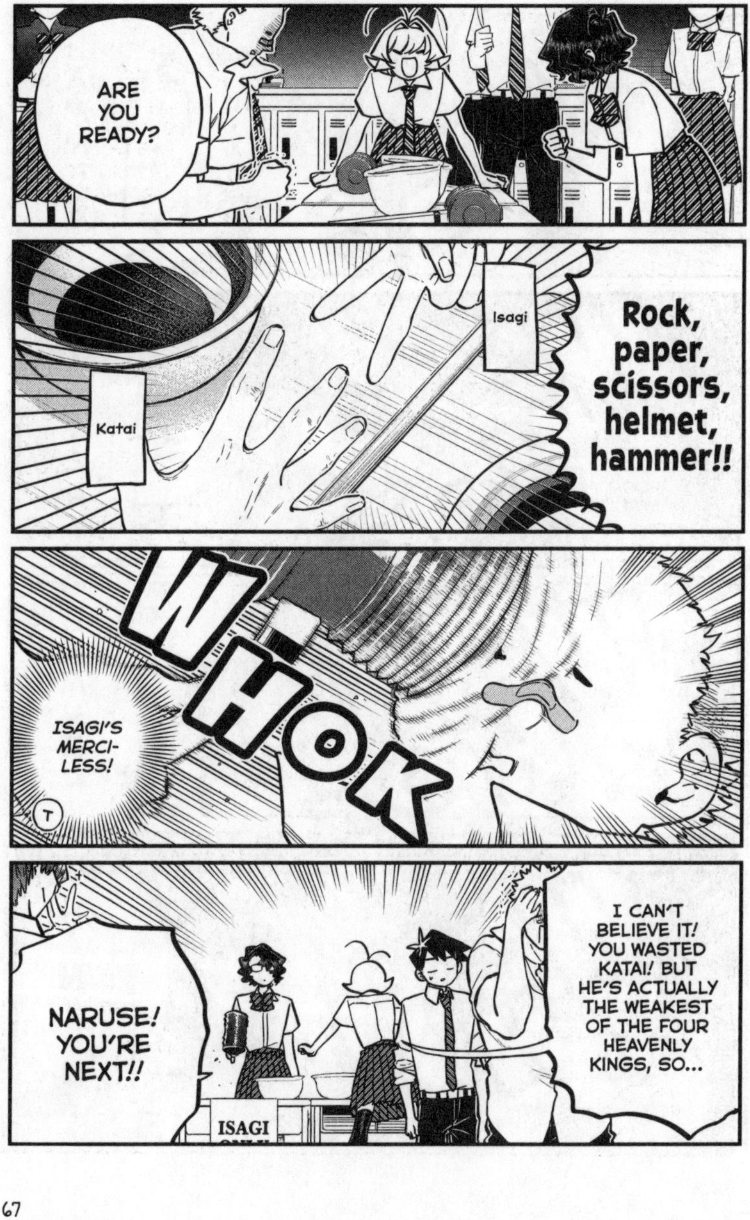
ARE YOU READY?
Rock, paper, scissors, helmet, hammer!!
Isagi
Katai
WHOK
ISAGI'S MERCI-LESS!
I CAN'T BELIEVE IT! YOU WASTED KATAI! BUT HE'S ACTUALLY THE WEAKEST OF THE FOUR HEAVENLY KINGS, SO...
NARUSE! YOU'RE NEXT!!
ISAGI

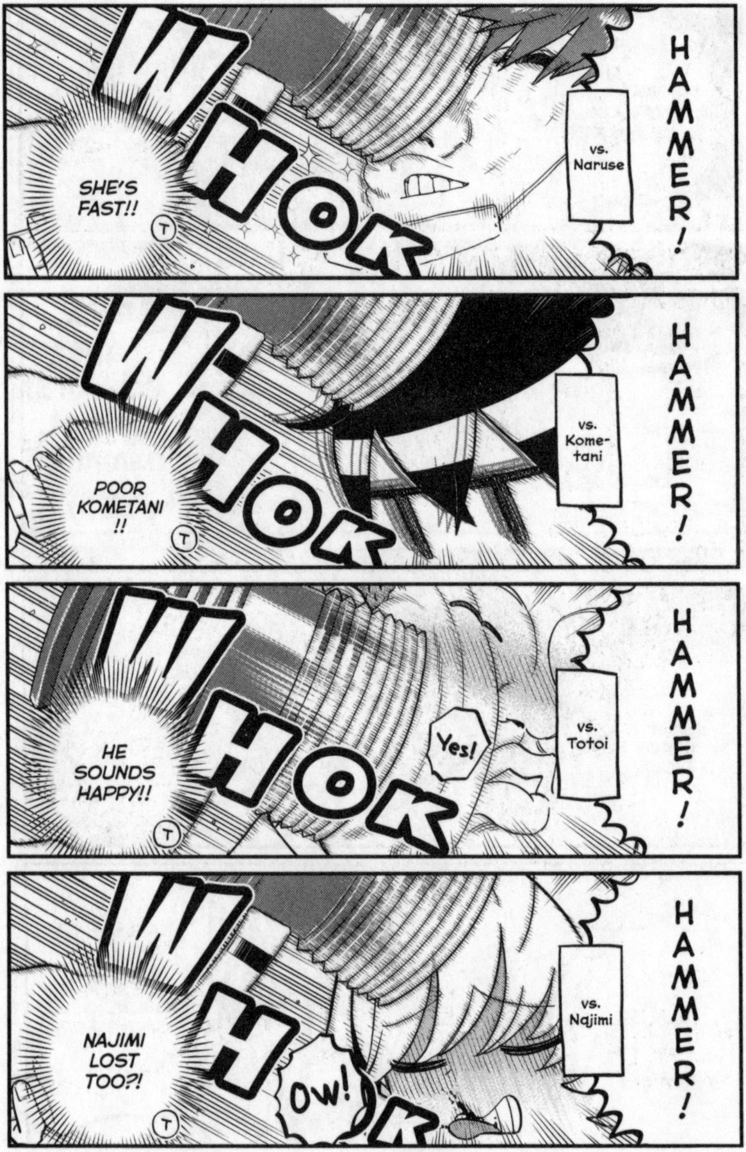
HAMMER!
vs. Naruse
WHOK
SHE'S FAST!!
HAMMER!
vs. Kome-tani
WHOK
POOR KOMETANI !!
HAMMER!
vs. Totoi
Yes!
WHOK
HE SOUNDS HAPPY!!
HAMMER!
vs. Najimi
OW!
NAJIMI LOST TOO?!

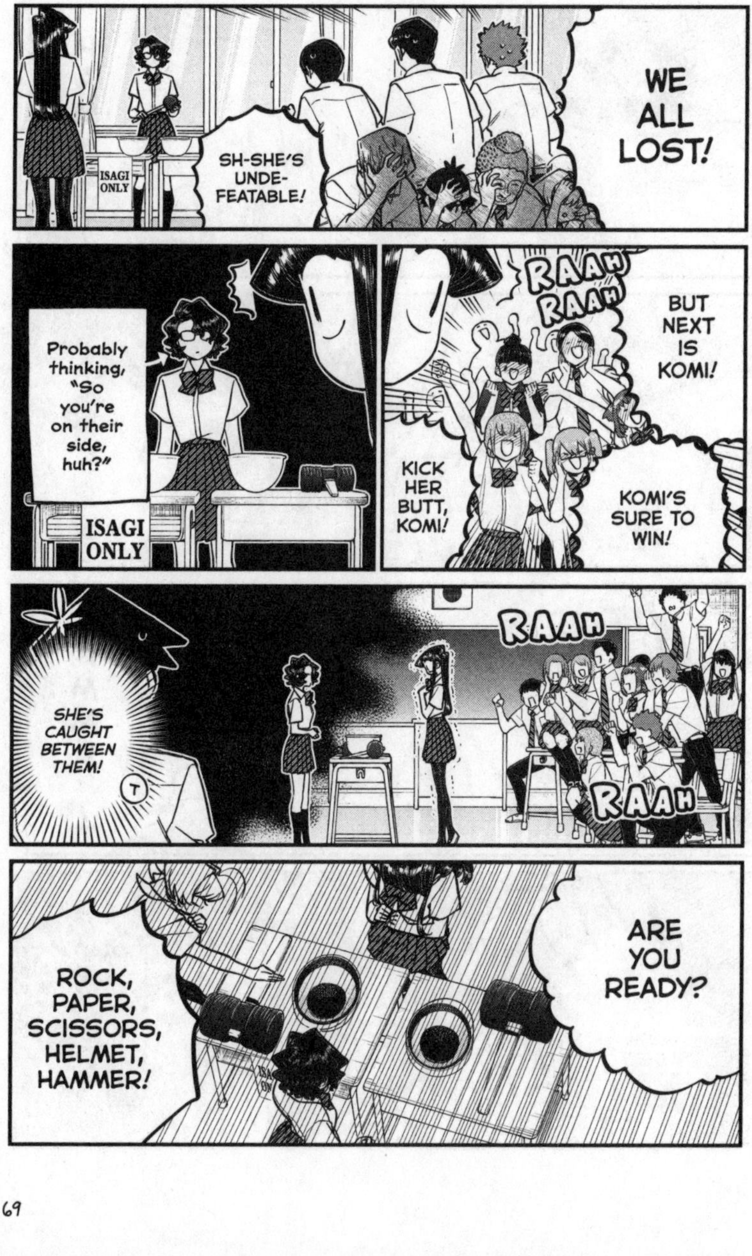

WE ALL LOST!
SH-SHE'S UNDE-FEATABLE!
ISAGI ONLY
RAAH RAAH
BUT NEXT IS KOMI!
KOMI'S SURE TO WIN!
KICK HER BUTT, KOMI!
Probably thinking, "So you're on their side, huh?"
ISAGI ONLY
RAAH
RAAH
SHE'S CAUGHT BETWEEN THEM!
T
ARE YOU READY?
ROCK, PAPER, SCISSORS, HELMET, HAMMER!

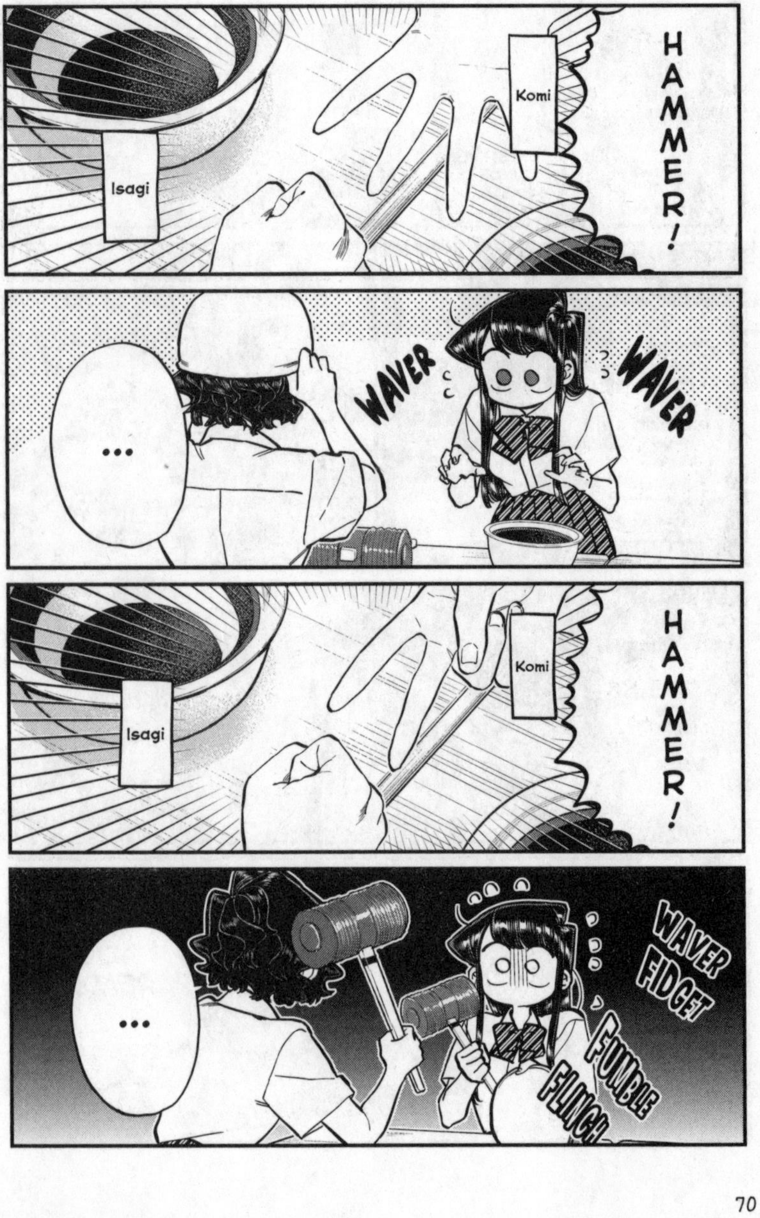
HAMMER!
Komi
Isagi
WAVER
WAVER
...
HAMMER!
Komi
Isagi
WAVER
FIDGET
FUMBLE
FLINCH
...

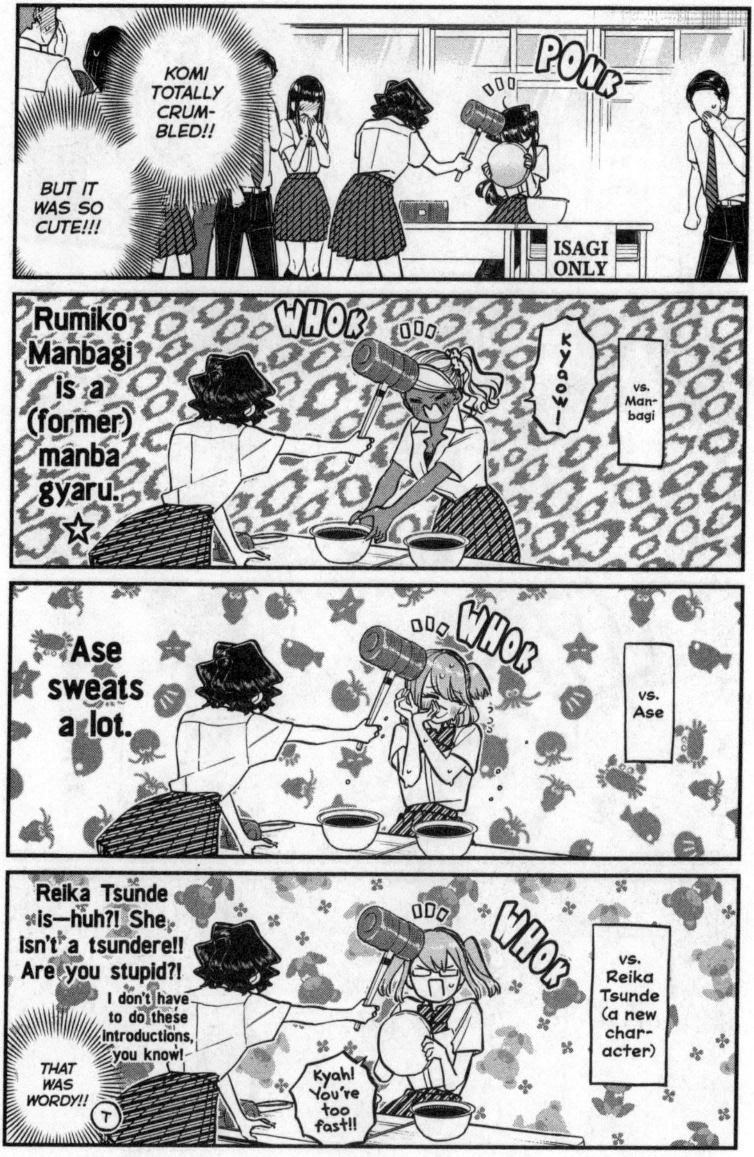
PONK
ISAGI ONLY
KOMI TOTALLY CRUMBLED!!
BUT IT WAS SO CUTE!!!
vs. Manbagi
Kyaow!
WHOK
Rumiko Manbagi is a (former) manba gyaru. ☆
vs. Ase
WHOK
Ase sweats a lot.
vs. Reika Tsunde (a new character)
WHOK
Kyah! You're too fast!!
Reika Tsunde is—huh?! She isn't a tsundere!! Are you stupid?!
I don't have to do these introductions, you know!
THAT WAS WORDY!!

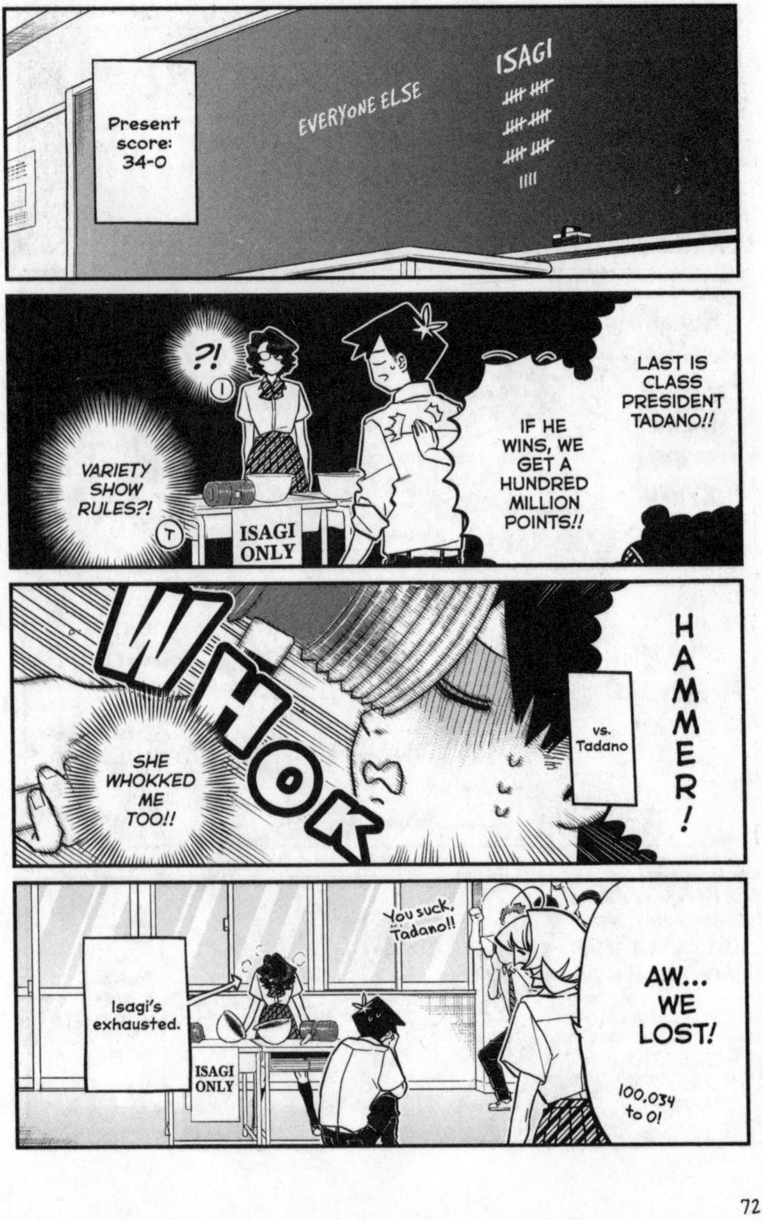
ISAGI
EVERYONE ELSE
Present score: 34-0
LAST IS CLASS PRESIDENT TADANO!!
IF HE WINS, WE GET A HUNDRED MILLION POINTS!!
?!
I
VARIETY SHOW RULES?!
T
ISAGI ONLY
HAMMER!
vs. Tadano
WHOK
SHE WHOKKED ME TOO!!
AW... WE LOST!
100,034 to 0!
You suck, Tadano!!
Isagi's exhausted.
ISAGI ONLY

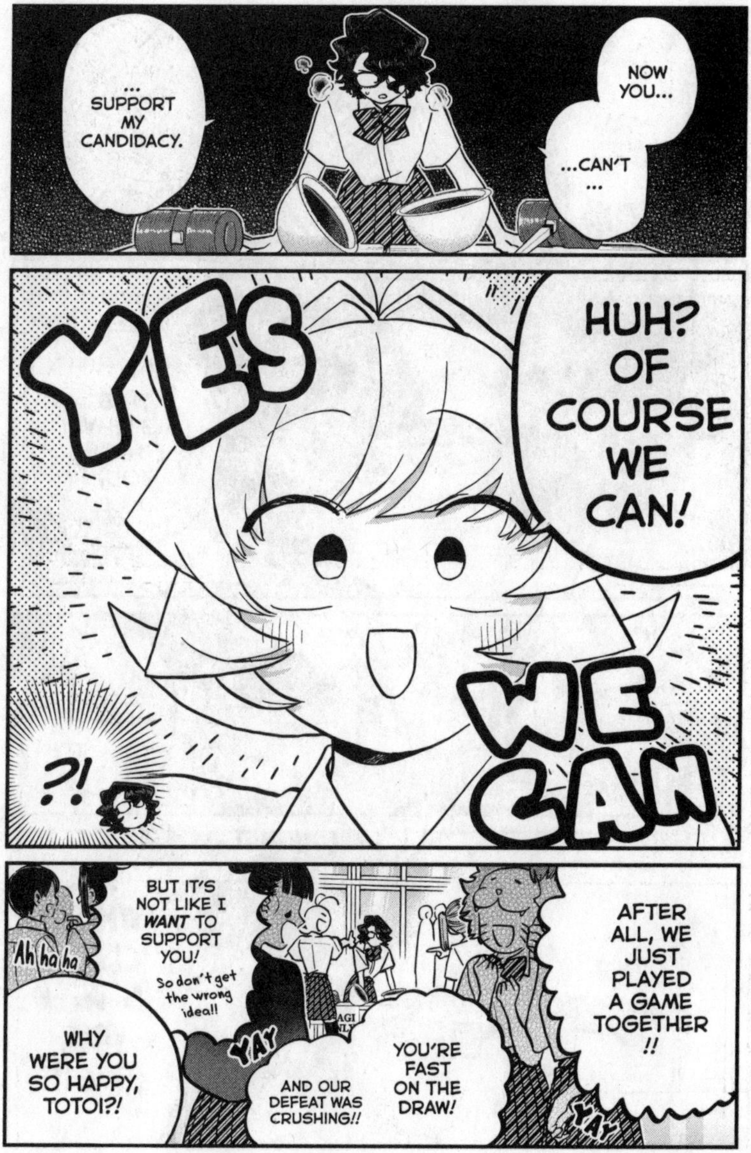
NOW YOU...
...CAN'T ...
... SUPPORT MY CANDIDACY.
HUH? OF COURSE WE CAN!
YES WE CAN
?!
AFTER ALL, WE JUST PLAYED A GAME TOGETHER!!
YAY
YOU'RE FAST ON THE DRAW!
AND OUR DEFEAT WAS CRUSHING!!
YAY
BUT IT'S NOT LIKE I *WANT* TO SUPPORT YOU!
So don't get the wrong idea!!
WHY WERE YOU SO HAPPY, TOTOI?!
Ah ha ha

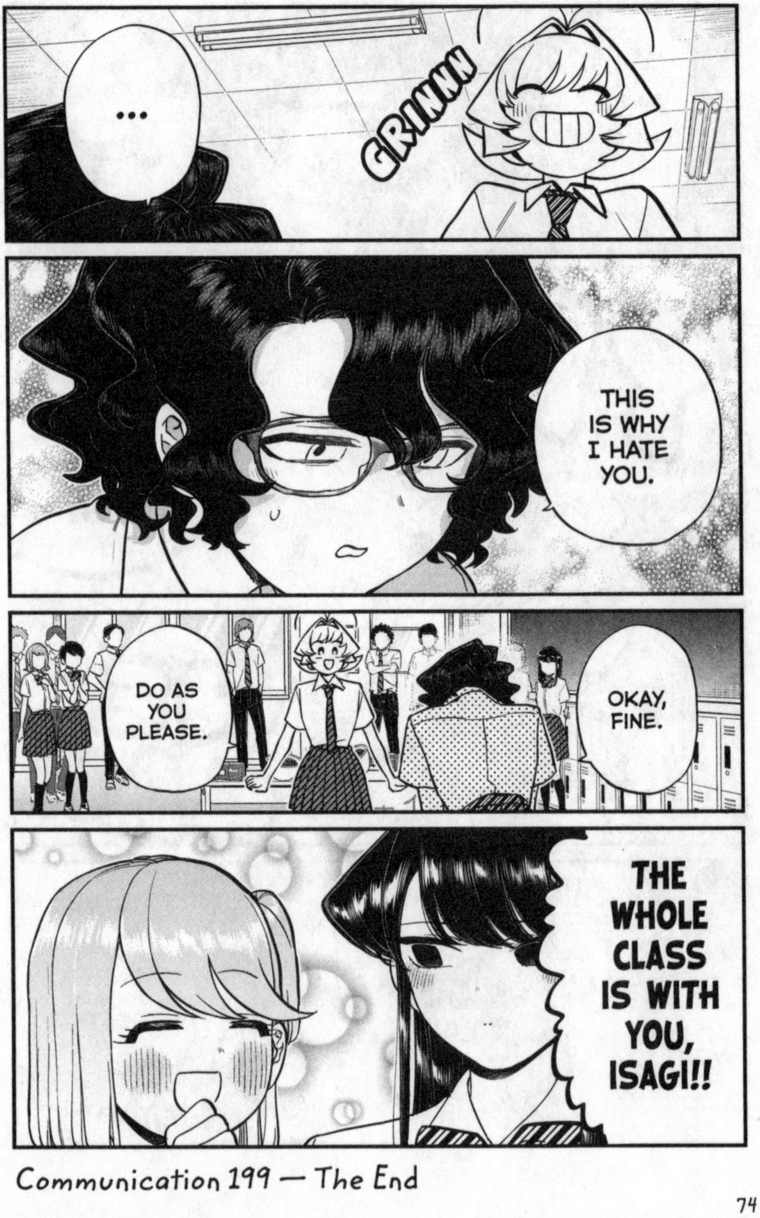
GRINNN
...
THIS IS WHY I HATE YOU.
OKAY, FINE.
DO AS YOU PLEASE.
THE WHOLE CLASS IS WITH YOU, ISAGI!!

Communication 199 — The End

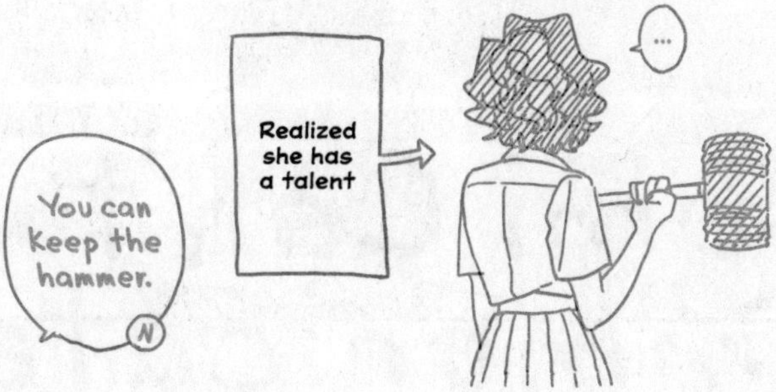
...
Realized she has a talent
You can keep the hammer.
N

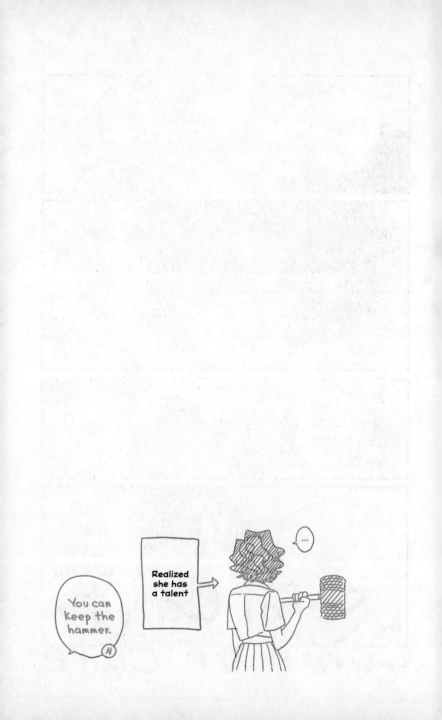

# Komi Can't
# Communicate

# Komi Can’t Communicate

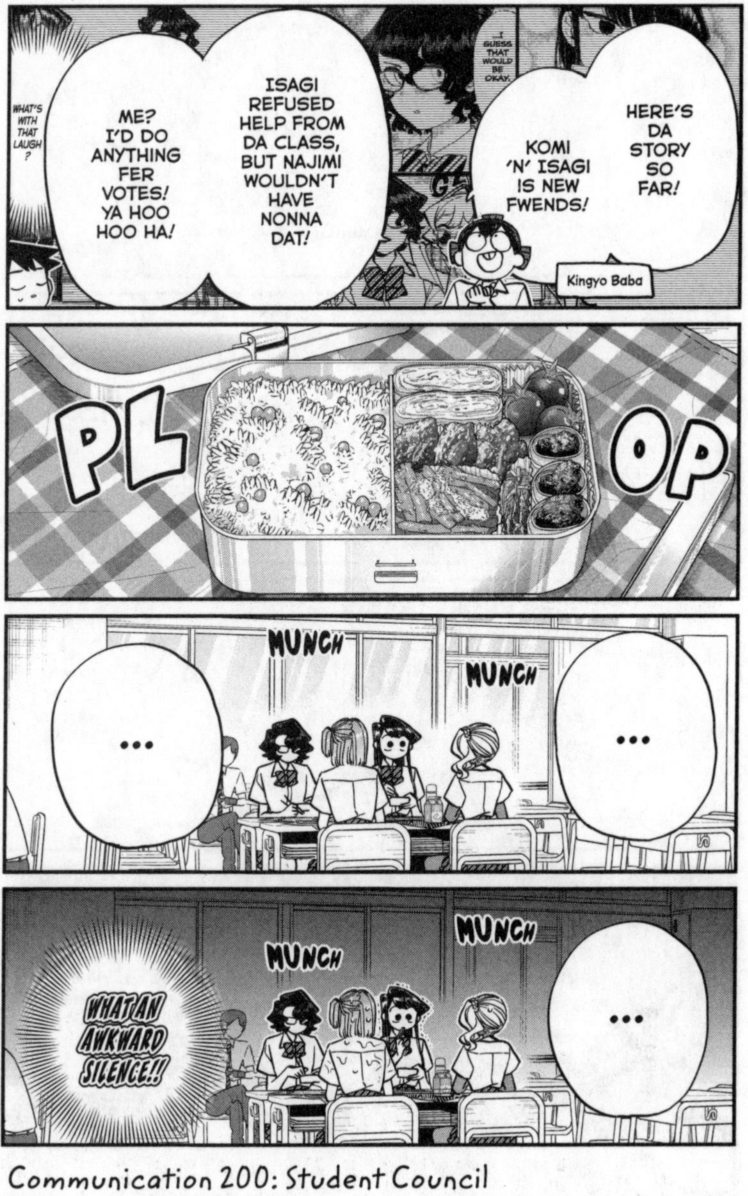
HERE’S DA STORY SO FAR!
KOMI ’N’ ISAGI IS NEW FWENDS!
Kingyo Baba
...I GUESS THAT WOULD BE OKAY.
ISAGI REFUSED HELP FROM DA CLASS, BUT NAJIMI WOULDN’T HAVE NONNA DAT!
ME? I’D DO ANYTHING FER VOTES! YA HOO HOO HA!
WHAT’S WITH THAT LAUGH?
PL OP
...
MUNCH
MUNCH
...
...
MUNCH
MUNCH
WHAT AN AWKWARD SILENCE!!

Communication 200: Student Council

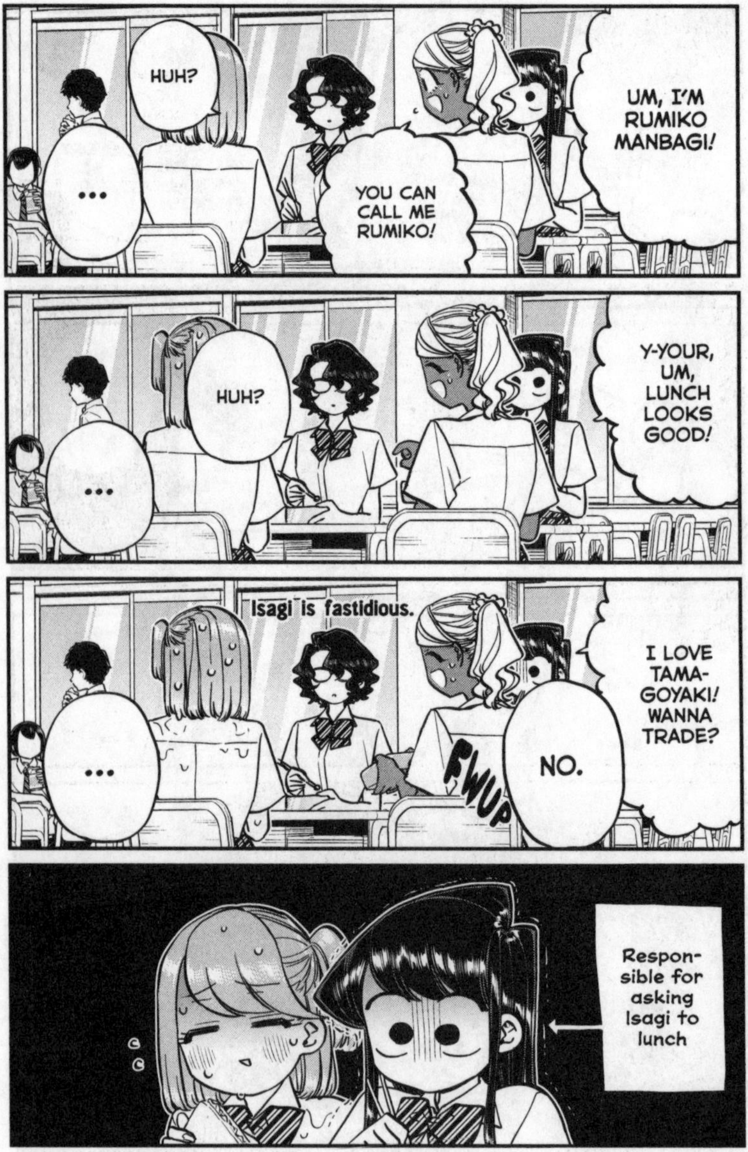
UM, I'M RUMIKO MANBAGI!
YOU CAN CALL ME RUMIKO!
HUH?
...
Y-YOUR, UM, LUNCH LOOKS GOOD!
HUH?
...
I LOVE TAMA-GOYAKI! WANNA TRADE?
NO.
FWUP
Isagi is fastidious.
...
Respon-sible for asking Isagi to lunch

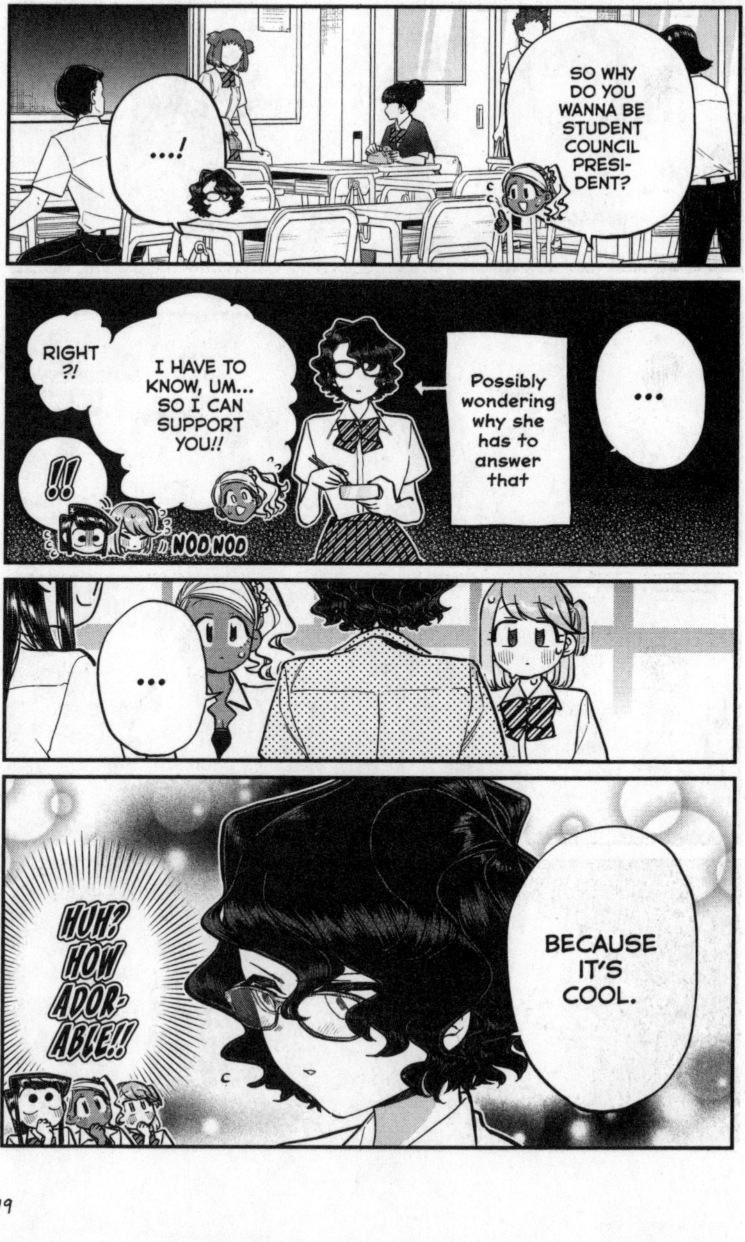
SO WHY DO YOU WANNA BE STUDENT COUNCIL PRESIDENT?
...!
...
Possibly wondering why she has to answer that
I HAVE TO KNOW, UM... SO I CAN SUPPORT YOU!!
RIGHT?!
!!
NOD NOD
...
BECAUSE IT'S COOL.
HUH? HOW ADORABLE!!

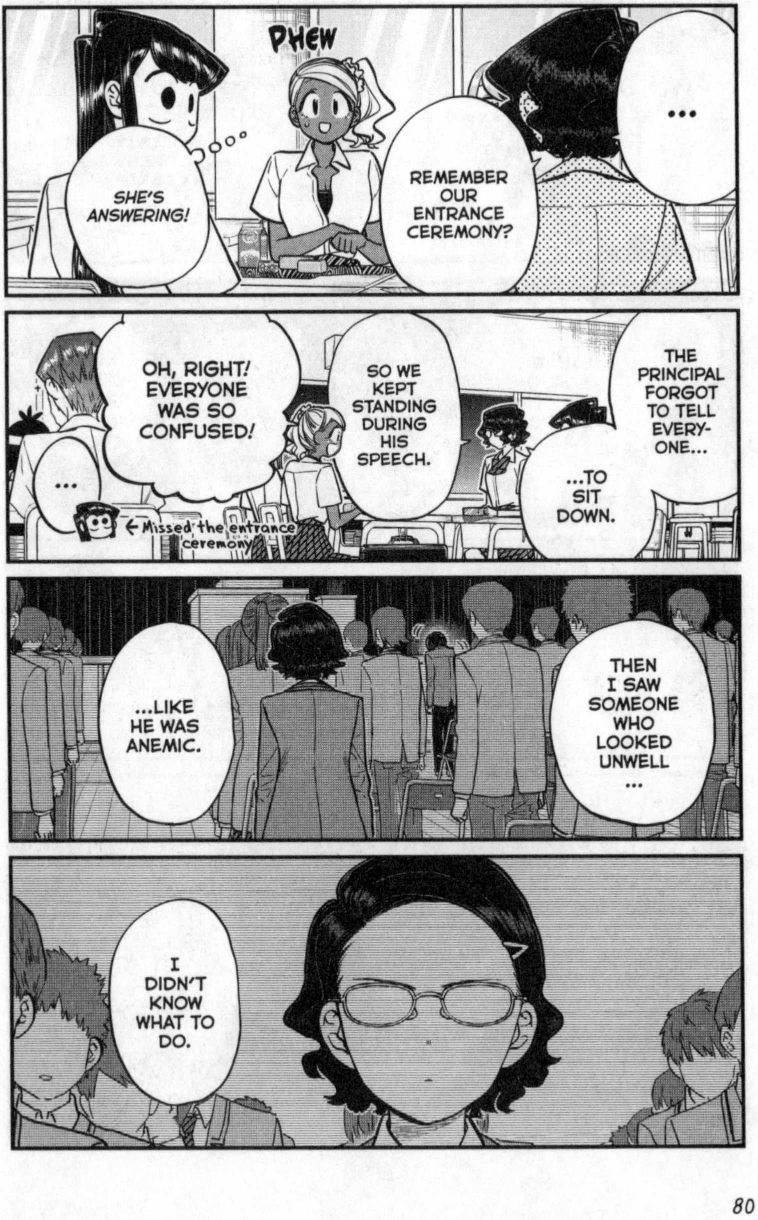
...
REMEMBER OUR ENTRANCE CEREMONY?
PHEW
SHE'S ANSWERING!
THE PRINCIPAL FORGOT TO TELL EVERY-ONE...
...TO SIT DOWN.
SO WE KEPT STANDING DURING HIS SPEECH.
OH, RIGHT! EVERYONE WAS SO CONFUSED!
...
← Missed the entrance ceremony
THEN I SAW SOMEONE WHO LOOKED UNWELL ...
...LIKE HE WAS ANEMIC.
I DIDN'T KNOW WHAT TO DO.

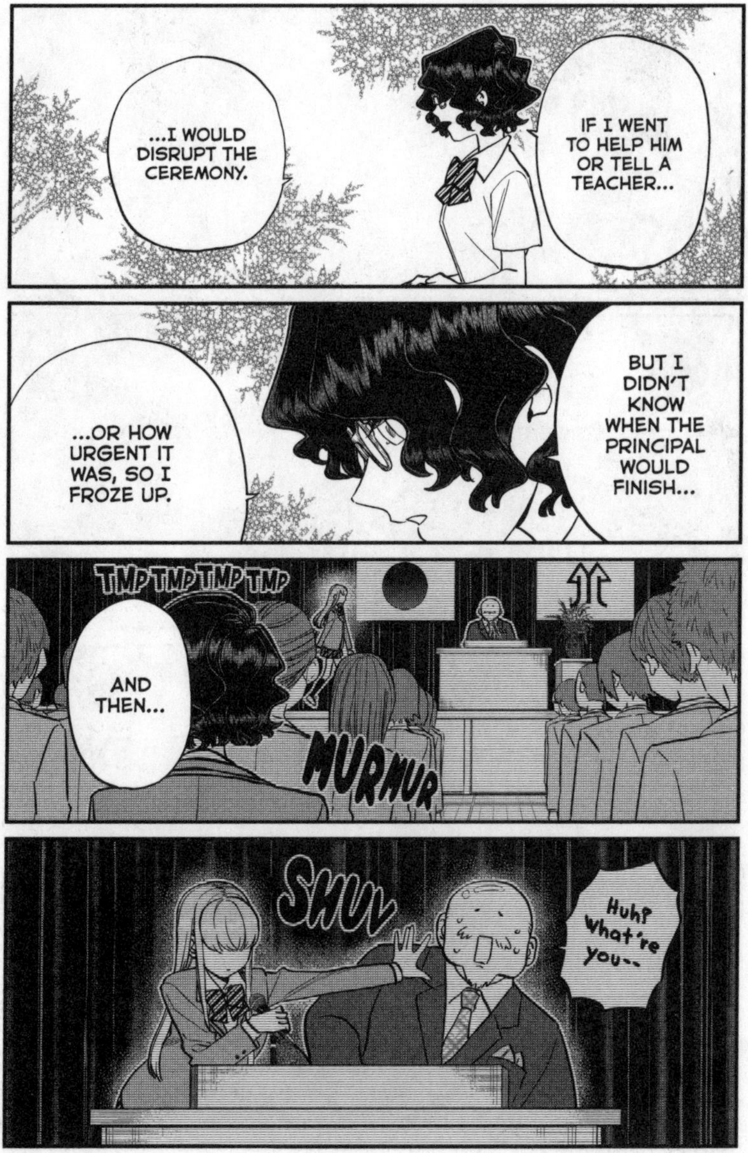
IF I WENT TO HELP HIM OR TELL A TEACHER...
...I WOULD DISRUPT THE CEREMONY.
BUT I DIDN'T KNOW WHEN THE PRINCIPAL WOULD FINISH...
...OR HOW URGENT IT WAS, SO I FROZE UP.
TMP TMP TMP TMP
AND THEN...
MURMUR
Huh? What're you--
SHUV

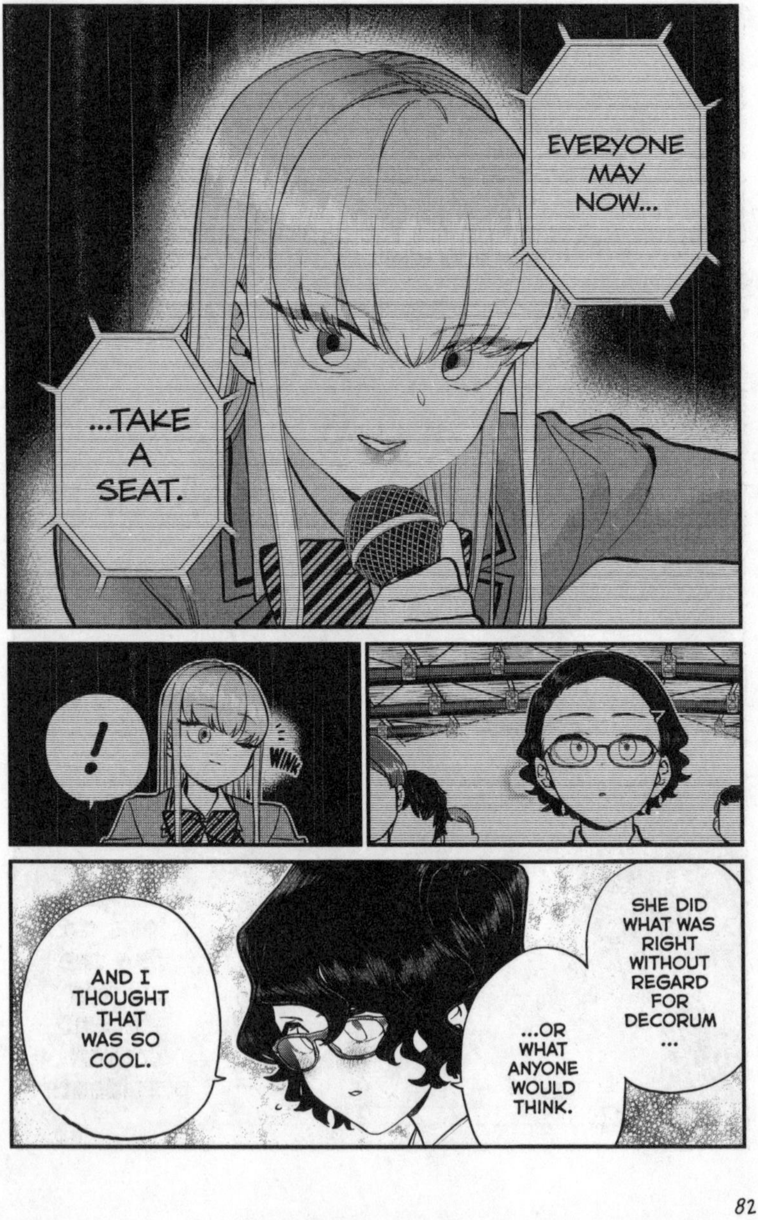
EVERYONE MAY NOW...
...TAKE A SEAT.
!
WINK
SHE DID WHAT WAS RIGHT WITHOUT REGARD FOR DECORUM ...
...OR WHAT ANYONE WOULD THINK.
AND I THOUGHT THAT WAS SO COOL.

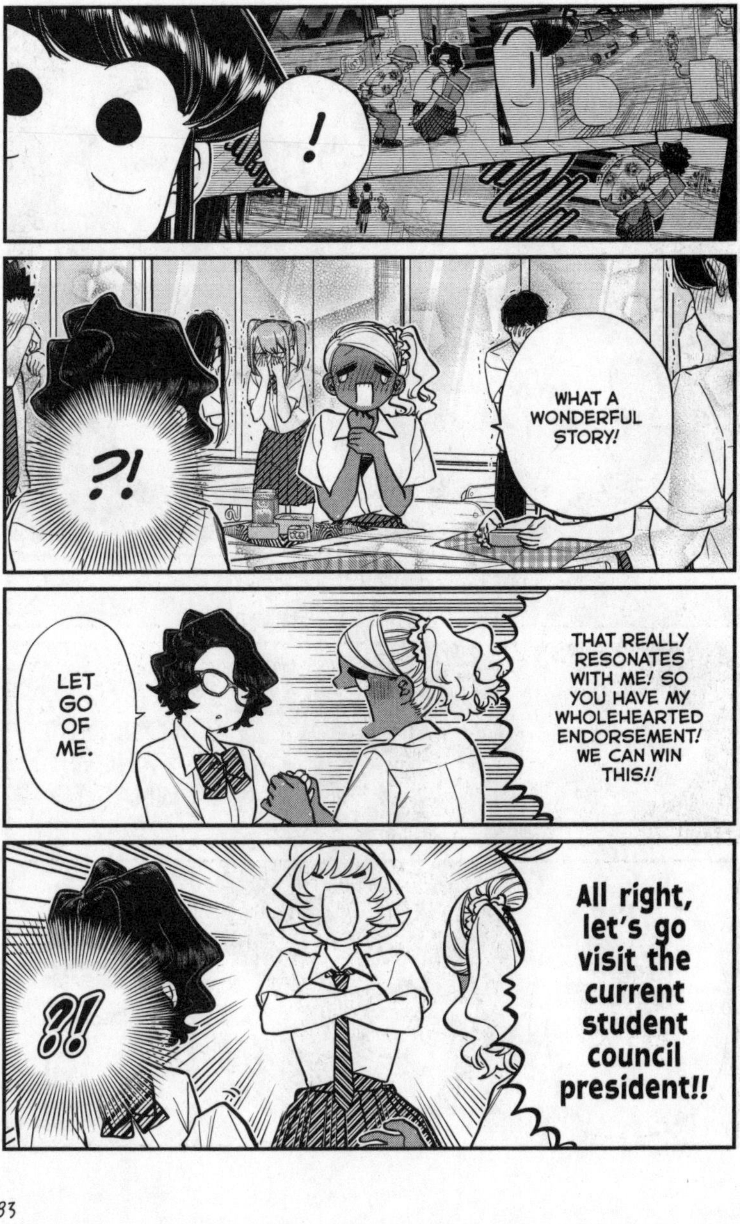
!
WHAT A WONDERFUL STORY!
?!
THAT REALLY RESONATES WITH ME! SO YOU HAVE MY WHOLEHEARTED ENDORSEMENT! WE CAN WIN THIS!!
LET GO OF ME.
All right, let's go visit the current student council president!!
?!

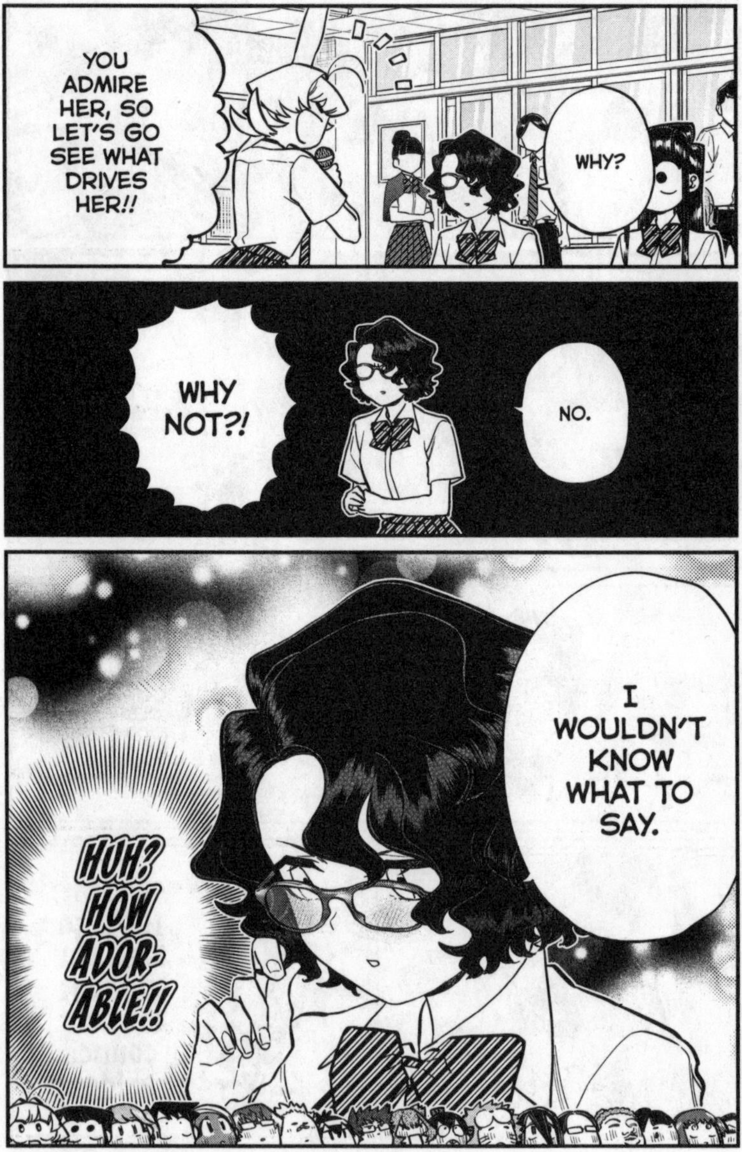
WHY?
YOU ADMIRE HER, SO LET'S GO SEE WHAT DRIVES HER!!
NO.
WHY NOT?!
I WOULDN'T KNOW WHAT TO SAY.
HUH? HOW ADOR-ABLE!!

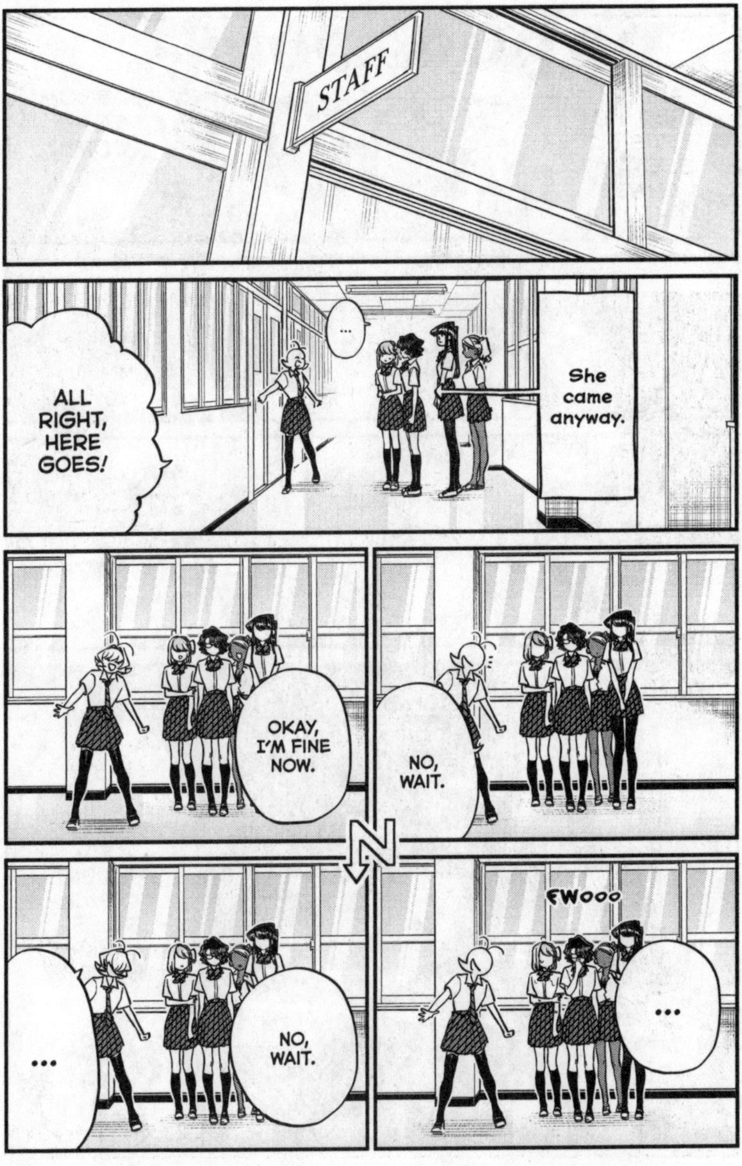
STAFF
She came anyway.
...
ALL RIGHT, HERE GOES!
NO, WAIT.
OKAY, I'M FINE NOW.
FWOOO
...
NO, WAIT.
...

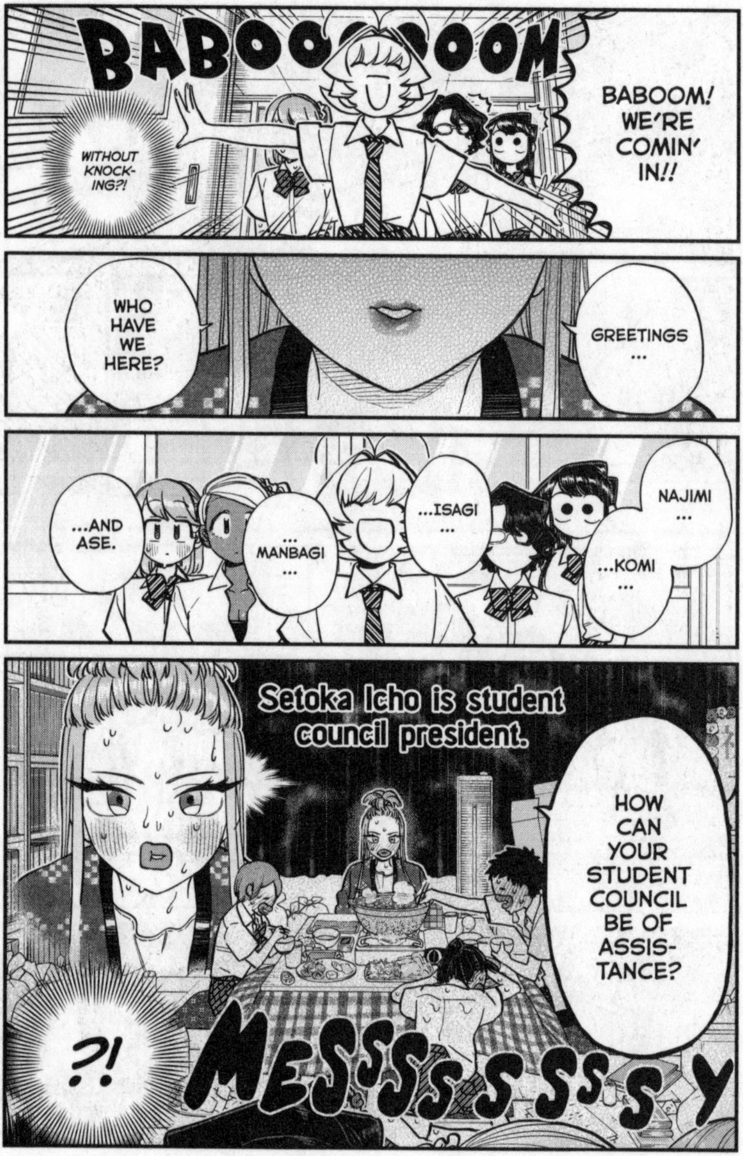
BABOOM! WE'RE COMIN' IN!!
BABOOOOOM
WITHOUT KNOCK-ING?!
GREETINGS ...
WHO HAVE WE HERE?
NAJIMI ...
...KOMI ...
...ISAGI ...
... MANBAGI ...
...AND ASE.
Setoka Icho is student council president.
HOW CAN YOUR STUDENT COUNCIL BE OF ASSIS-TANCE?
MESSSSSSSY
?!

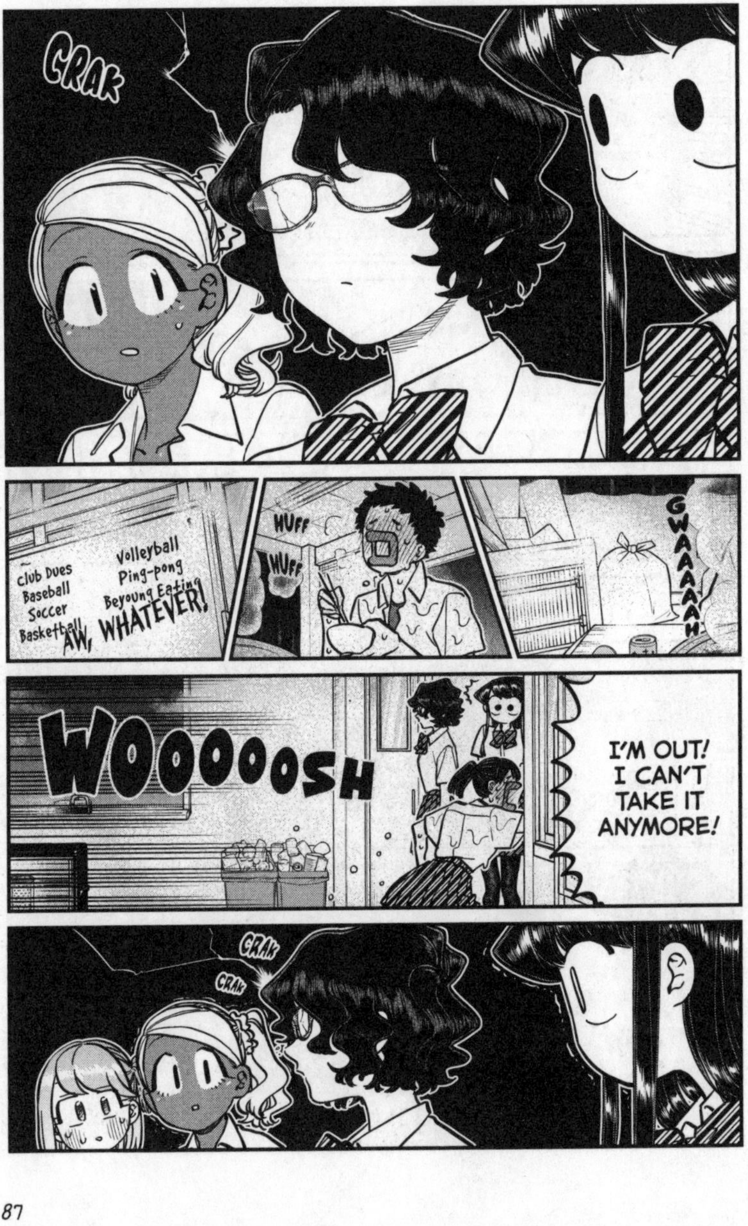
CRAK
GWAAAAAH
HUFF
HUFF
~ Club Dues
Baseball
Soccer
Basketball
Volleyball
Ping-pong
Beyoung Eating
AW, WHATEVER!
I'M OUT! I CAN'T TAKE IT ANYMORE!
WOOOOOSH
CRAK
CRAK

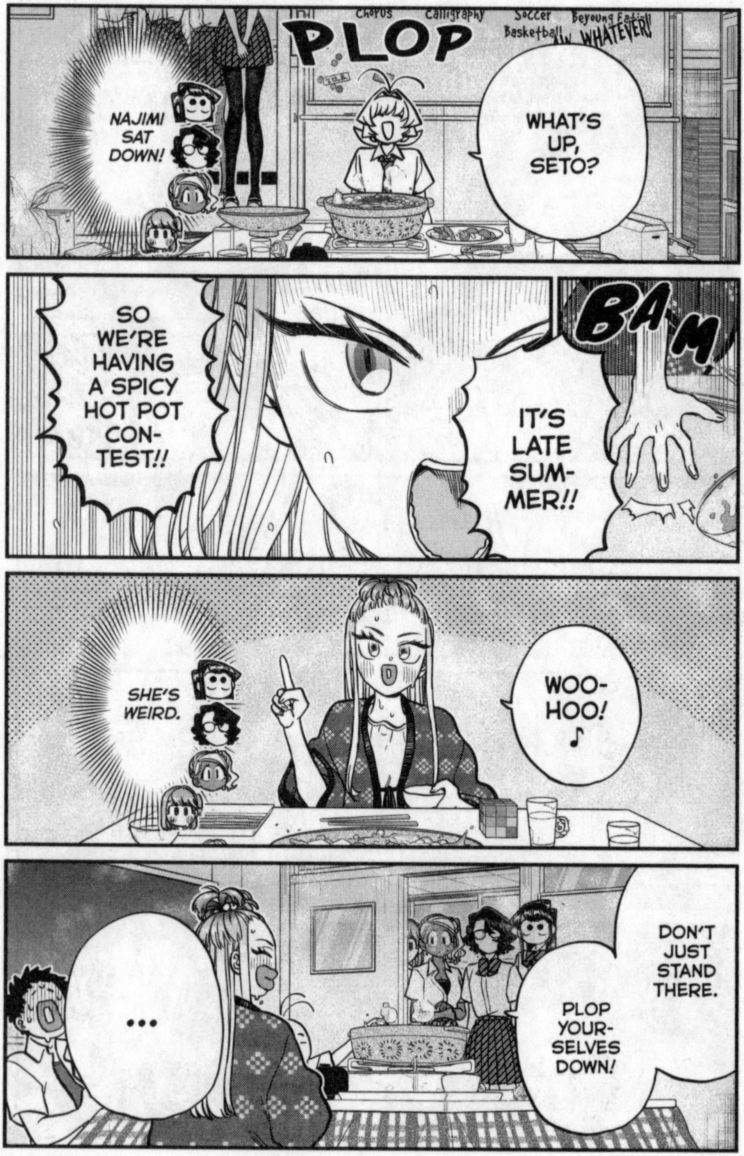

Chorus Calligraphy Soccer Basketball Aw WHATEVER!
PLOP
WHAT'S UP, SETO?
NAJIMI SAT DOWN!
BAM
IT'S LATE SUMMER!!
SO WE'RE HAVING A SPICY HOT POT CON-TEST!!
WOO-HOO! ♪
SHE'S WEIRD.
DON'T JUST STAND THERE.
PLOP YOUR-SELVES DOWN!
...

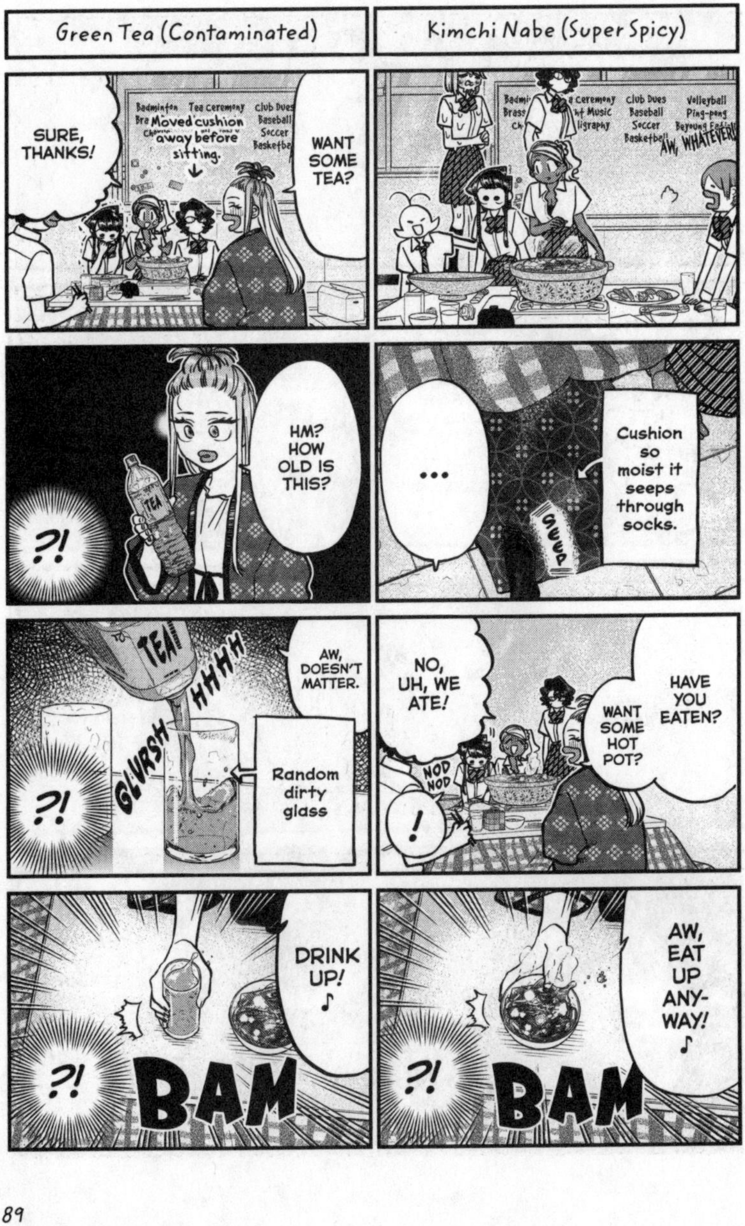
Kimchi Nabe (Super Spicy)
Club Dues
Baseball
Soccer
Basketball
Volleyball
Ping-pong
AW, WHATEVER!
...
Cushion so moist it seeps through socks.
SEEP
HAVE YOU EATEN?
WANT SOME HOT POT?
NO, UH, WE ATE!
NOD NOD
!
AW, EAT UP ANYWAY! ♪
?!
BAM
Green Tea (Contaminated)
WANT SOME TEA?
SURE, THANKS!
Badminton
Tea Ceremony
Club Dues
Baseball
Soccer
Moved cushion away before sitting.
HM? HOW OLD IS THIS?
TEA
?!
AW, DOESN'T MATTER.
TEA
GLURSHHHH
Random dirty glass
?!
DRINK UP! ♪
?!
BAM

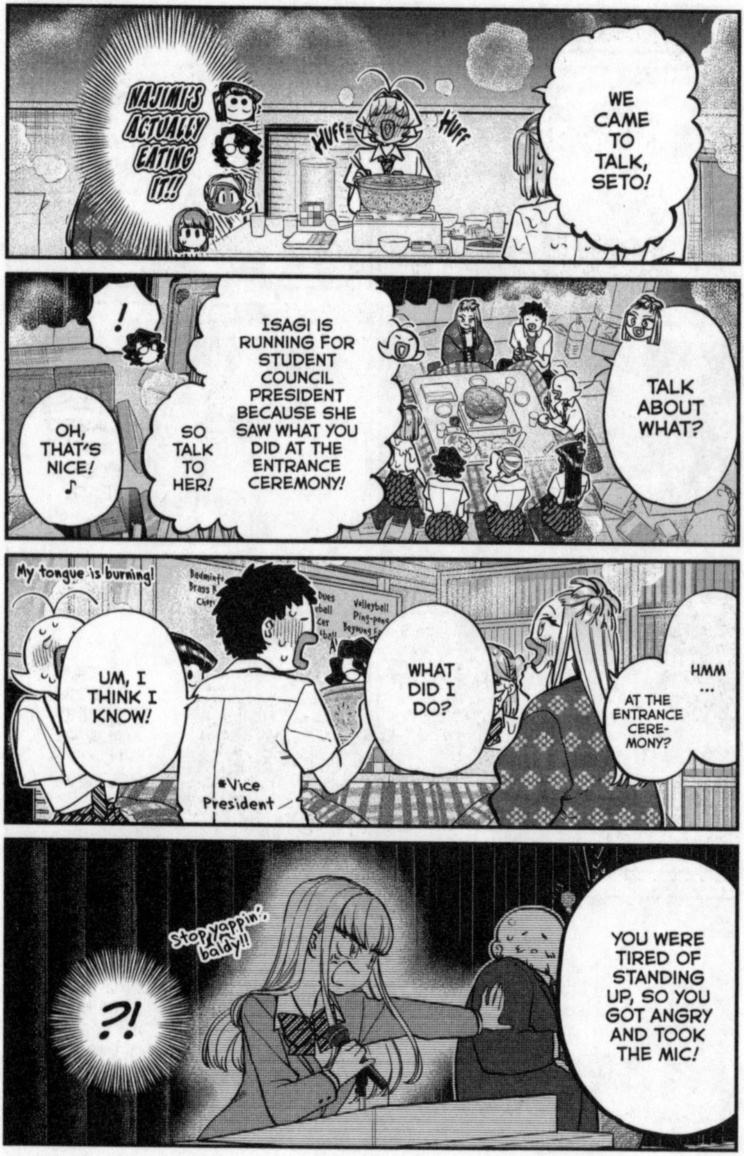
WE CAME TO TALK, SETO!
HUFF
HUFF
NAJIMI'S ACTUALLY EATING IT!!
TALK ABOUT WHAT?
ISAGI IS RUNNING FOR STUDENT COUNCIL PRESIDENT BECAUSE SHE SAW WHAT YOU DID AT THE ENTRANCE CEREMONY!
SO TALK TO HER!
!
OH, THAT'S NICE! ♪
HMM...
AT THE ENTRANCE CERE-MONY?
WHAT DID I DO?
UM, I THINK I KNOW!
#Vice President
My tongue is burning!
Volleyball
Ping-pong
YOU WERE TIRED OF STANDING UP, SO YOU GOT ANGRY AND TOOK THE MIC!
Stop yappin', baldy!!
?!

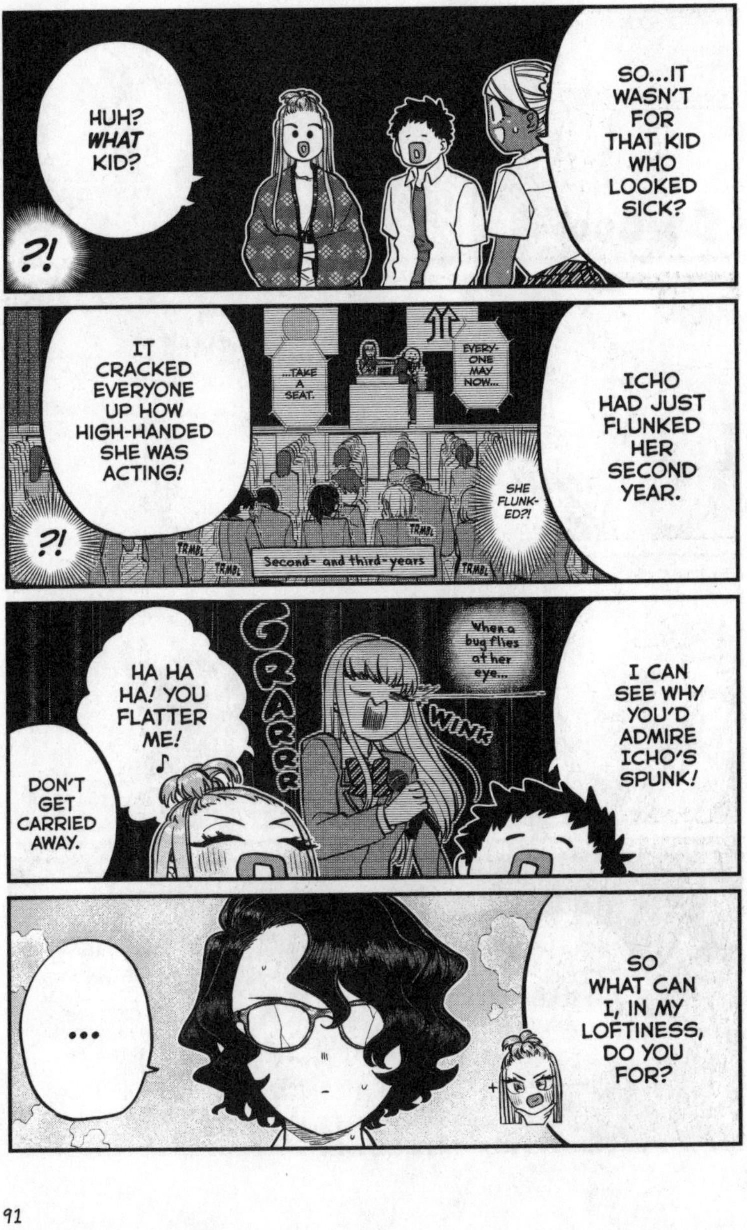

SO...IT WASN'T FOR THAT KID WHO LOOKED SICK?
HUH? WHAT KID?
?!
ICHO HAD JUST FLUNKED HER SECOND YEAR.
SHE FLUNKED?!
EVERYONE MAY NOW...
...TAKE A SEAT.
IT CRACKED EVERYONE UP HOW HIGH-HANDED SHE WAS ACTING!
TRMBL
TRMBL
Second- and third-years
TRMBL
TRMBL
?!
I CAN SEE WHY YOU'D ADMIRE ICHO'S SPUNK!
When a bug flies at her eye...
WINK
GRARRR
HA HA HA! YOU FLATTER ME! ♪
DON'T GET CARRIED AWAY.
SO WHAT CAN I, IN MY LOFTINESS, DO YOU FOR?
...

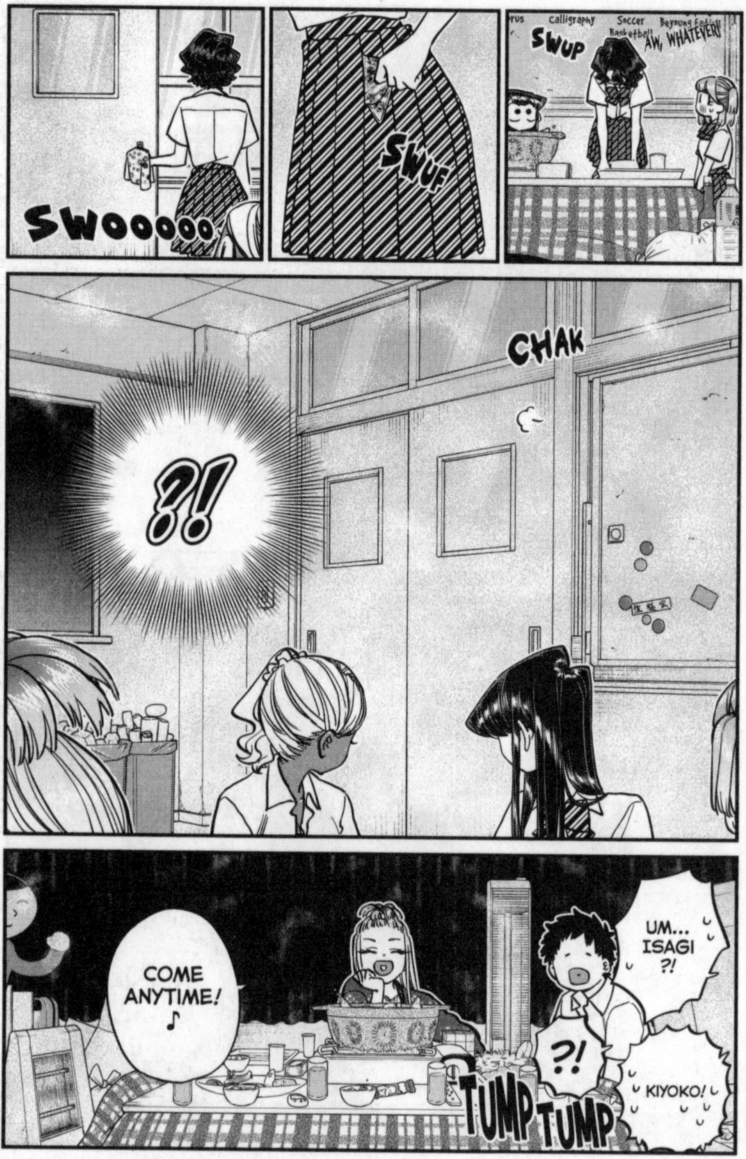
Calligraphy
Soccer
Basketball
SWUP
AW, WHATEVER!
SWUF
SWOOOOO
CHAK
?!
UM... ISAGI ?!
KIYOKO!
?!
TUMP TUMP
COME ANYTIME! ♪

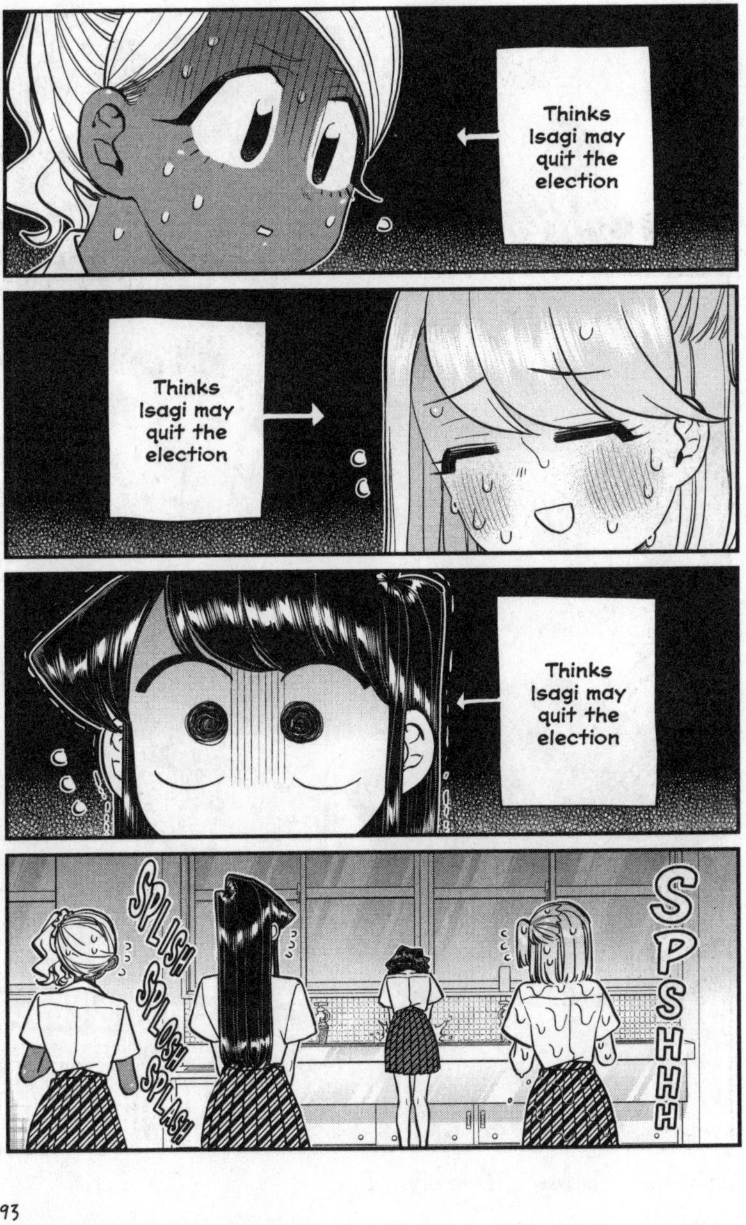
Thinks Isagi may quit the election
Thinks Isagi may quit the election
Thinks Isagi may quit the election
SPSHHH
SPLISH
SPLOSH
SPLASH

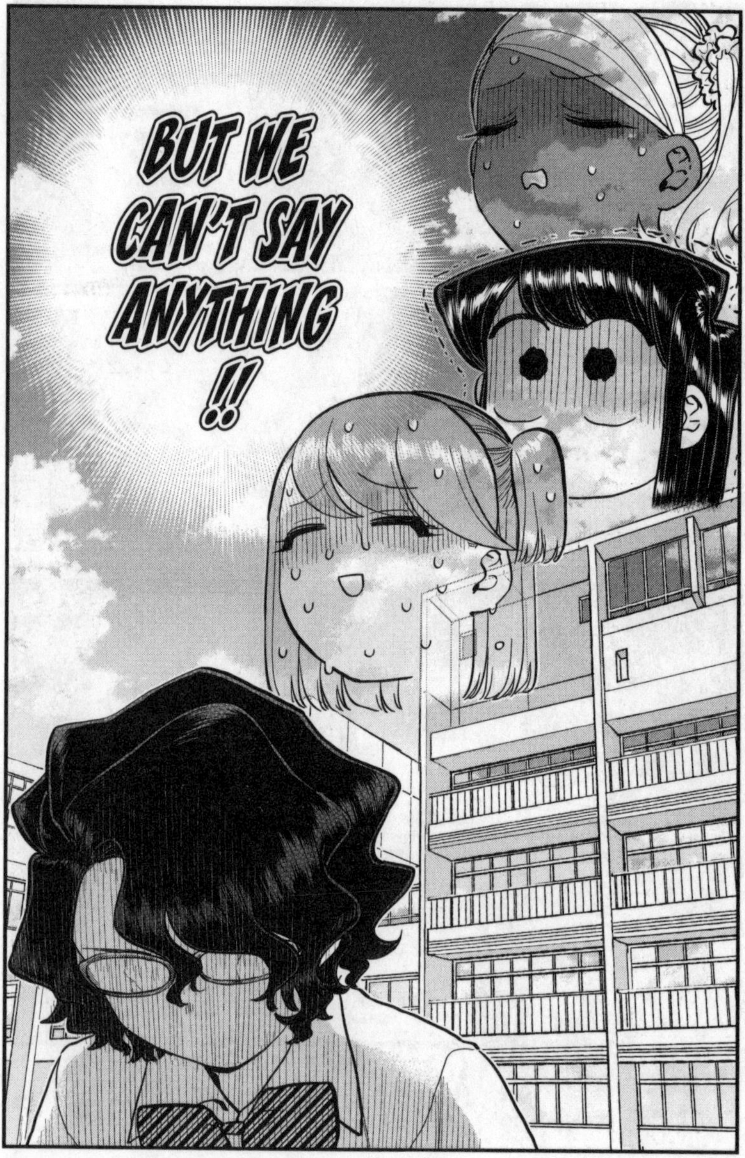
BUT WE CAN'T SAY ANYTHING !!

Communication 200 — The End

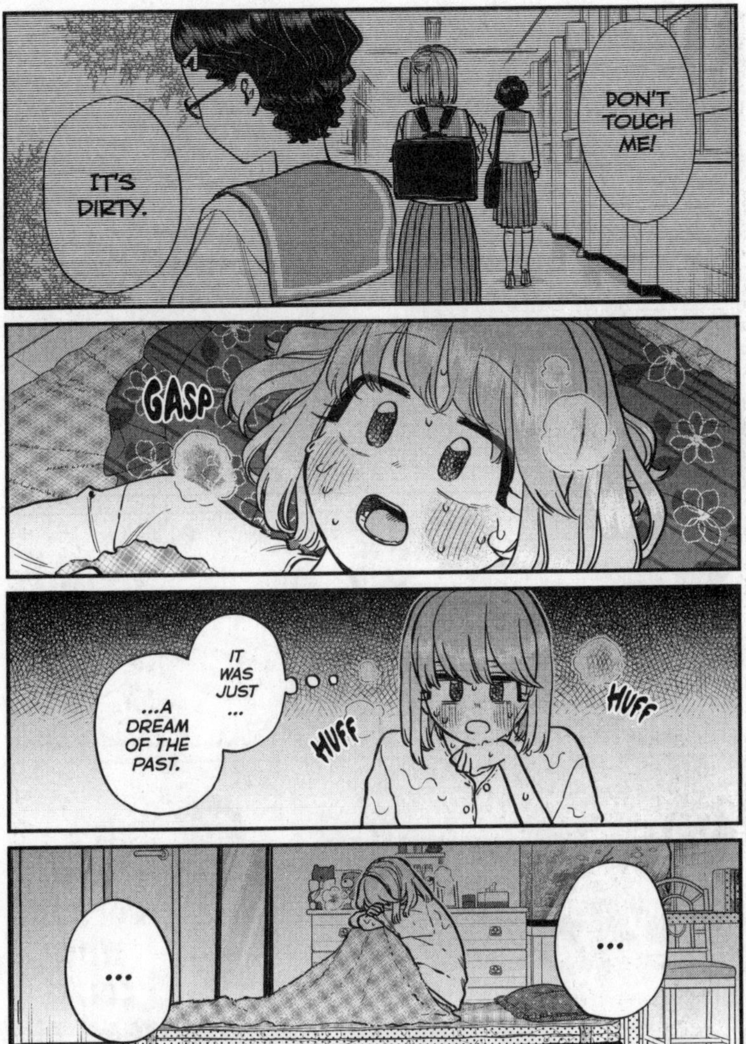
DON'T TOUCH ME!
IT'S DIRTY.
GASP
HUFF
HUFF
IT WAS JUST ...
...A DREAM OF THE PAST.
...
...

# Komi Can't Communicate

## Communication 201: Smile

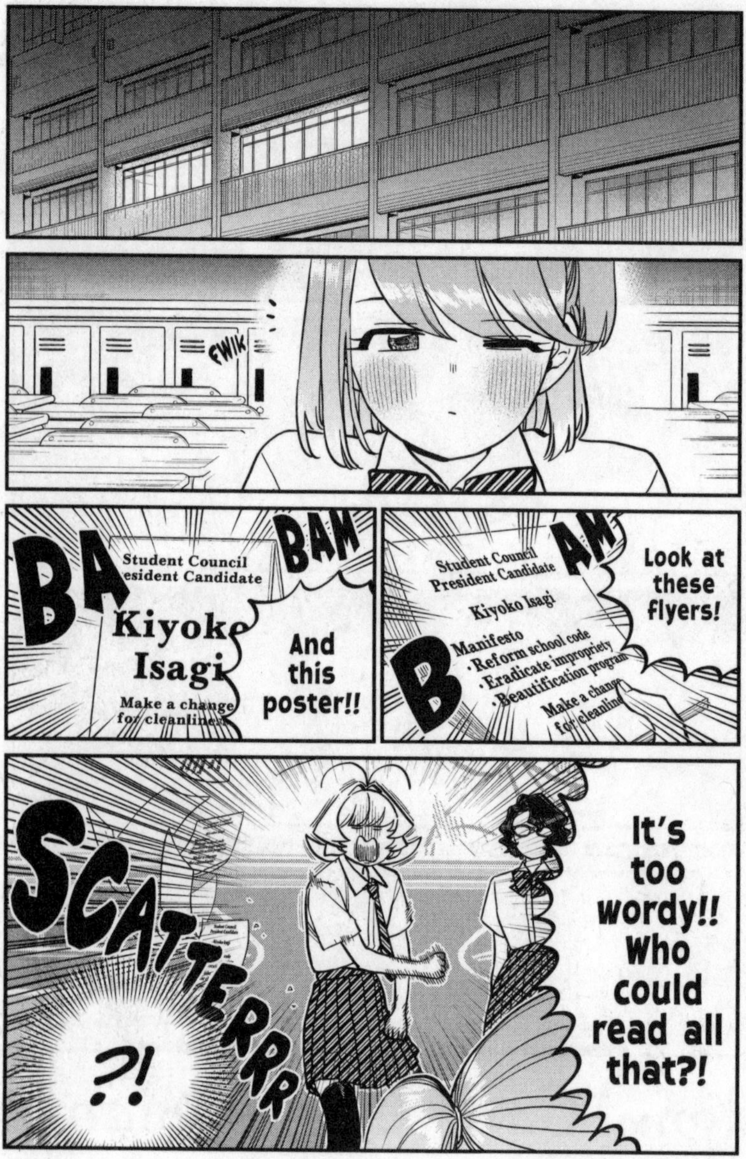
FWIK
Look at these flyers!
AM
B
Student Council President Candidate
Kiyoko Isagi
Manifesto
· Reform school code
· Eradicate impropriety
· Beautification program
BAM
BA
Student Council
Kiyoko Isagi
Make a change
And this poster!!
It's too wordy!! Who could read all that?!
SCATTERRR
?!

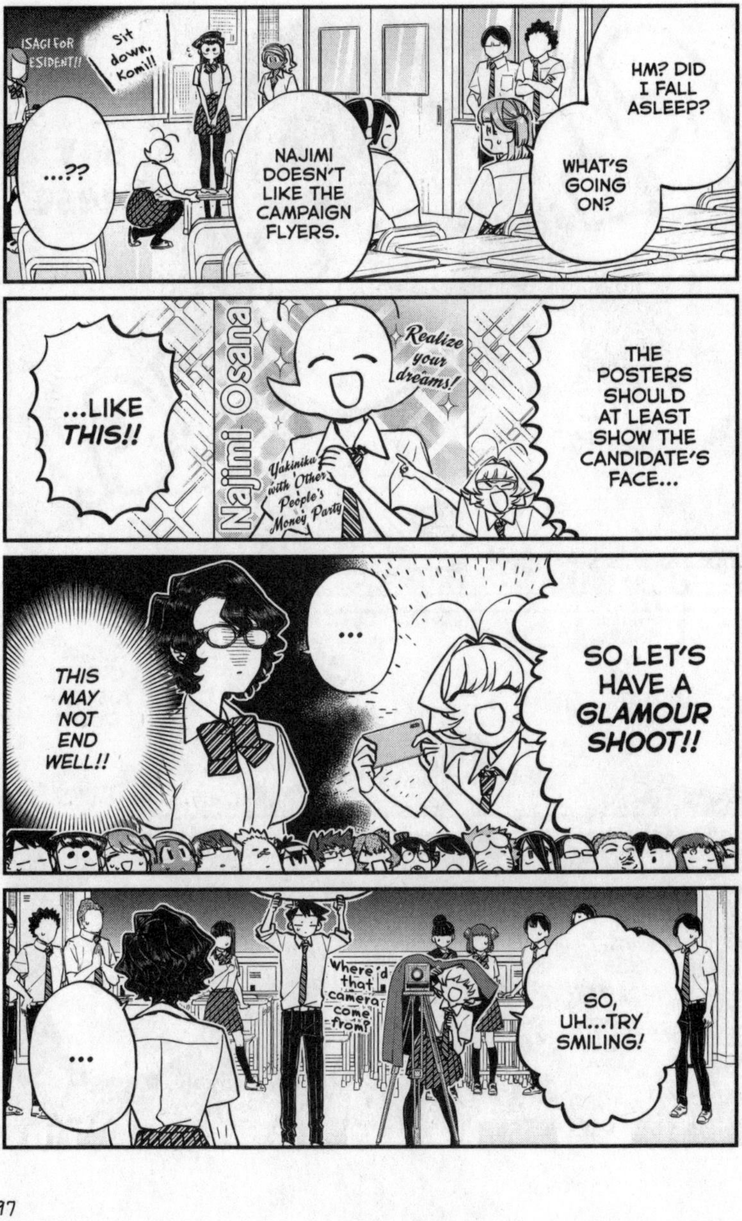
HM? DID I FALL ASLEEP?
WHAT'S GOING ON?
NAJIMI DOESN'T LIKE THE CAMPAIGN FLYERS.
Sit down, Komi!!
ISAGI FOR ESIDENT!!
...??
THE POSTERS SHOULD AT LEAST SHOW THE CANDIDATE'S FACE...
Realize your dreams!
Najimi Osana
Yakiniku with Other People's Money Party
...LIKE THIS!!
SO LET'S HAVE A GLAMOUR SHOOT!!
...
THIS MAY NOT END WELL!!
SO, UH...TRY SMILING!
Where'd that camera come from?
...

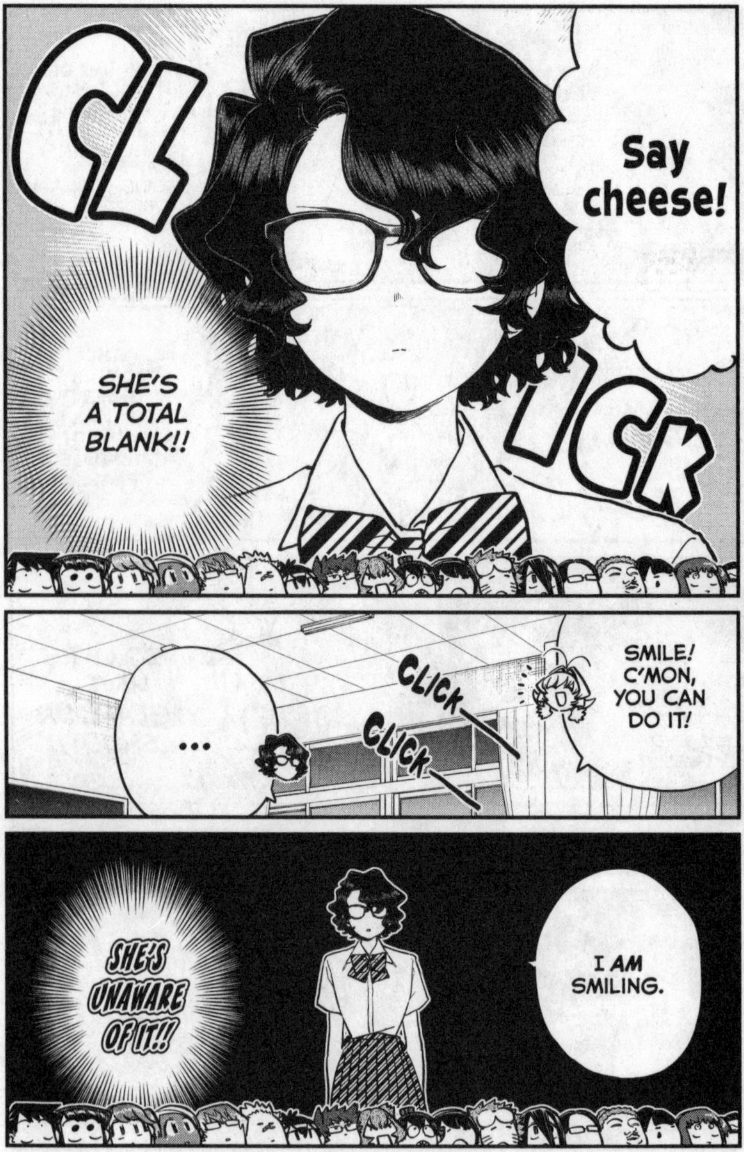
Say cheese!
CLICK
SHE'S A TOTAL BLANK!!
SMILE! C'MON, YOU CAN DO IT!
CLICK—
CLICK—
...
I AM SMILING.
SHE'S UNAWARE OF IT!!

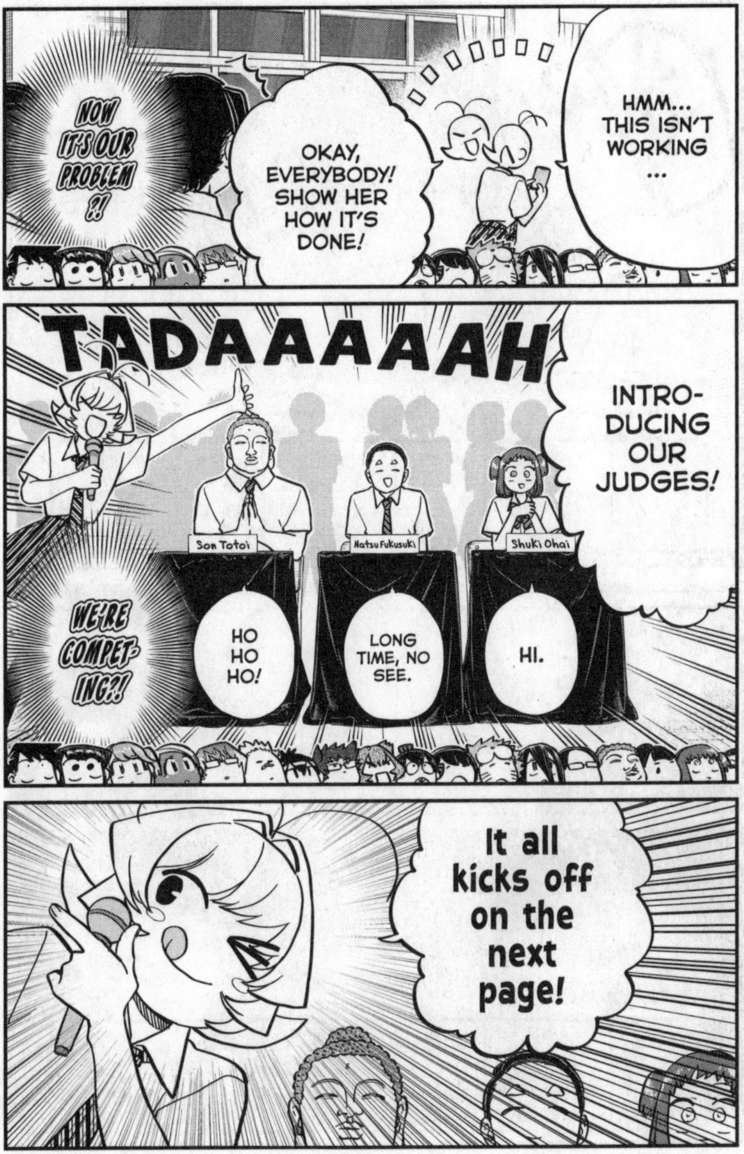
HMM... THIS ISN'T WORKING ...
OKAY, EVERYBODY! SHOW HER HOW IT'S DONE!
NOW IT'S OUR PROBLEM?!
TADAAAAAAH
INTRO-DUCING OUR JUDGES!
Shuki Ohai
Natsu Fukusuki
Son Totoi
HI.
LONG TIME, NO SEE.
HO HO HO!
WE'RE COMPET-ING?!
It all kicks off on the next page!

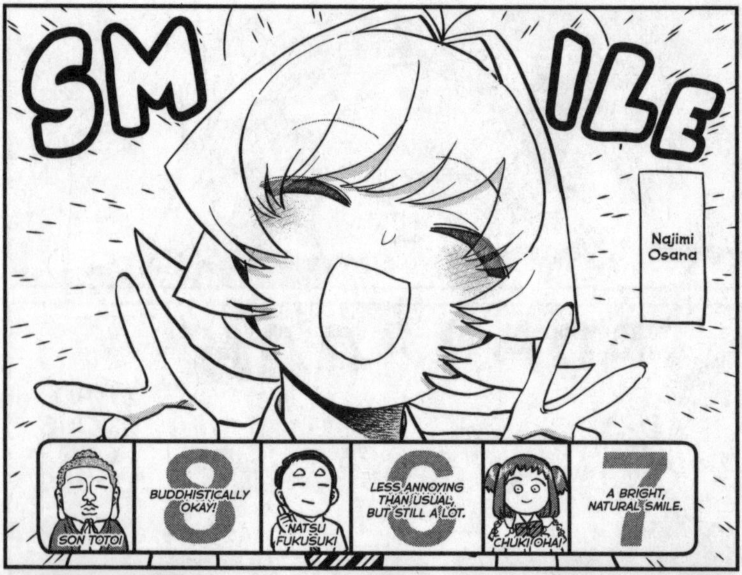
Najimi Osana
SMILE
7
A BRIGHT, NATURAL SMILE.
CHUKI OHAI
6
LESS ANNOYING THAN USUAL, BUT STILL A LOT.
NATSU FUKUSUKI
8
BUDDHISTICALLY OKAY!
SON TOTOI

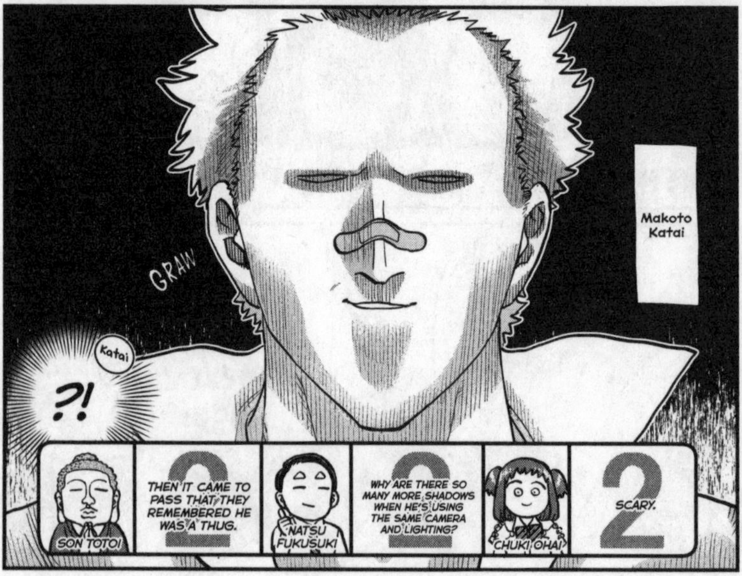
Makoto Katai
GRAW
Katai
?!
2
SCARY.
CHUKI OHAI
2
WHY ARE THERE SO MANY MORE SHADOWS WHEN HE'S USING THE SAME CAMERA AND LIGHTING?
NATSU FUKUSUKI
2
THEN IT CAME TO PASS THAT THEY REMEMBERED HE WAS A THUG.
SON TOTOI

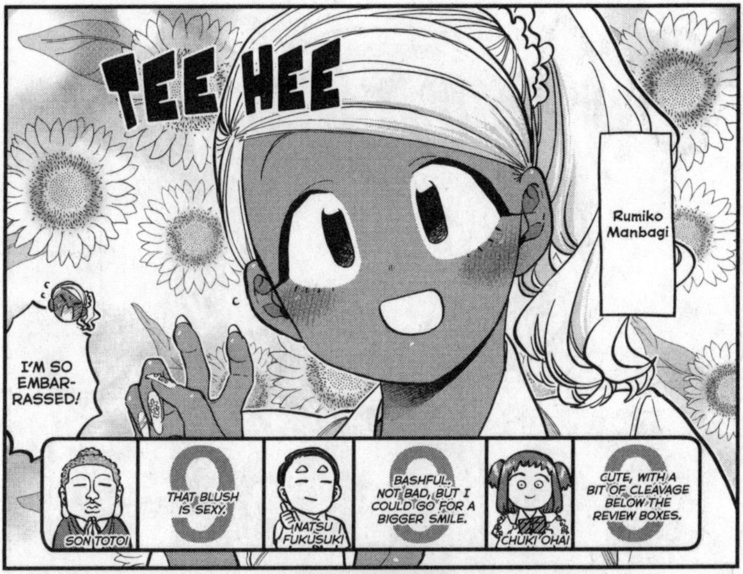
Rumiko Manbagi
TEE HEE
I'M SO EMBAR-RASSED!
SON TOTOI
9
THAT BLUSH IS SEXY.
NATSU FUKUSUKI
9
BASHFUL. NOT BAD, BUT I COULD GO FOR A BIGGER SMILE.
CHUKI OHAI
9
CUTE, WITH A BIT OF CLEAVAGE BELOW THE REVIEW BOXES.

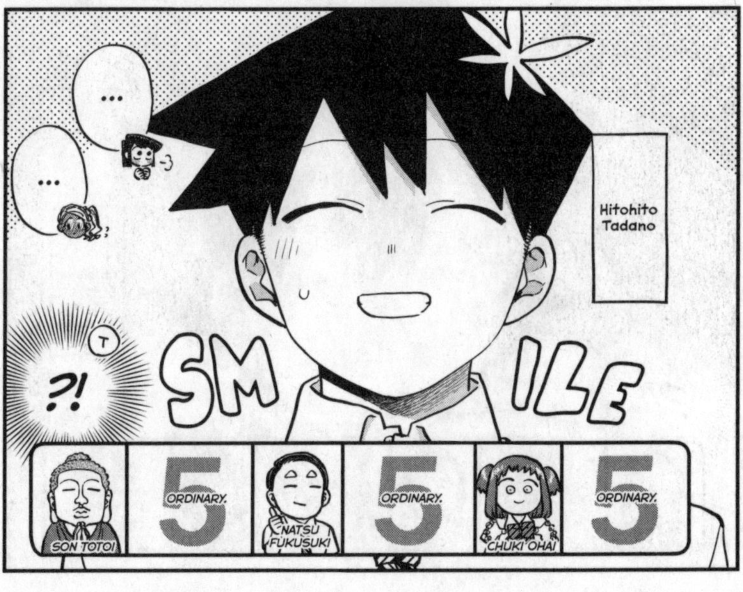
Hitohito Tadano
...
...
SMILE
T
?!
SON TOTOI
5
ORDINARY.
NATSU FUKUSUKI
5
ORDINARY.
CHUKI OHAI
5
ORDINARY.

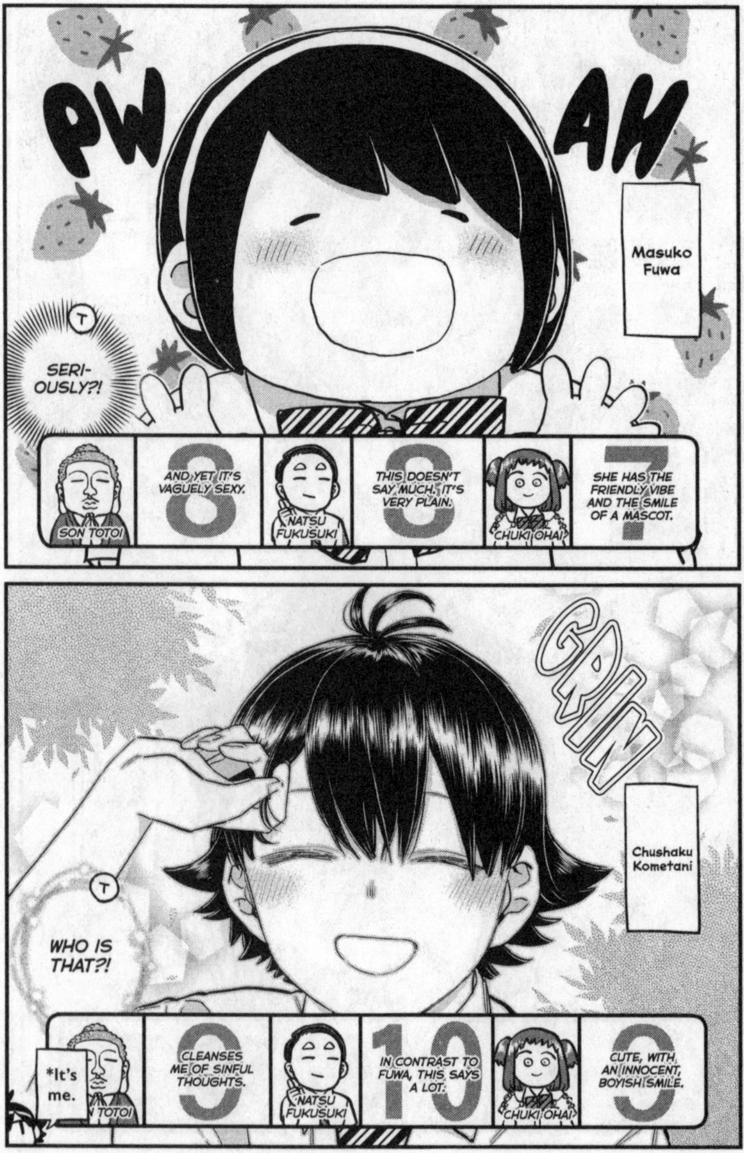
PWAH
Masuko Fuwa
SERI-OUSLY?!
SON TOTOI
8
AND YET IT'S VAGUELY SEXY.
NATSU FUKUSUKI
3
THIS DOESN'T SAY MUCH. IT'S VERY PLAIN.
CHUKI OHAI
7
SHE HAS THE FRIENDLY VIBE AND THE SMILE OF A MASCOT.
GRIN
Chushaku Kometani
WHO IS THAT?!
*It's me.
9
CLEANSES ME OF SINFUL THOUGHTS.
NATSU FUKUSUKI
10
IN CONTRAST TO FUWA, THIS SAYS A LOT.
CHUKI OHAI
9
CUTE, WITH AN INNOCENT, BOYISH SMILE.

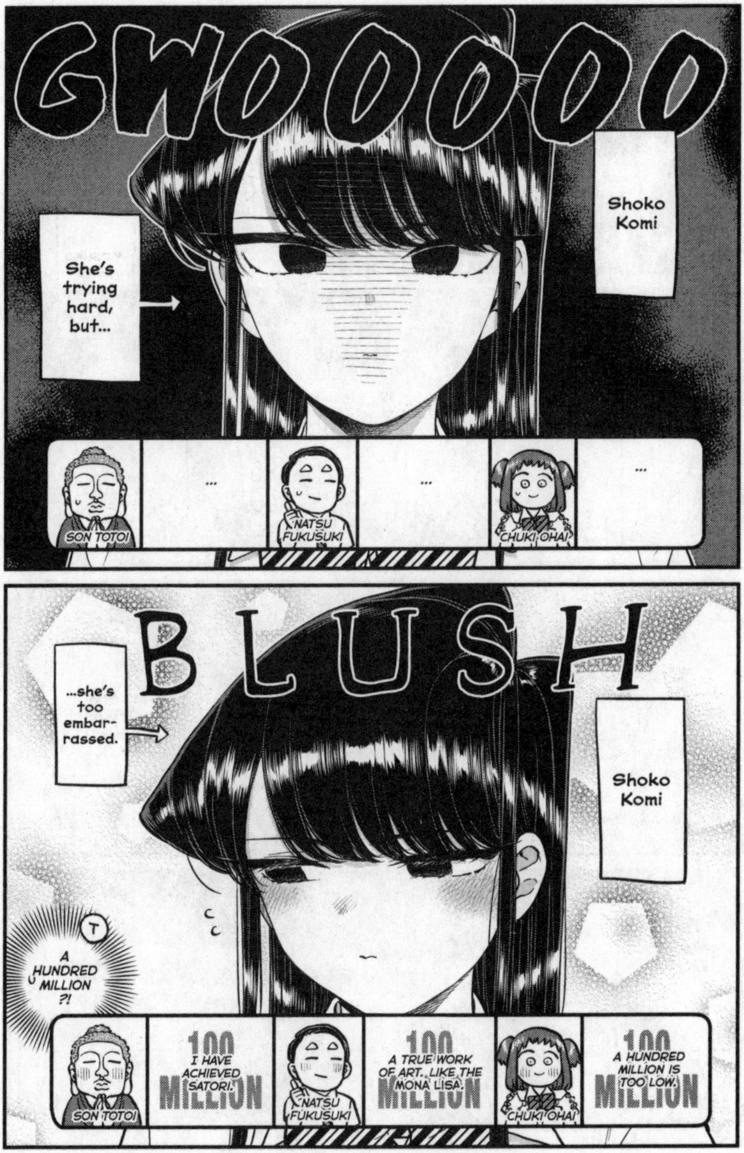
GWOOOOO
Shoko Komi
She's trying hard, but...
...
CHUKI OHAI
...
NATSU FUKUSUKI
...
SON TOTOI
BLUSH
Shoko Komi
...she's too embarrassed.
T
A HUNDRED MILLION ?!
100 MILLION
A HUNDRED MILLION IS TOO LOW.
CHUKI OHAI
100 MILLION
A TRUE WORK OF ART. LIKE THE MONA LISA.
NATSU FUKUSUKI
100 MILLION
I HAVE ACHIEVED SATORI.
SON TOTOI

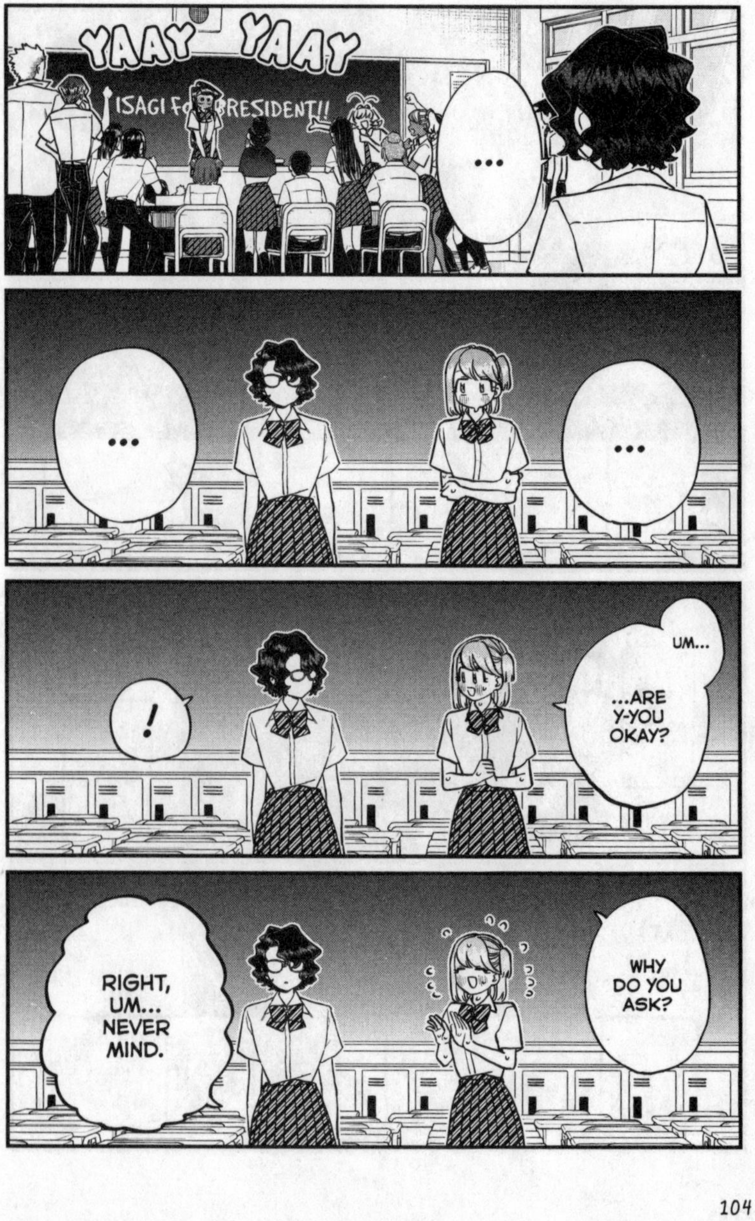
...
YAAY YAAY
ISAGI FOR PRESIDENT!!
...
...
UM...
...ARE Y-YOU OKAY?
!
WHY DO YOU ASK?
RIGHT, UM... NEVER MIND.

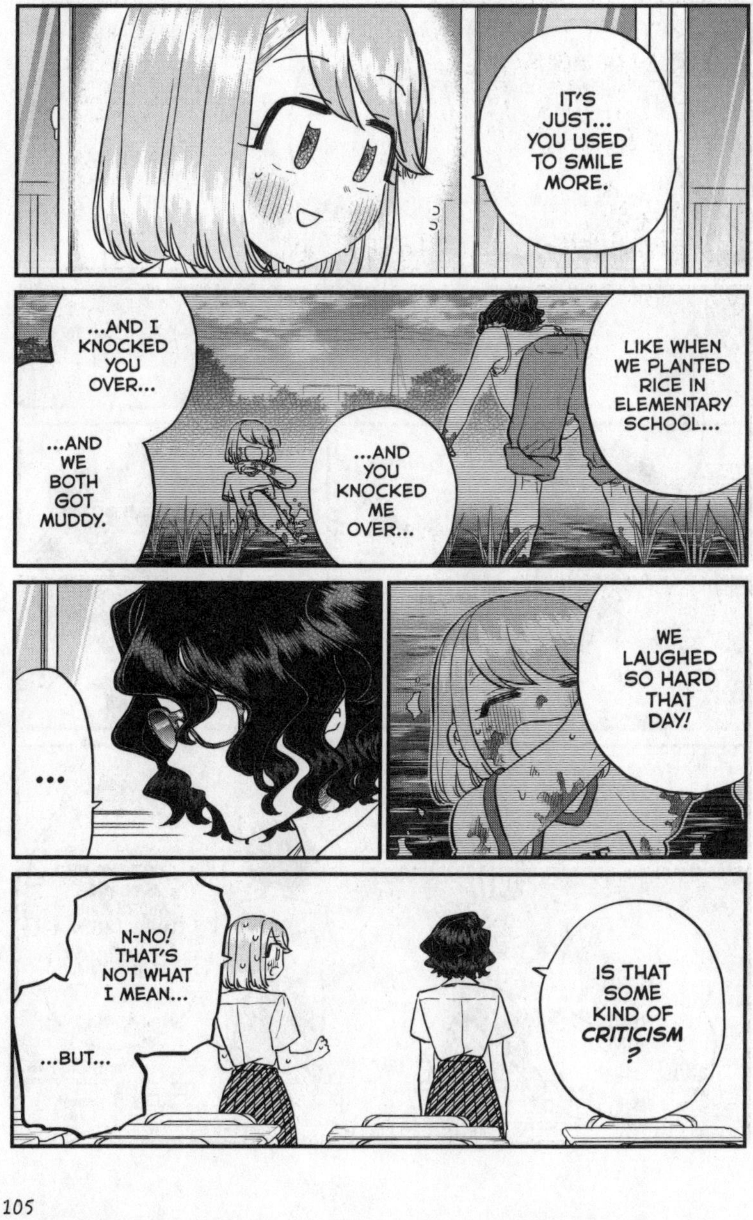
IT'S JUST... YOU USED TO SMILE MORE.
LIKE WHEN WE PLANTED RICE IN ELEMENTARY SCHOOL...
...AND YOU KNOCKED ME OVER...
...AND I KNOCKED YOU OVER...
...AND WE BOTH GOT MUDDY.
WE LAUGHED SO HARD THAT DAY!
...
IS THAT SOME KIND OF *CRITICISM*?
N-NO! THAT'S NOT WHAT I MEAN...
...BUT...

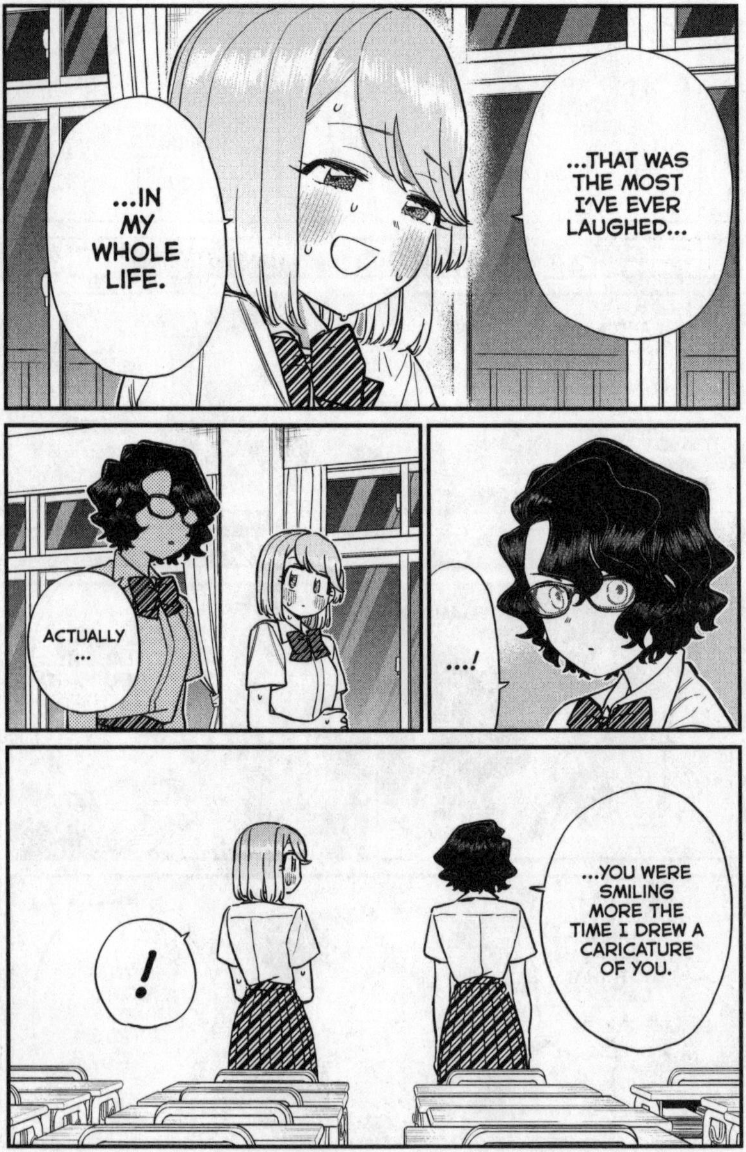
...THAT WAS THE MOST I'VE EVER LAUGHED...
...IN MY WHOLE LIFE.
...!
ACTUALLY ...
...YOU WERE SMILING MORE THE TIME I DREW A CARICATURE OF YOU.
!

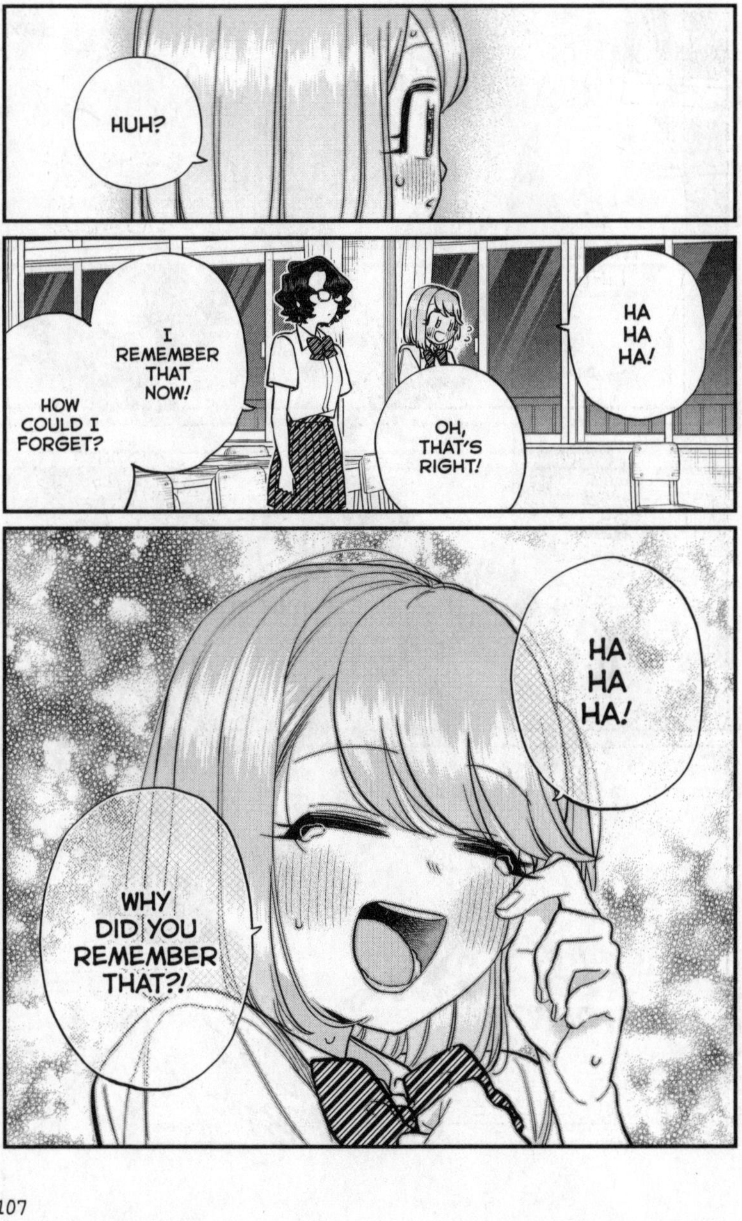
HUH?
HA HA HA!
OH, THAT'S RIGHT!
I REMEMBER THAT NOW!
HOW COULD I FORGET?
HA HA HA!
WHY DID YOU REMEMBER THAT?!

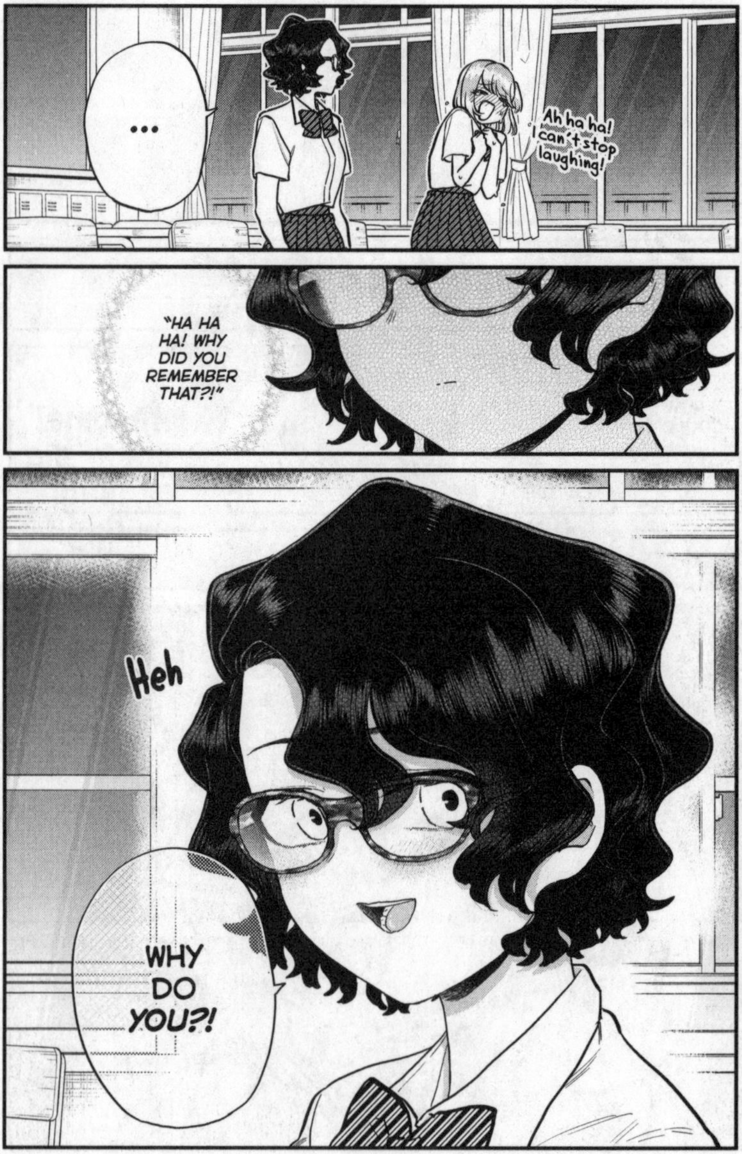
Ah ha ha! I can't stop laughing!
...
"HA HA HA! WHY DID YOU REMEMBER THAT?!"
Heh
WHY DO YOU?!

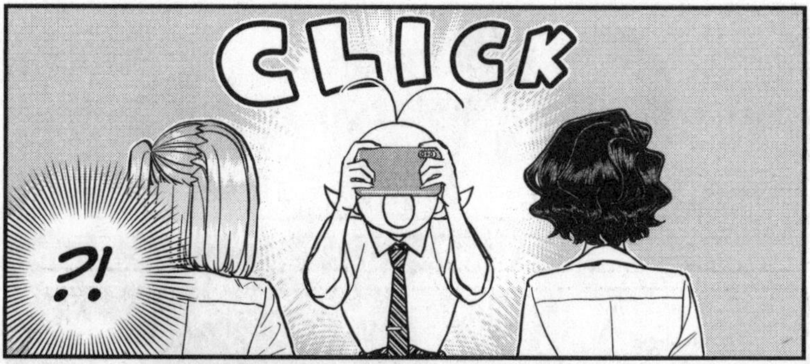
CLICK
?!

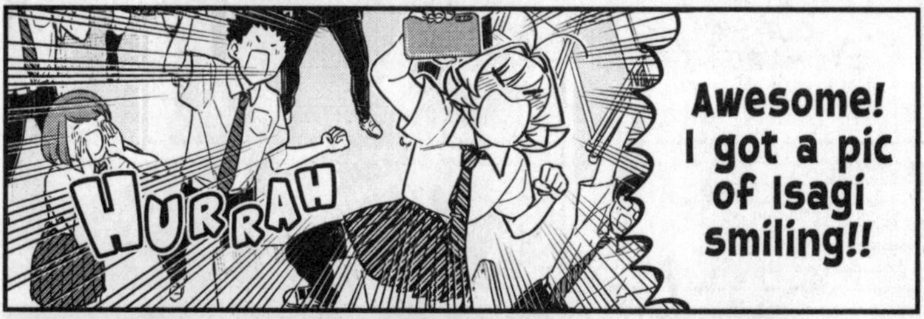
Awesome! I got a pic of Isagi smiling!!
HURRAH

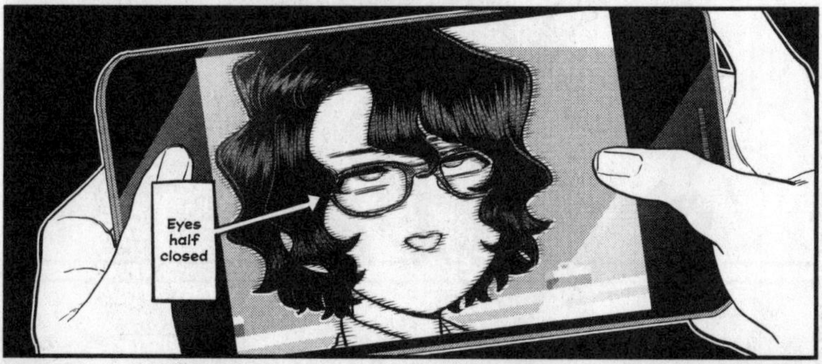
Eyes half closed

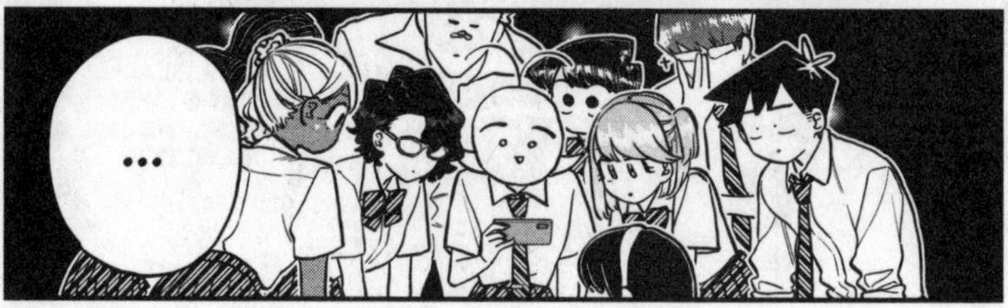
...

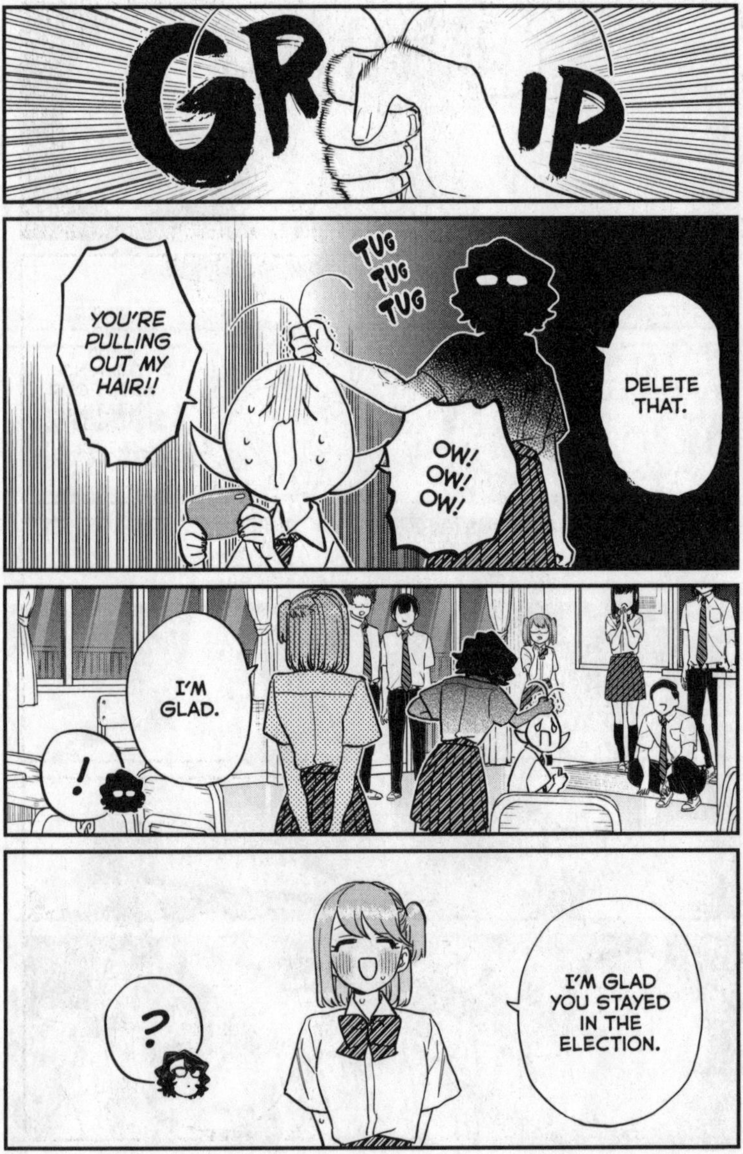
GRIP
DELETE THAT.
TUG TUG TUG
OW! OW! OW!
YOU'RE PULLING OUT MY HAIR!!
I'M GLAD.
!
I'M GLAD YOU STAYED IN THE ELECTION.
?

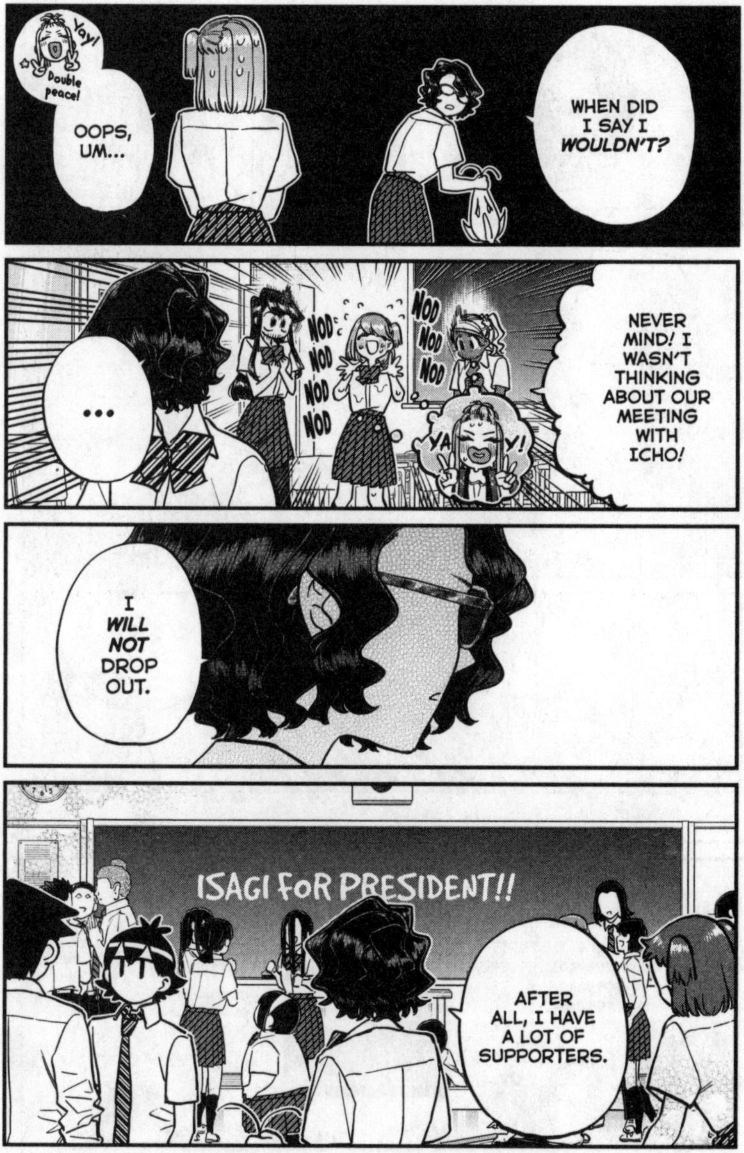
WHEN DID I SAY I *WOULDN'T?*
Yay! Double peace!
OOPS, UM...
NEVER MIND! I WASN'T THINKING ABOUT OUR MEETING WITH ICHO!
NOD NOD NOD
NOD NOD NOD NOD
YAY!
...
I *WILL NOT* DROP OUT.
ISAGI FOR PRESIDENT!!
AFTER ALL, I HAVE A LOT OF SUPPORTERS.

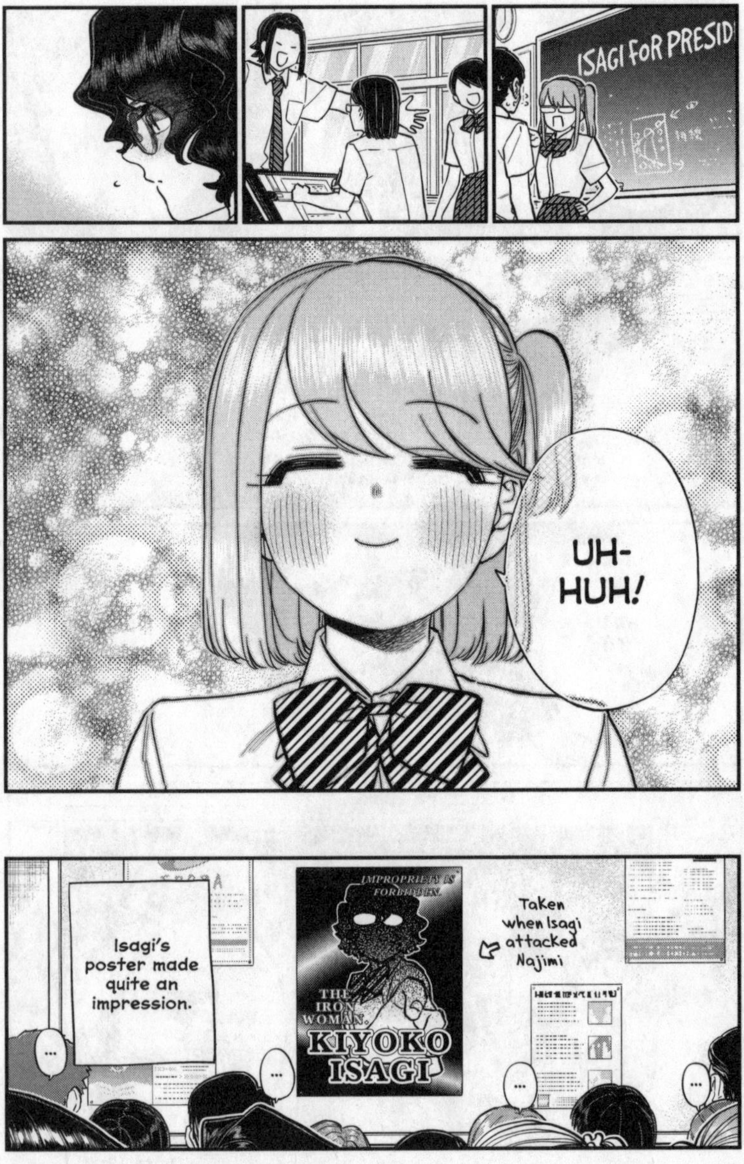
ISAGI FOR PRESID
UH-HUH!
Taken when Isagi attacked Najimi
IMPROPRIETY IS FORBIDDEN.
THE IRON WOMAN.
KIYOKO ISAGI
Isagi's poster made quite an impression.
...
...
...
...

Communication 201 — The End

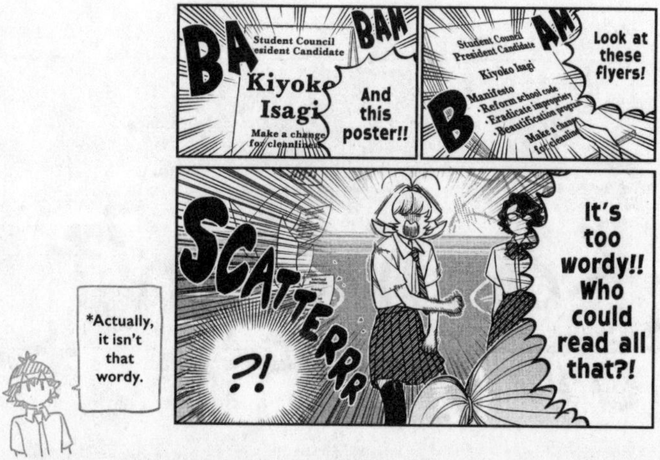
AM
B
Student Council
President Candidate
Kiyoko Isagi
Manifesto
· Reform school code
· Eradicate impropriety
· Beautification progra
Make a chan
for cleanlin
Look at these flyers!
BA
BAM
Student Council
esident Candidate
Kiyoke
Isagi
Make a change
And this poster!!
SCATTERRR
?!
It's too wordy!! Who could read all that?!
*Actually, it isn't that wordy.

Komi Can't Communicate

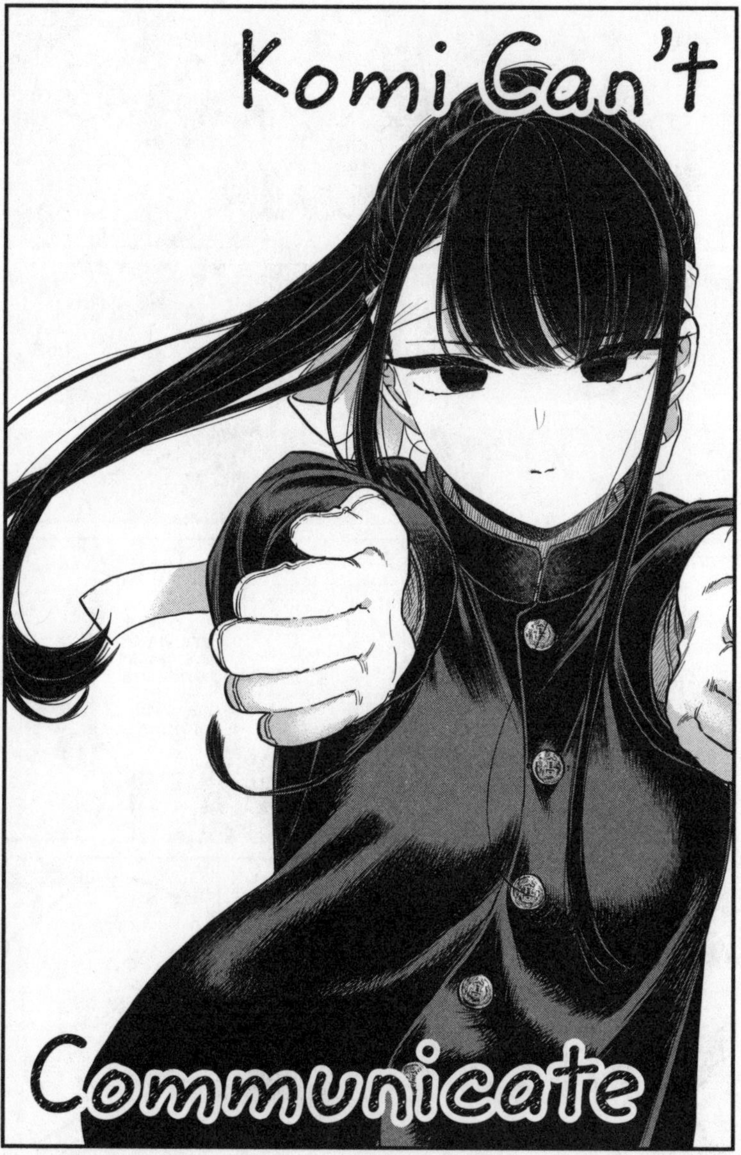
Komi Can't
Communicate

Communication 202: Campaign Rep

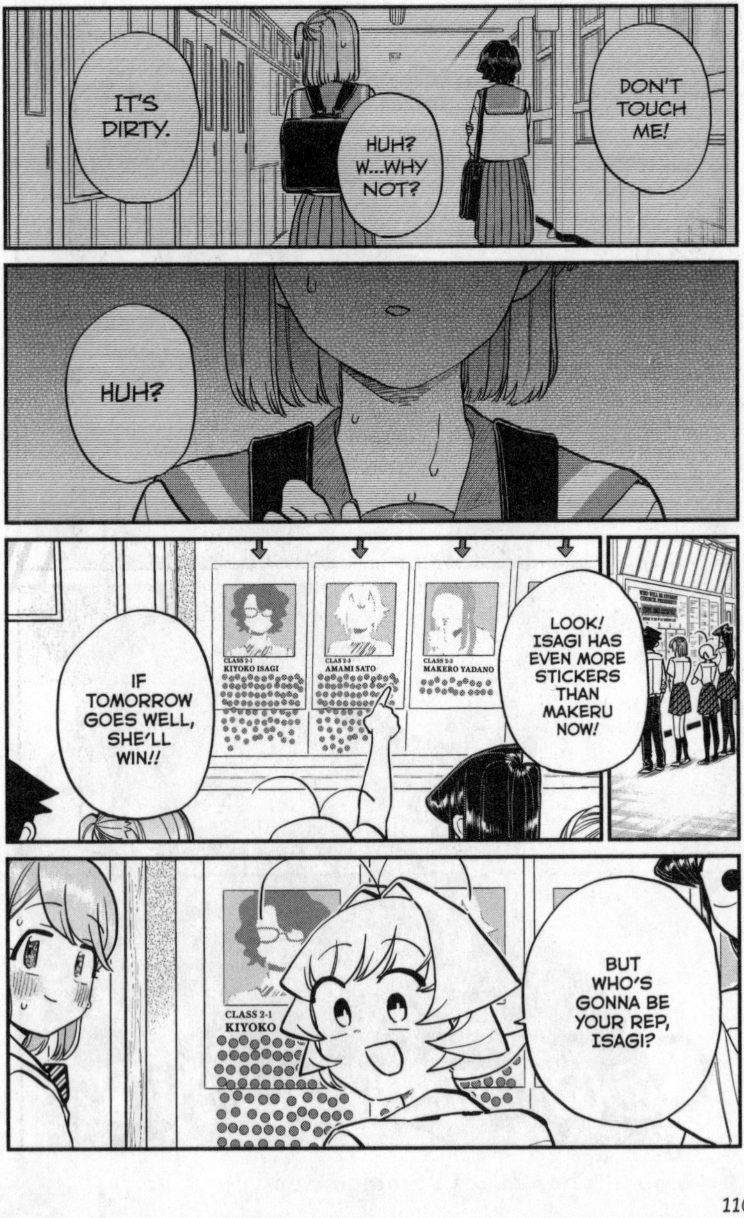
DON'T TOUCH ME!
HUH? W...WHY NOT?
IT'S DIRTY.
HUH?
LOOK! ISAGI HAS EVEN MORE STICKERS THAN MAKERU NOW!
CLASS 2-3 MAKERO YADANO
CLASS 2-3 AMAMI SATO
CLASS 2-1 KIYOKO ISAGI
IF TOMORROW GOES WELL, SHE'LL WIN!!
BUT WHO'S GONNA BE YOUR REP, ISAGI?
CLASS 2-1 KIYOKO

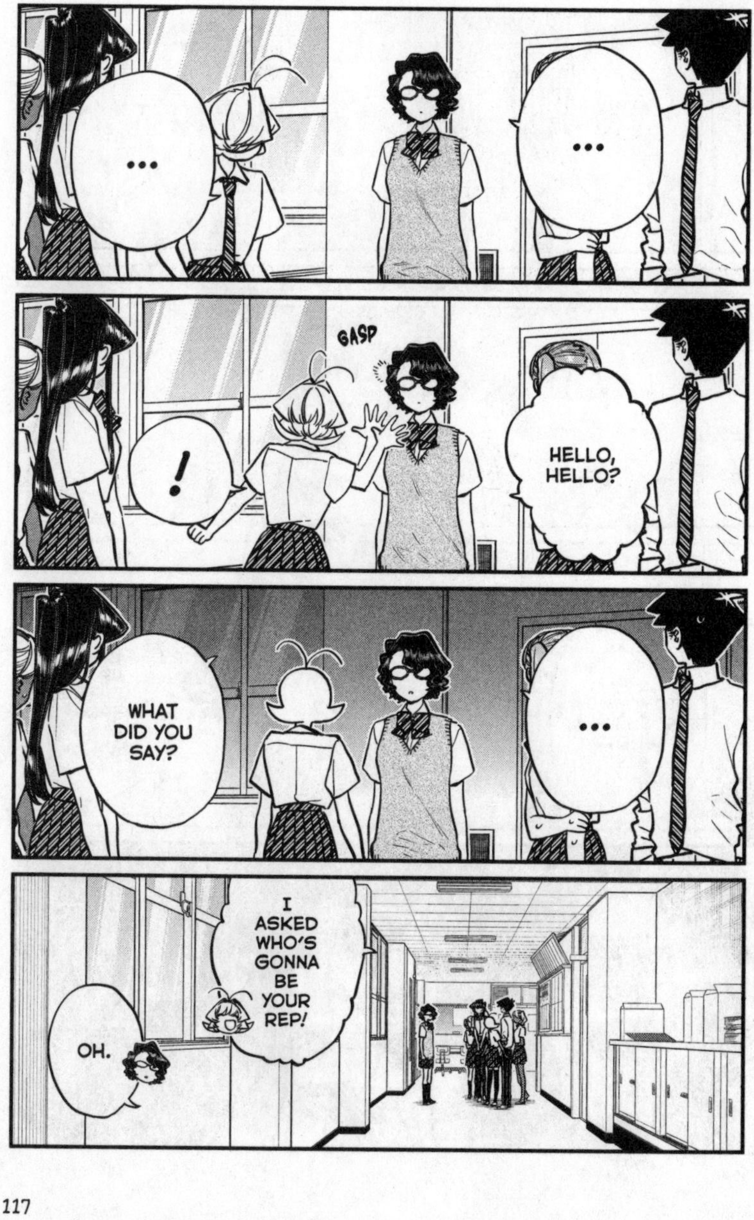
...
...
HELLO, HELLO?
GASP
!
...
WHAT DID YOU SAY?
I ASKED WHO'S GONNA BE YOUR REP!
OH.

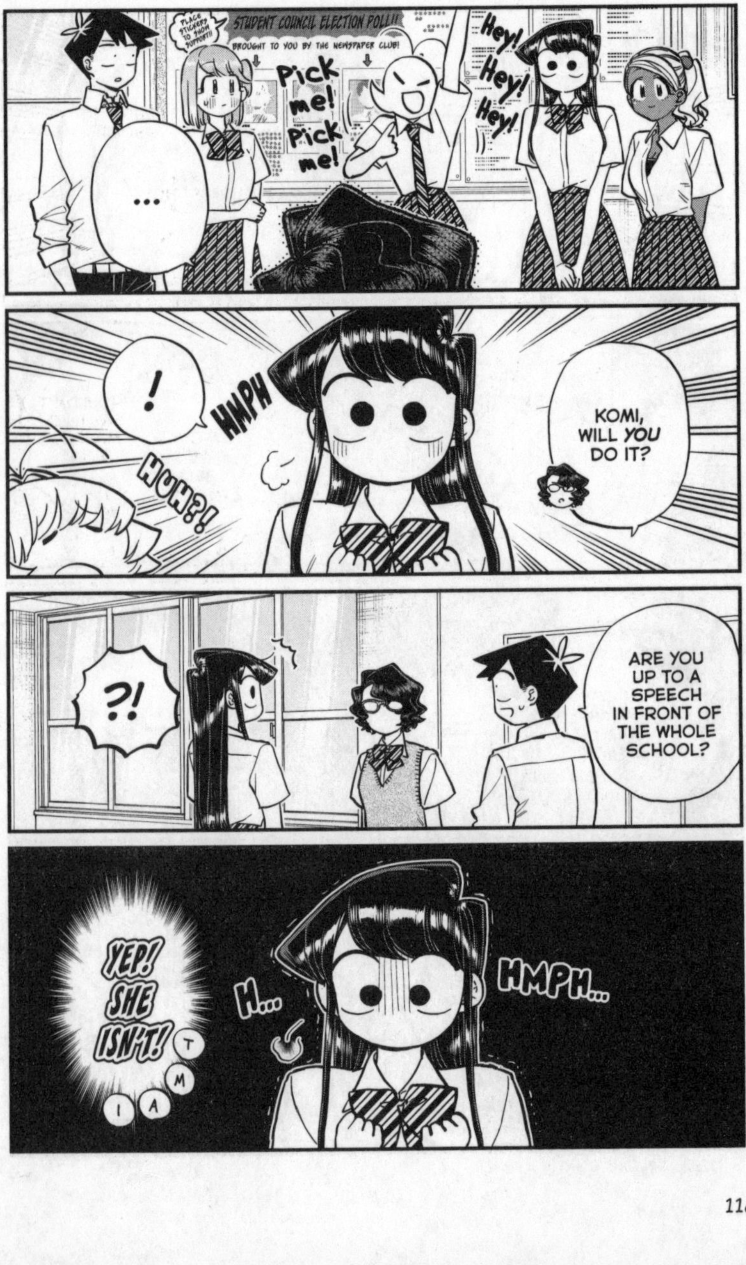
Hey! Hey! Hey!
STUDENT COUNCIL ELECTION POLL!!
BROUGHT TO YOU BY THE NEWSPAPER CLUB!
Pick me! Pick me!
PLACE STICKERS TO SHOW SUPPORT!!
...
KOMI, WILL YOU DO IT?
HMPH
!
HUH?!
ARE YOU UP TO A SPEECH IN FRONT OF THE WHOLE SCHOOL?
?!
HMPH...
H...
YEP! SHE ISN'T!
T
M
A
I

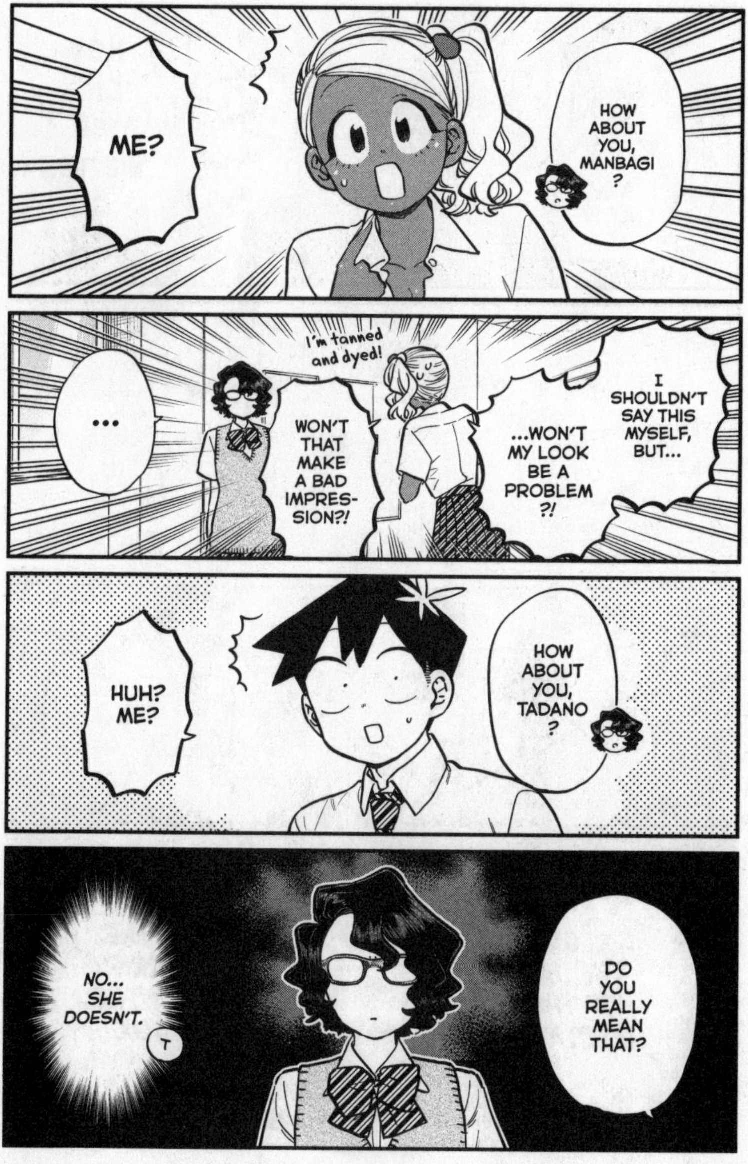
HOW ABOUT YOU, MANBAGI?
ME?
I SHOULDN'T SAY THIS MYSELF, BUT...
...WON'T MY LOOK BE A PROBLEM?!
I'm tanned and dyed!
WON'T THAT MAKE A BAD IMPRES-SION?!
...
HOW ABOUT YOU, TADANO?
HUH? ME?
DO YOU REALLY MEAN THAT?
NO... SHE DOESN'T.
T

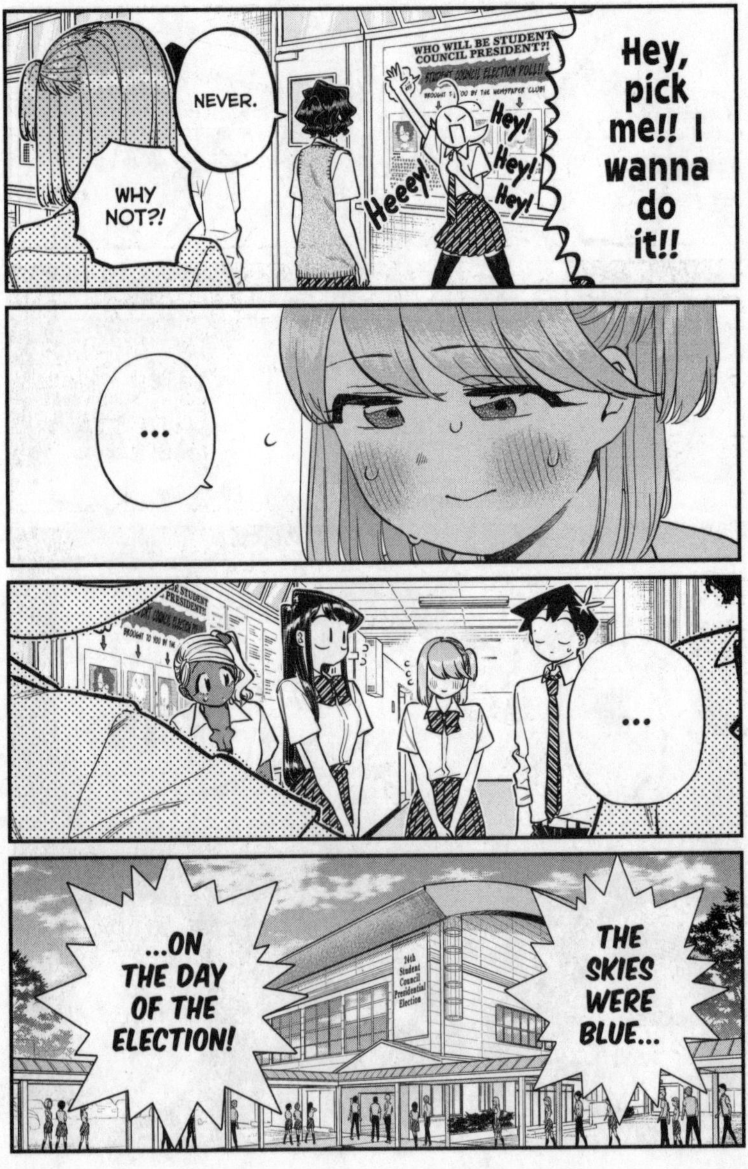
Hey, pick me!! I wanna do it!!
WHO WILL BE STUDENT COUNCIL PRESIDENT?!
STUDENT COUNCIL ELECTION POLL!!
Hey!
Hey!
Hey!
Heeey
NEVER.
WHY NOT?!
...
...
THE SKIES WERE BLUE...
24th Student Council Presidential Election
...ON THE DAY OF THE ELECTION!

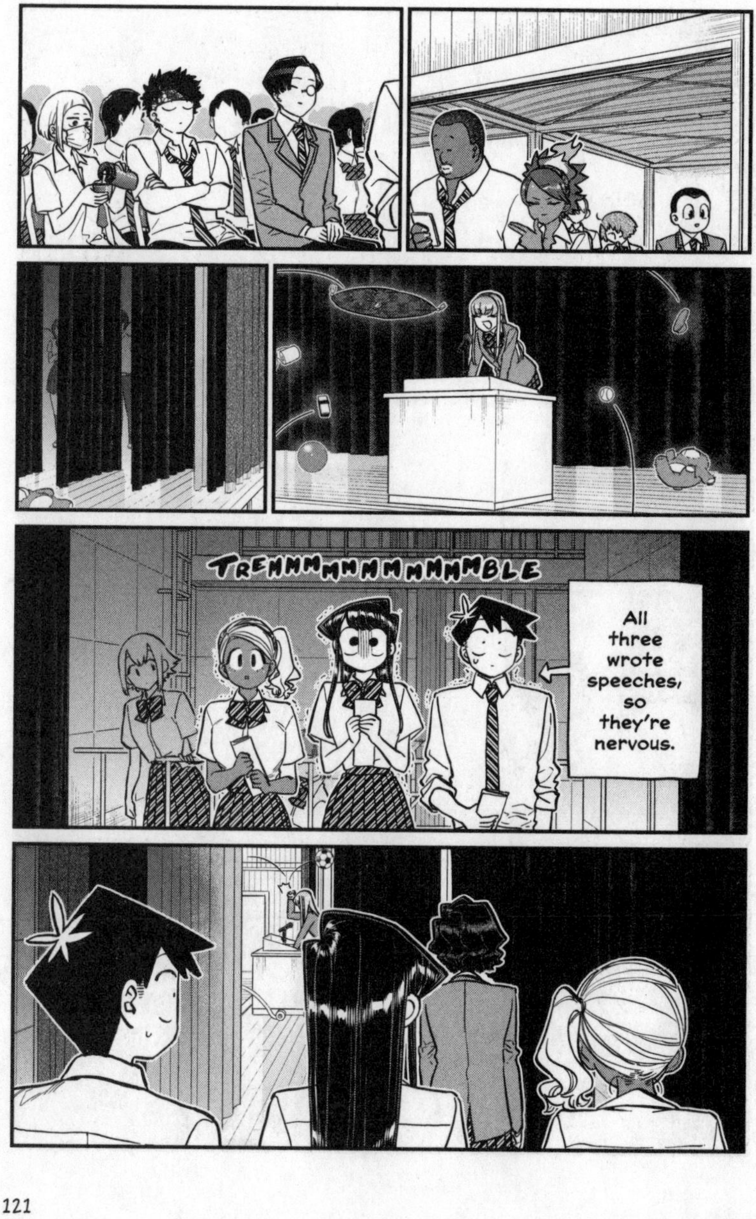
TREMMMMMMMMMMMMBLE
All three wrote speeches, so they're nervous.

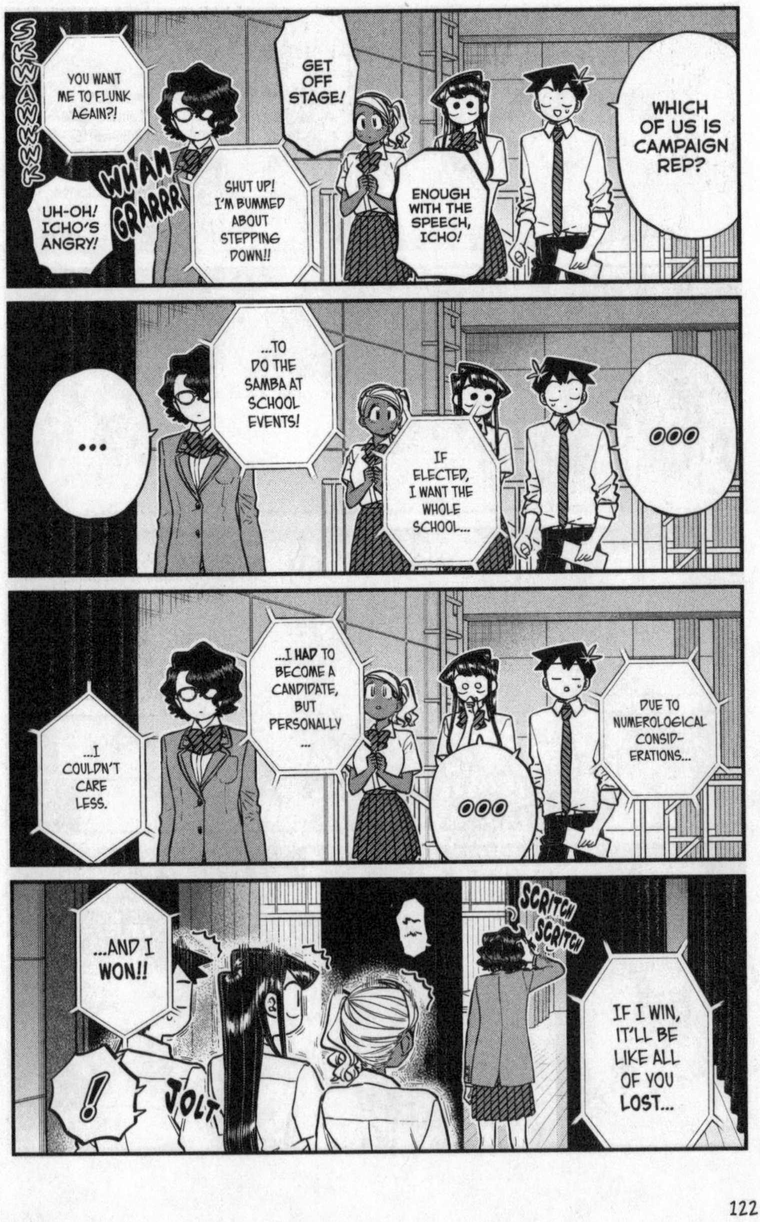

WHICH OF US IS CAMPAIGN REP?
GET OFF STAGE!
ENOUGH WITH THE SPEECH, ICHO!
SHUT UP! I'M BUMMED ABOUT STEPPING DOWN!!
YOU WANT ME TO FLUNK AGAIN?!
WHAM
GRARRR
SKWAWWWK
UH-OH! ICHO'S ANGRY!
OOO
...TO DO THE SAMBA AT SCHOOL EVENTS!
IF ELECTED, I WANT THE WHOLE SCHOOL...
...
DUE TO NUMEROLOGICAL CONSID-ERATIONS...
...I HAD TO BECOME A CANDIDATE, BUT PERSONALLY ...
OOO
...I COULDN'T CARE LESS.
SCRITCH SCRITCH
IF I WIN, IT'LL BE LIKE ALL OF YOU LOST...
...AND I WON!!
JOLT
!

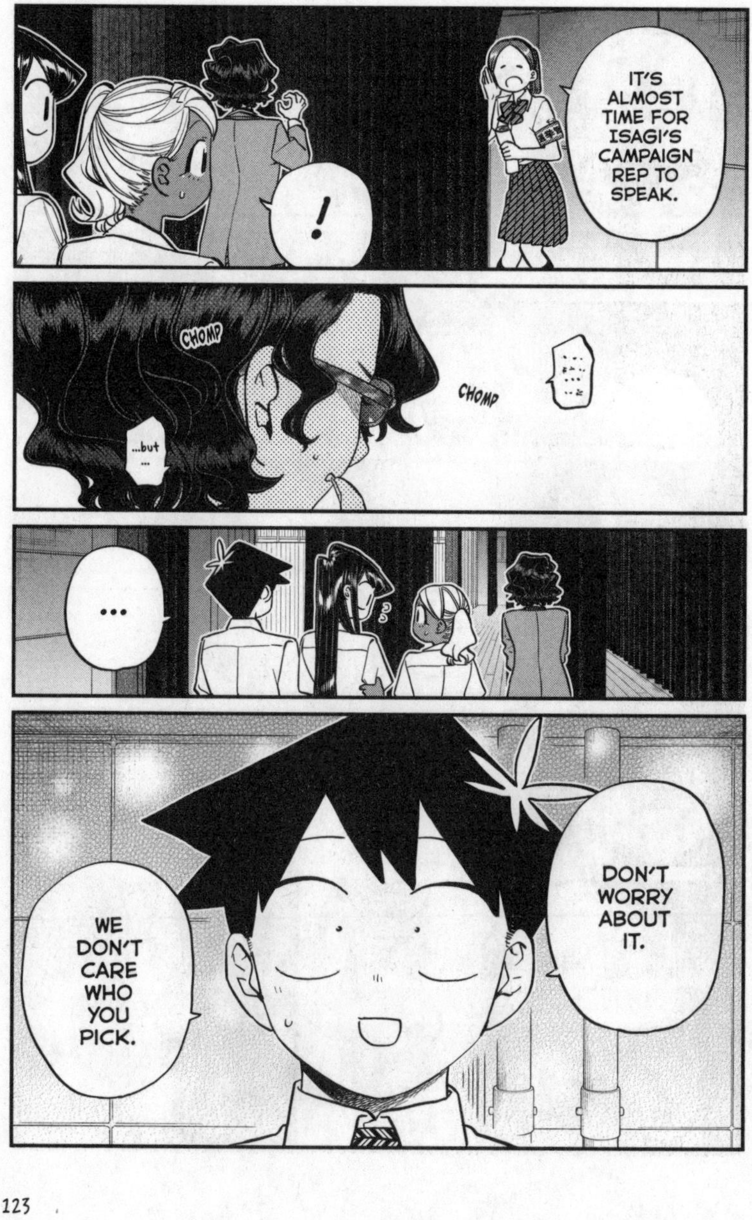
IT'S ALMOST TIME FOR ISAGI'S CAMPAIGN REP TO SPEAK.
!
CHOMP
CHOMP
...but ...
...
DON'T WORRY ABOUT IT.
WE DON'T CARE WHO YOU PICK.

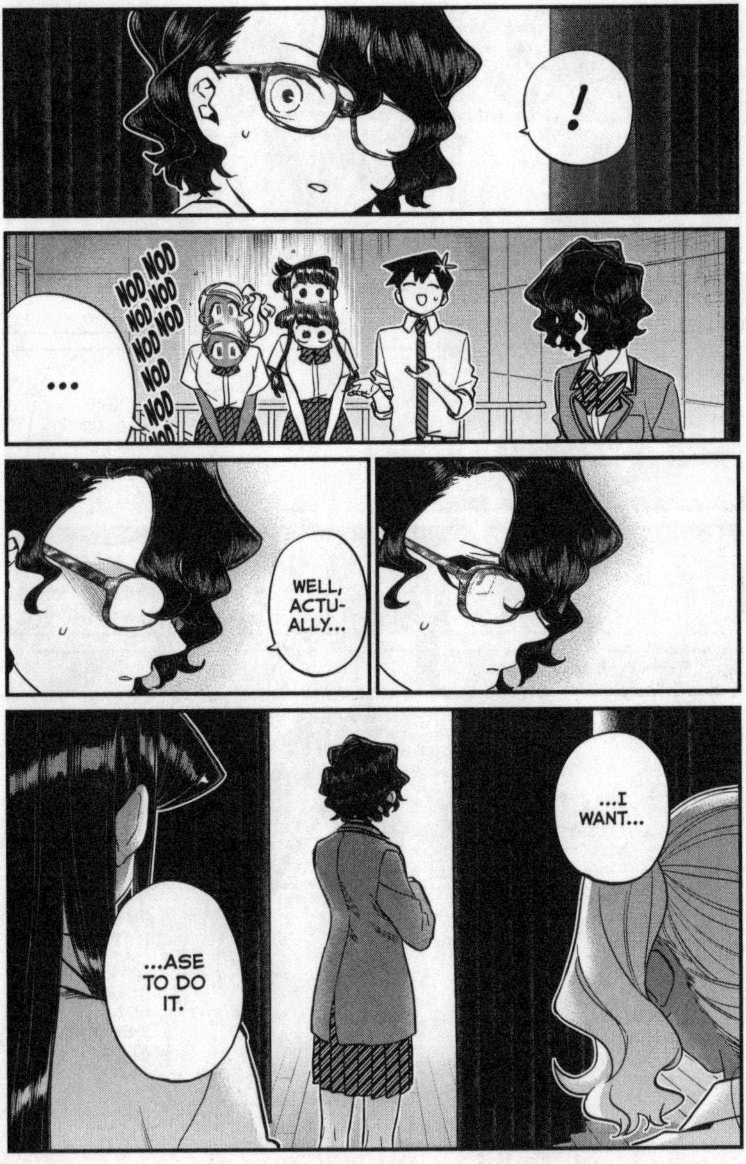
!
NOD NOD NOD NOD NOD NOD NOD NOD NOD NOD
...
WELL, ACTU-ALLY...
...I WANT...
...ASE TO DO IT.

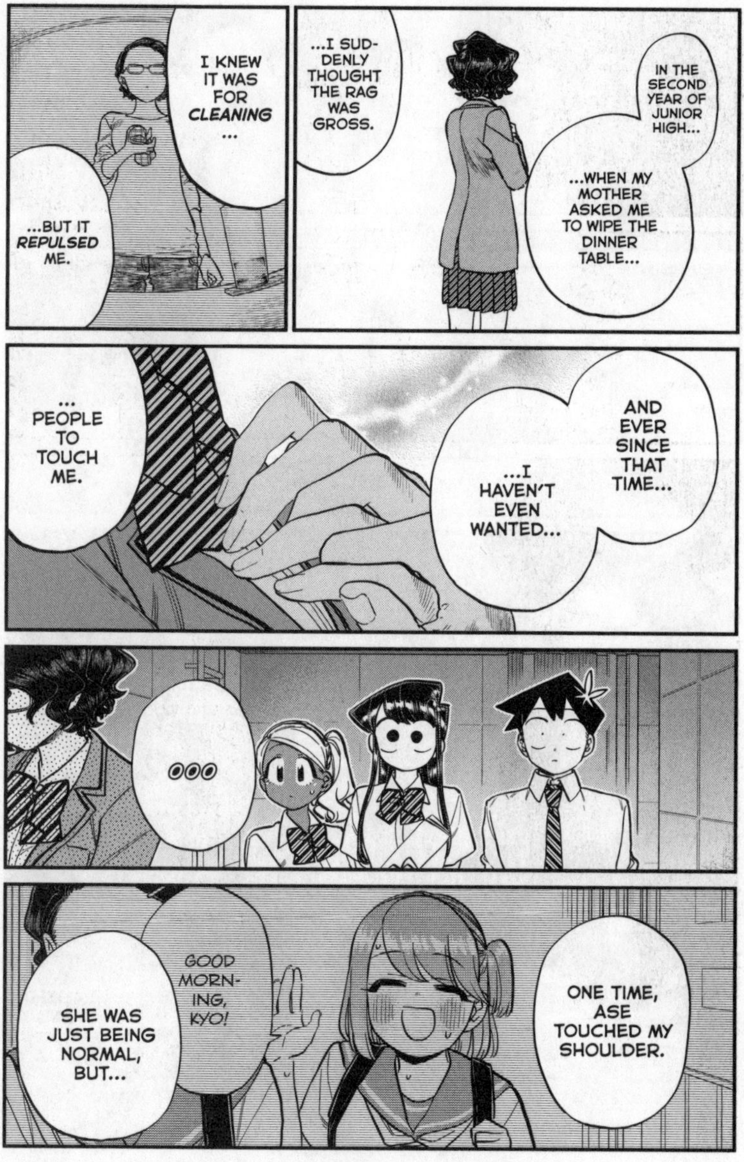
IN THE SECOND YEAR OF JUNIOR HIGH...
...WHEN MY MOTHER ASKED ME TO WIPE THE DINNER TABLE...
...I SUDDENLY THOUGHT THE RAG WAS GROSS.
I KNEW IT WAS FOR *CLEANING*...
...BUT IT *REPULSED* ME.
AND EVER SINCE THAT TIME...
...I HAVEN'T EVEN WANTED...
...PEOPLE TO TOUCH ME.
○○○
ONE TIME, ASE TOUCHED MY SHOULDER.
GOOD MORNING, KYO!
SHE WAS JUST BEING NORMAL, BUT...

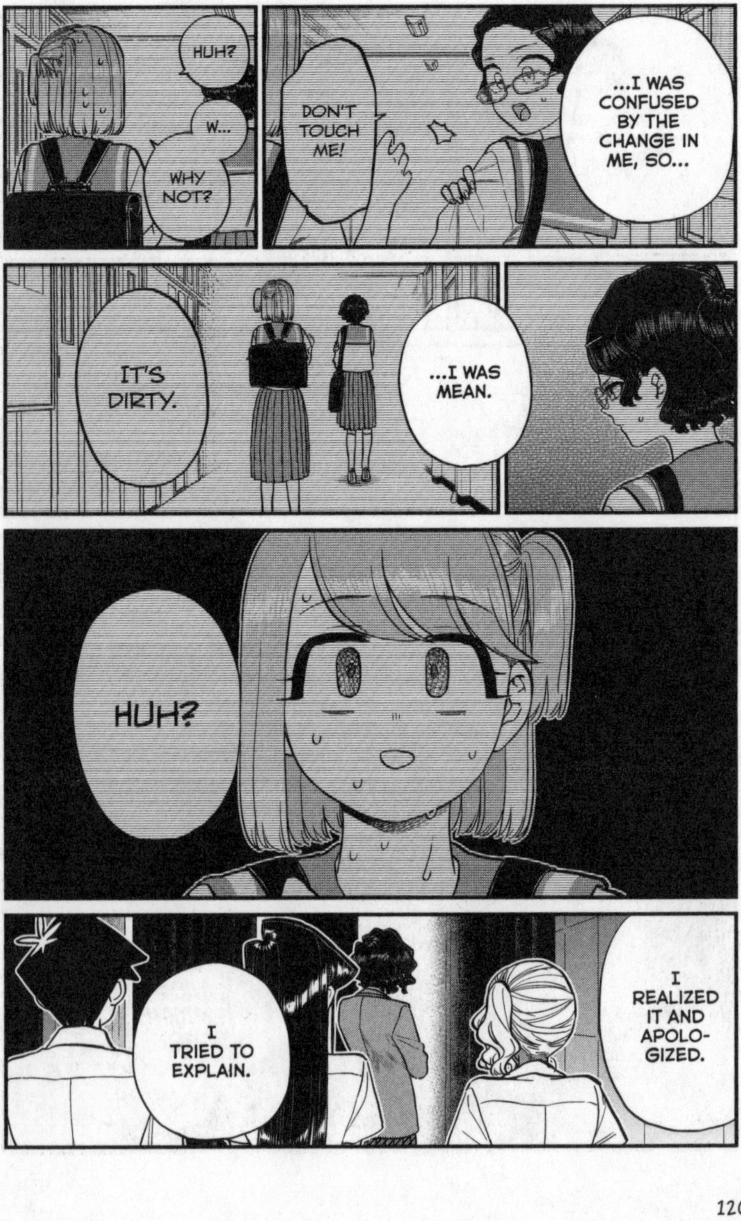
...I WAS CONFUSED BY THE CHANGE IN ME, SO...
DON'T TOUCH ME!
HUH?
W...
WHY NOT?
...I WAS MEAN.
IT'S DIRTY.
HUH?
I REALIZED IT AND APOLO-GIZED.
I TRIED TO EXPLAIN.

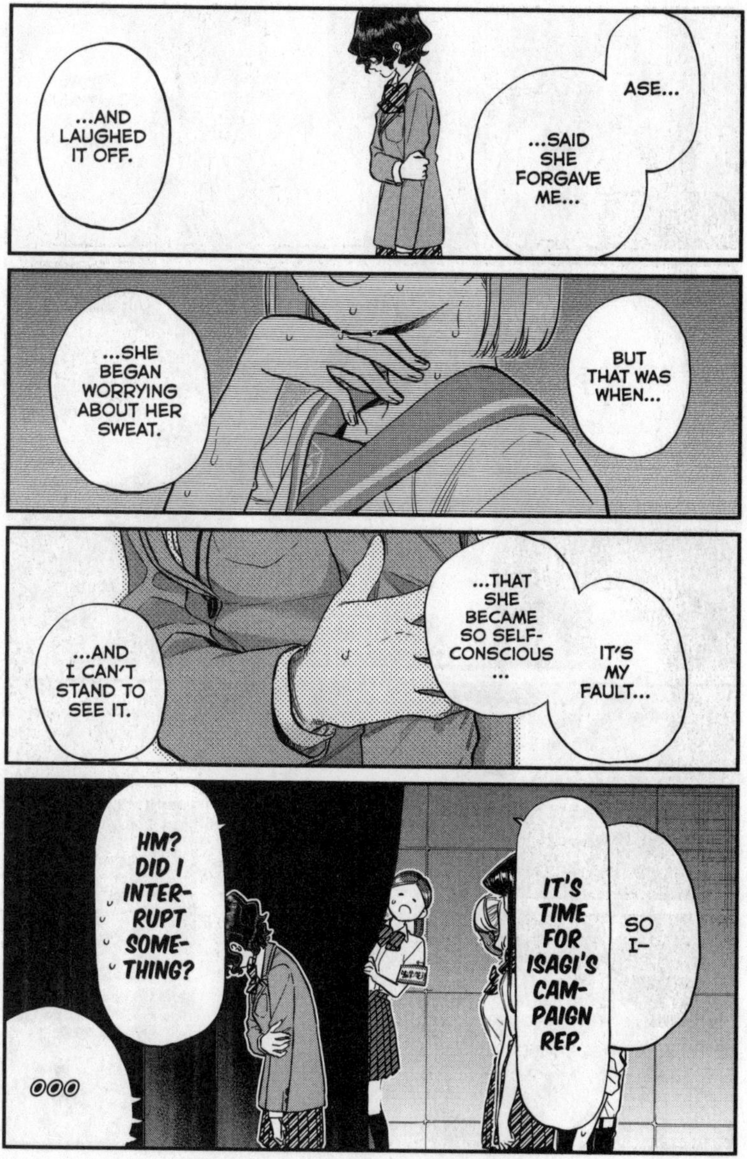
ASE...
...SAID SHE FORGAVE ME...
...AND LAUGHED IT OFF.
BUT THAT WAS WHEN...
...SHE BEGAN WORRYING ABOUT HER SWEAT.
IT'S MY FAULT...
...THAT SHE BECAME SO SELF-CONSCIOUS ...
...AND I CAN'T STAND TO SEE IT.
SO I—
IT'S TIME FOR ISAGI'S CAM-PAIGN REP.
HM? DID I INTER-RUPT SOME-THING?
OOO

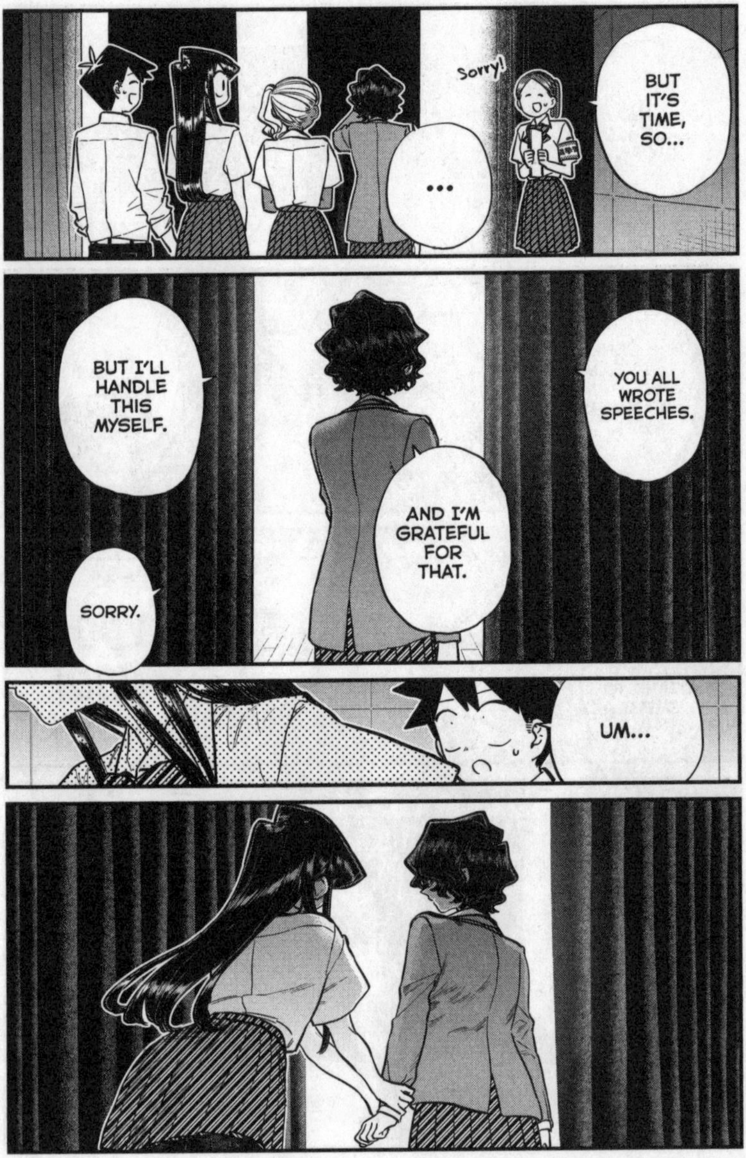
BUT IT'S TIME, SO...
Sorry!
...
YOU ALL WROTE SPEECHES.
AND I'M GRATEFUL FOR THAT.
BUT I'LL HANDLE THIS MYSELF.
SORRY.
UM...

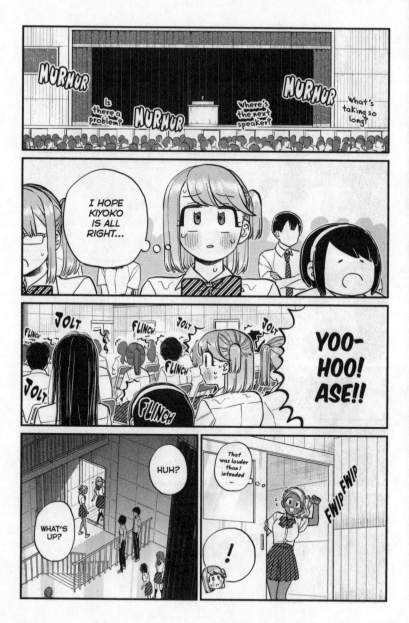

What's taking so long?
MURMUR
Where's the next speaker?
MURMUR
MURMUR
Is there a problem?
I HOPE KIYOKO IS ALL RIGHT...
YOO-HOO! ASE!!
JOLT
JOLT
FLINCH
FLINCH
JOLT
FLINCH
JOLT
FLINCH
FWIP FWIP
That was louder than I intended ...
!
HUH?
WHAT'S UP?

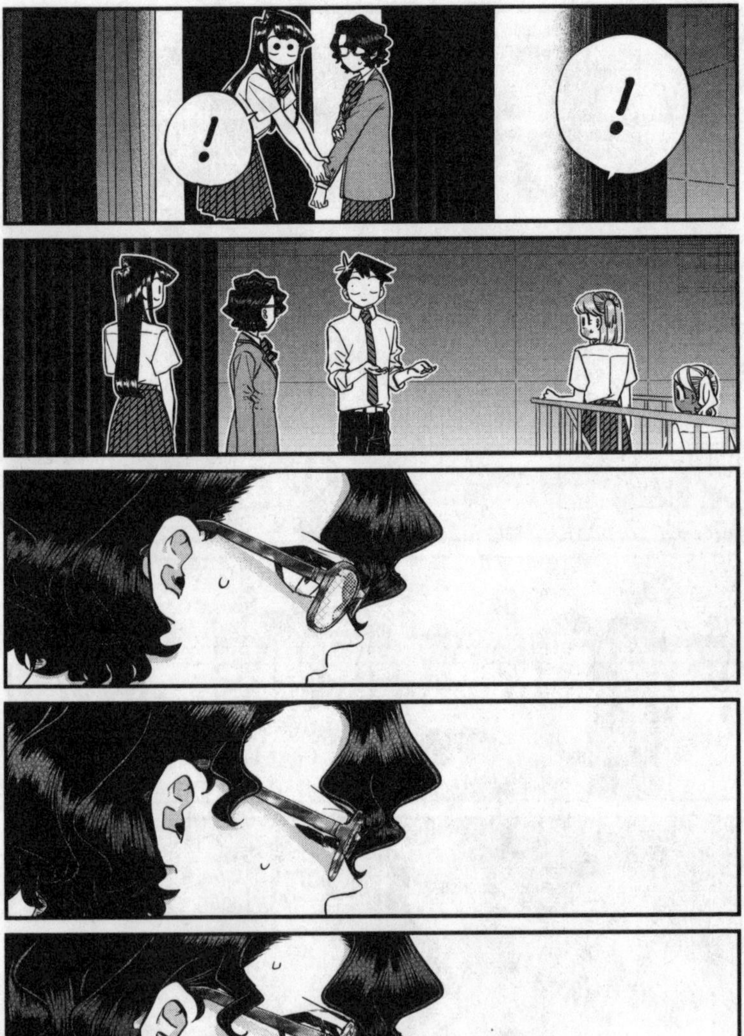
!
!

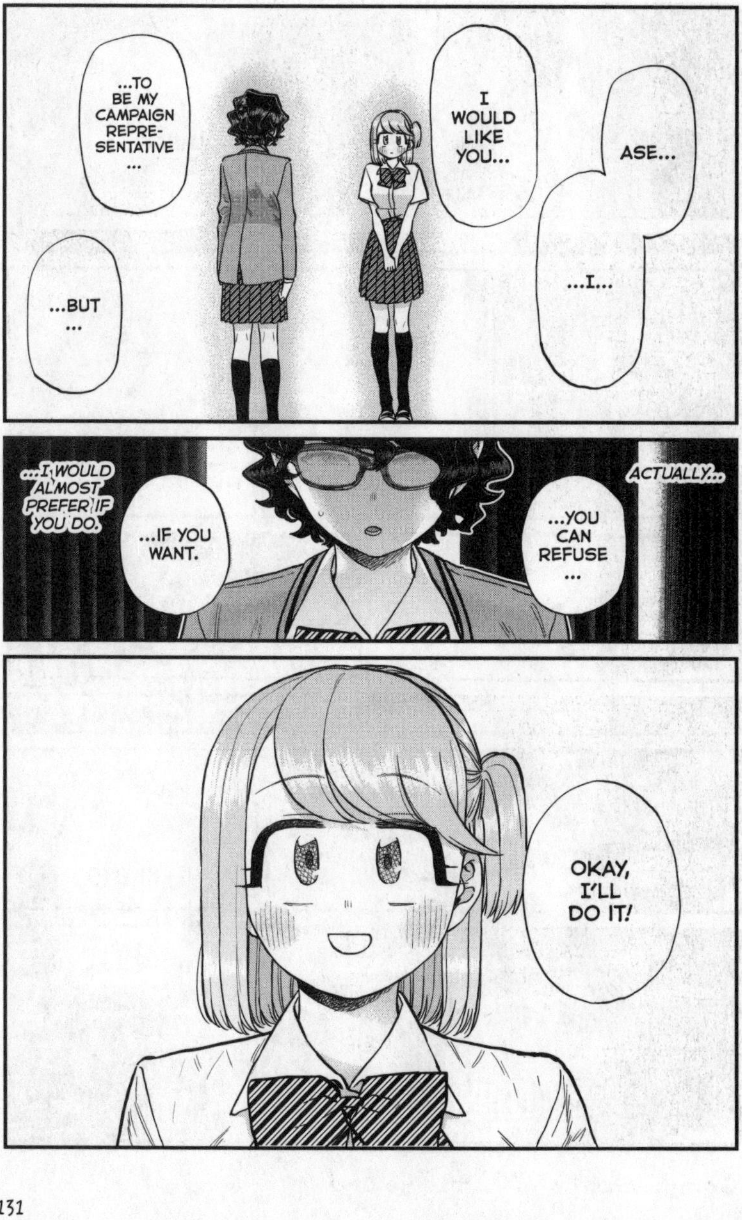
ASE...
...I...
I WOULD LIKE YOU...
...TO BE MY CAMPAIGN REPRESENTATIVE ...
...BUT ...
ACTUALLY...
...YOU CAN REFUSE ...
...IF YOU WANT.
...I WOULD ALMOST PREFER IF YOU DO.
OKAY, I'LL DO IT!

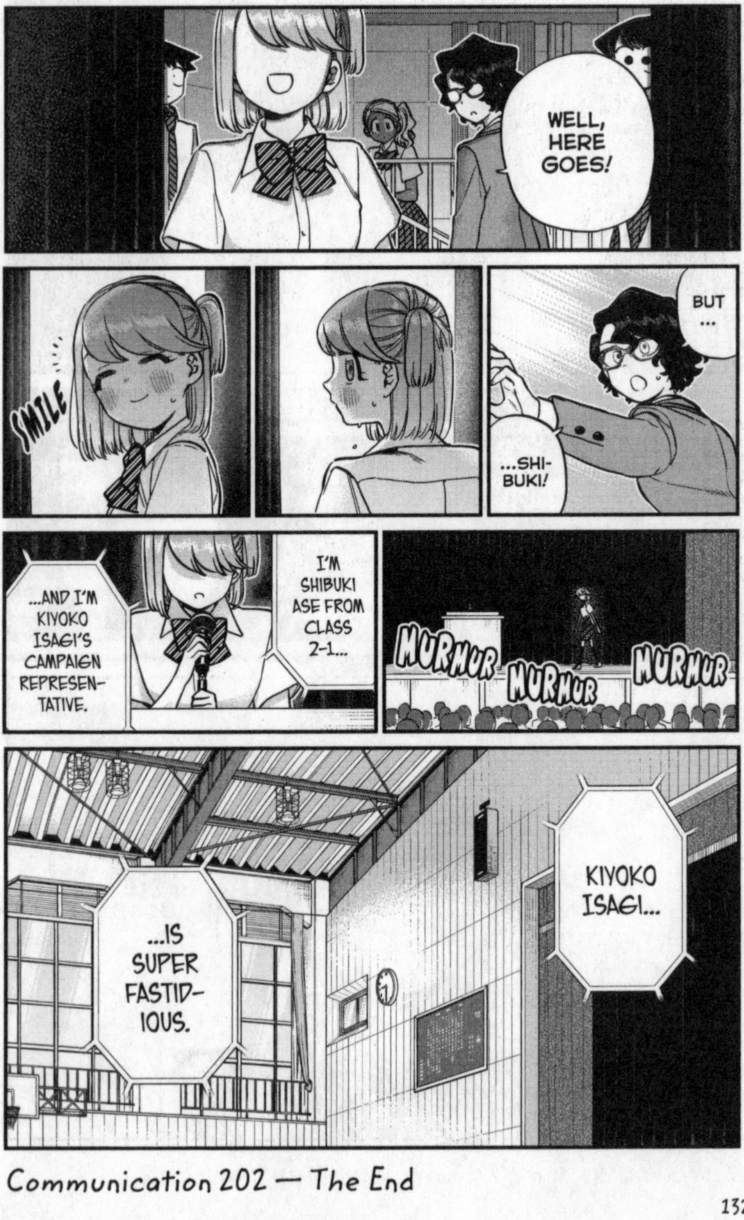
WELL, HERE GOES!
BUT ...
...SHI-BUKI!
SMILE
MURMUR
MURMUR
MURMUR
I'M SHIBUKI ASE FROM CLASS 2-1...
...AND I'M KIYOKO ISAGI'S CAMPAIGN REPRESEN-TATIVE.
KIYOKO ISAGI...
...IS SUPER FASTID-IOUS.

Communication 202 — The End

# Komi Can't Communicate

Communication 203: Campaign Rep, Part 2

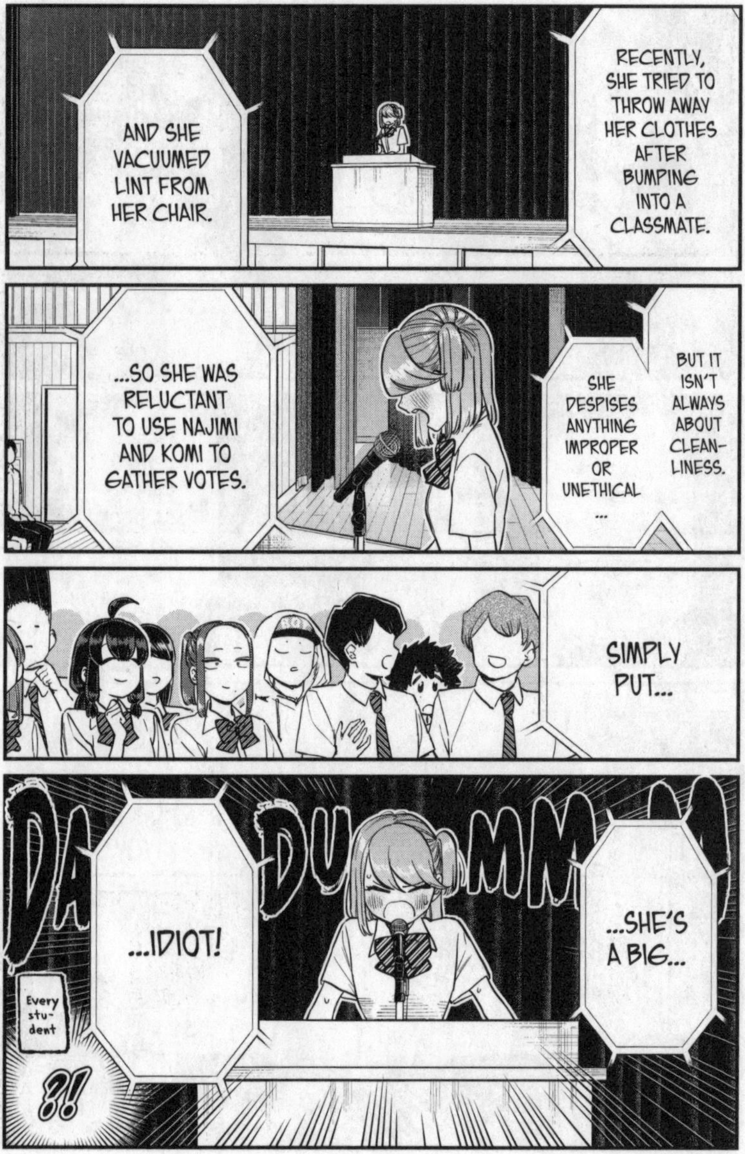
RECENTLY, SHE TRIED TO THROW AWAY HER CLOTHES AFTER BUMPING INTO A CLASSMATE.
AND SHE VACUUMED LINT FROM HER CHAIR.
BUT IT ISN'T ALWAYS ABOUT CLEANLINESS.
SHE DESPISES ANYTHING IMPROPER OR UNETHICAL...
...SO SHE WAS RELUCTANT TO USE NAJIMI AND KOMI TO GATHER VOTES.
SIMPLY PUT...
...SHE'S A BIG...
DA DU MM
...IDIOT!
Every student
?!

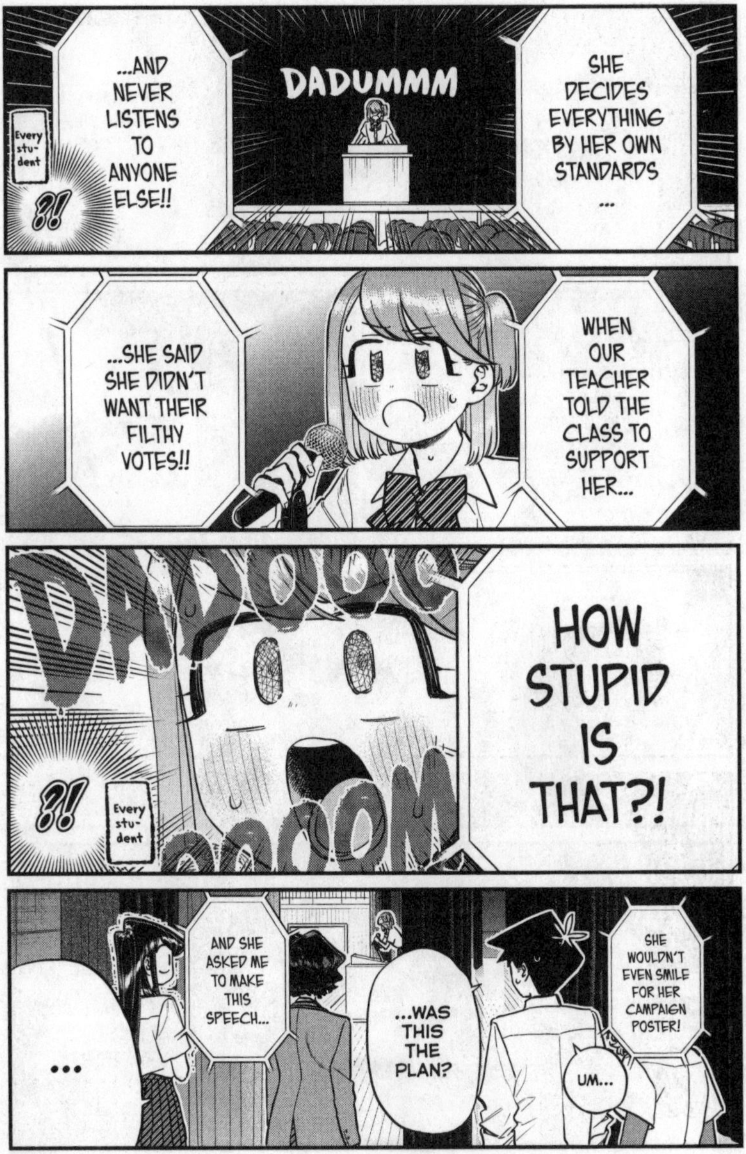
SHE DECIDES EVERYTHING BY HER OWN STANDARDS ...
DADUMMM
...AND NEVER LISTENS TO ANYONE ELSE!!
Every student
?!
WHEN OUR TEACHER TOLD THE CLASS TO SUPPORT HER...
...SHE SAID SHE DIDN'T WANT THEIR FILTHY VOTES!!
HOW STUPID IS THAT?!
?!
Every student
SHE WOULDN'T EVEN SMILE FOR HER CAMPAIGN POSTER!
UM...
...WAS THIS THE PLAN?
AND SHE ASKED ME TO MAKE THIS SPEECH...
...

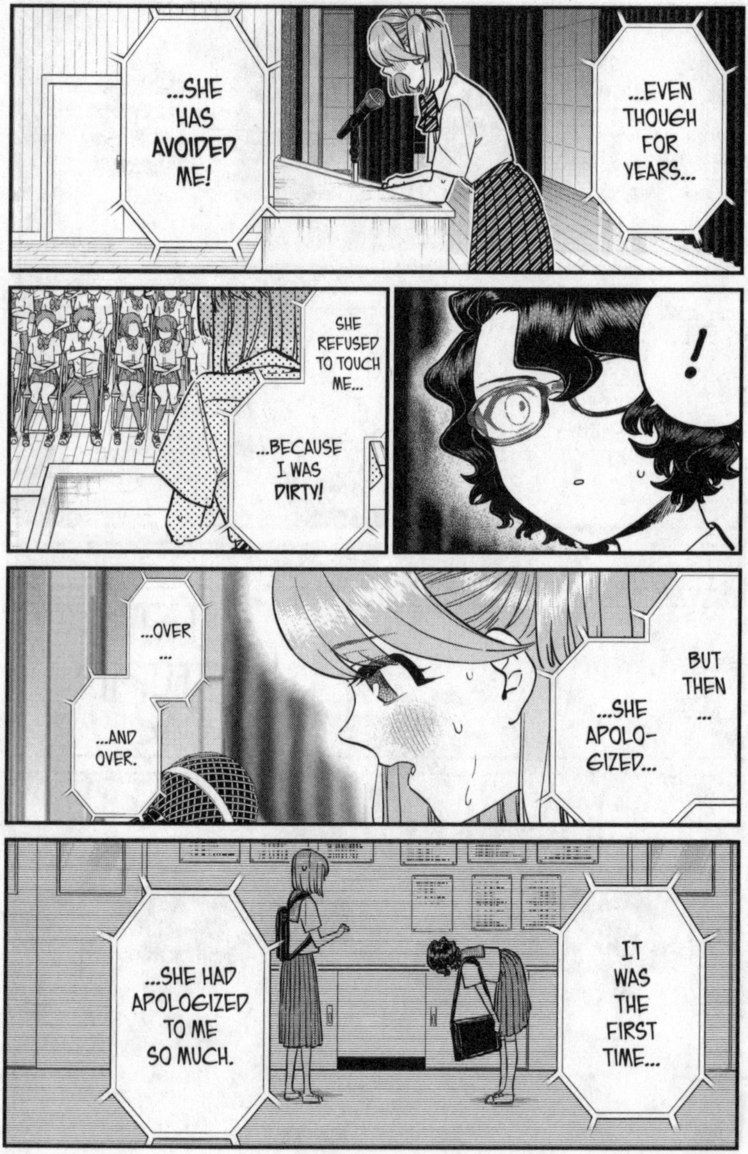
...EVEN THOUGH FOR YEARS...
...SHE HAS AVOIDED ME!
!
SHE REFUSED TO TOUCH ME...
...BECAUSE I WAS DIRTY!
BUT THEN ...
...SHE APOLOGIZED...
...OVER ...
...AND OVER.
IT WAS THE FIRST TIME...
...SHE HAD APOLOGIZED TO ME SO MUCH.

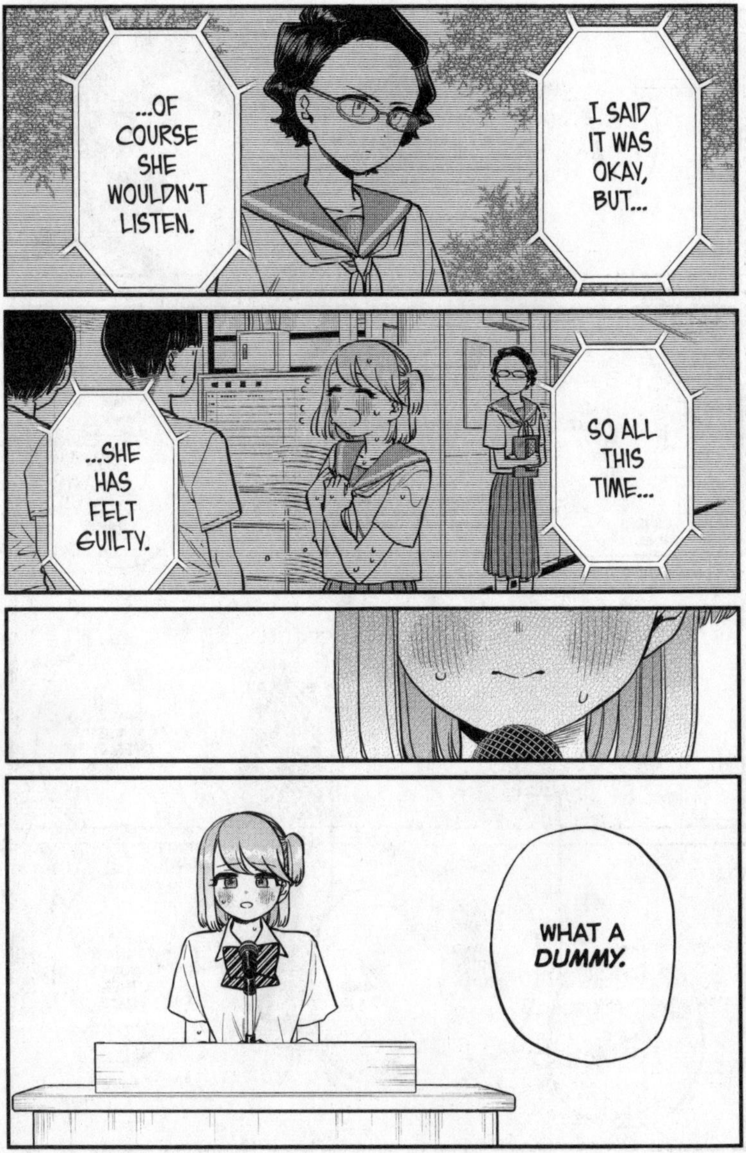
I SAID IT WAS OKAY, BUT...
...OF COURSE SHE WOULDN'T LISTEN.
SO ALL THIS TIME...
...SHE HAS FELT GUILTY.
WHAT A *DUMMY.*

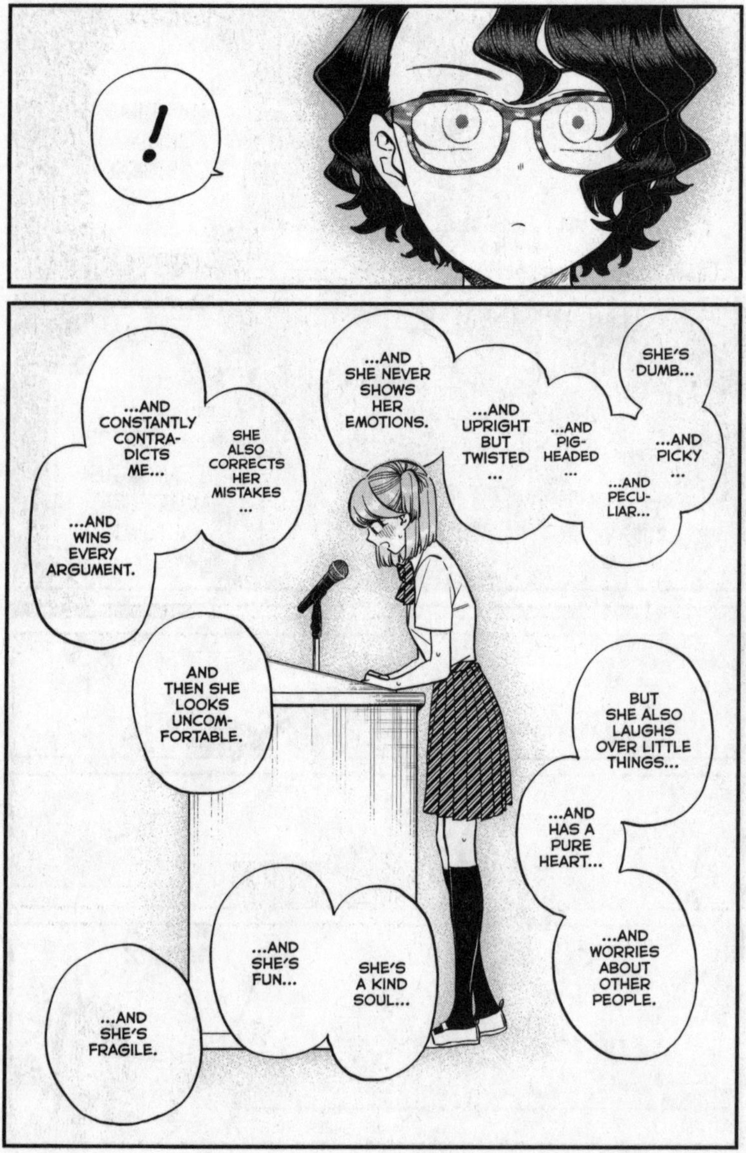
!
SHE'S DUMB...
...AND PICKY...
...AND PECULIAR...
...AND PIG-HEADED...
...AND UPRIGHT BUT TWISTED...
...AND SHE NEVER SHOWS HER EMOTIONS.
SHE ALSO CORRECTS HER MISTAKES...
...AND CONSTANTLY CONTRADICTS ME...
...AND WINS EVERY ARGUMENT.
AND THEN SHE LOOKS UNCOMFORTABLE.
BUT SHE ALSO LAUGHS OVER LITTLE THINGS...
...AND HAS A PURE HEART...
...AND WORRIES ABOUT OTHER PEOPLE.
SHE'S A KIND SOUL...
...AND SHE'S FUN...
...AND SHE'S FRAGILE.

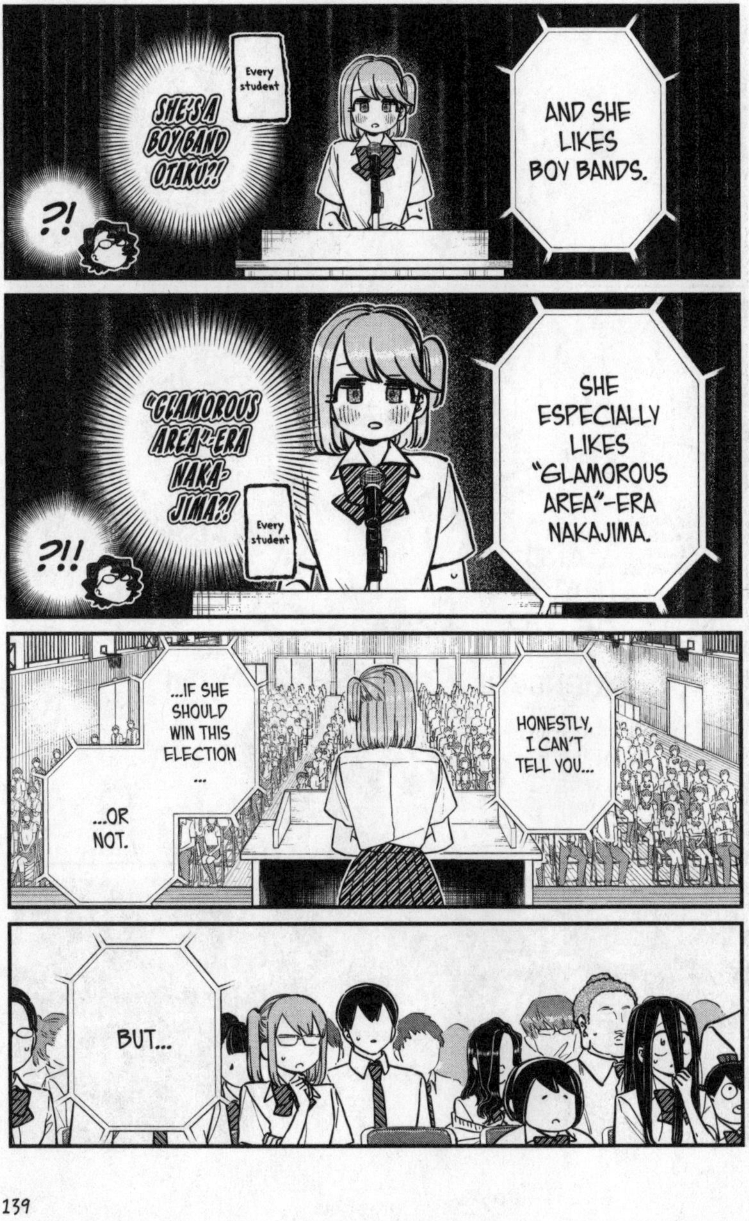
AND SHE LIKES BOY BANDS.
Every student
SHE'S A BOY BAND OTAKU?!
?!
SHE ESPECIALLY LIKES "GLAMOROUS AREA"-ERA NAKAJIMA.
Every student
"GLAMOROUS AREA"-ERA NAKA-JIMA?!
?!!
HONESTLY, I CAN'T TELL YOU...
...IF SHE SHOULD WIN THIS ELECTION...
...OR NOT.
BUT...

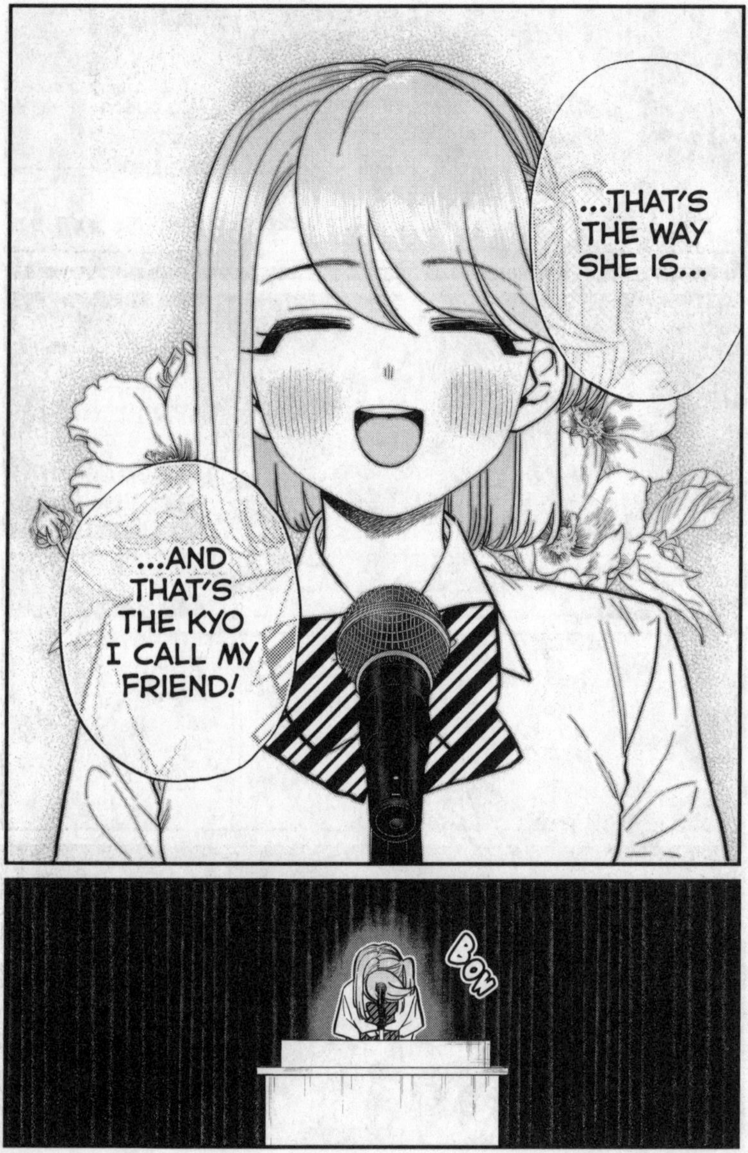
...THAT'S THE WAY SHE IS...
...AND THAT'S THE KYO I CALL MY FRIEND!
BOW

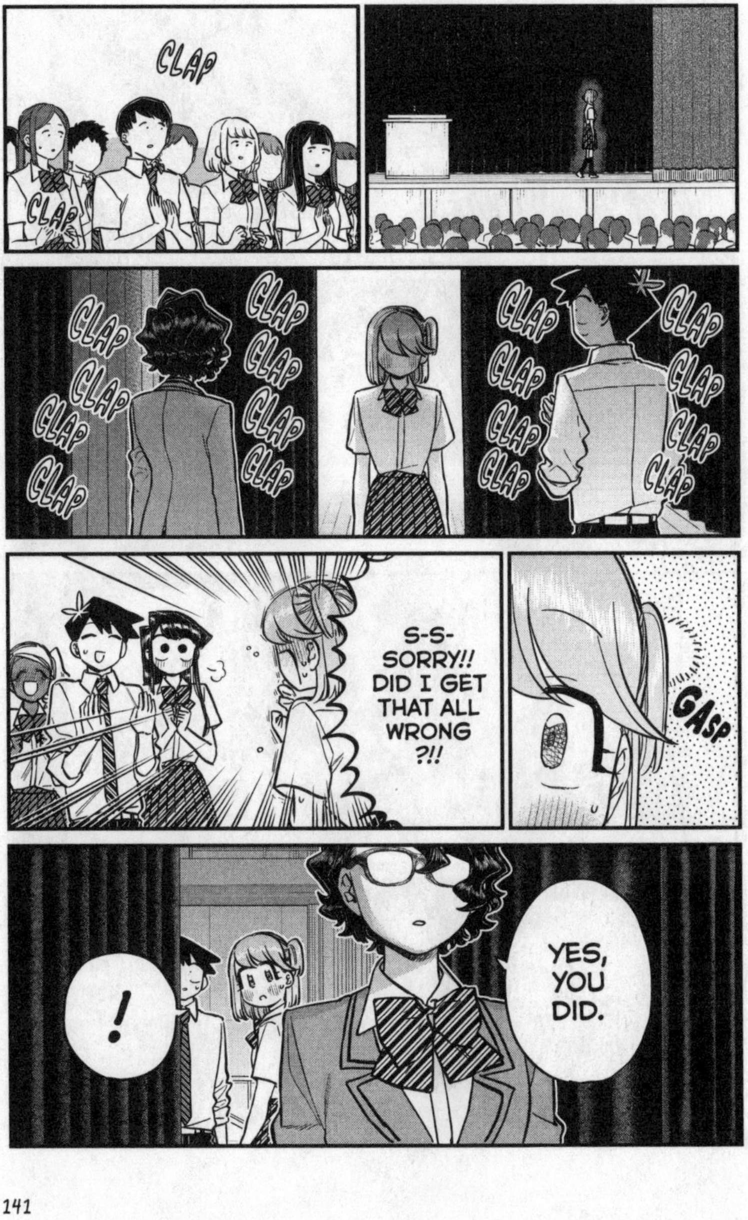

CLAP
CLAP
CLAP
CLAP
CLAP
CLAP
CLAP
CLAP
CLAP
CLAP
CLAP
CLAP
CLAP
CLAP
CLAP
CLAP
CLAP
CLAP
CLAP
GASP
S-S-SORRY!! DID I GET THAT ALL WRONG ?!!
YES, YOU DID.
!

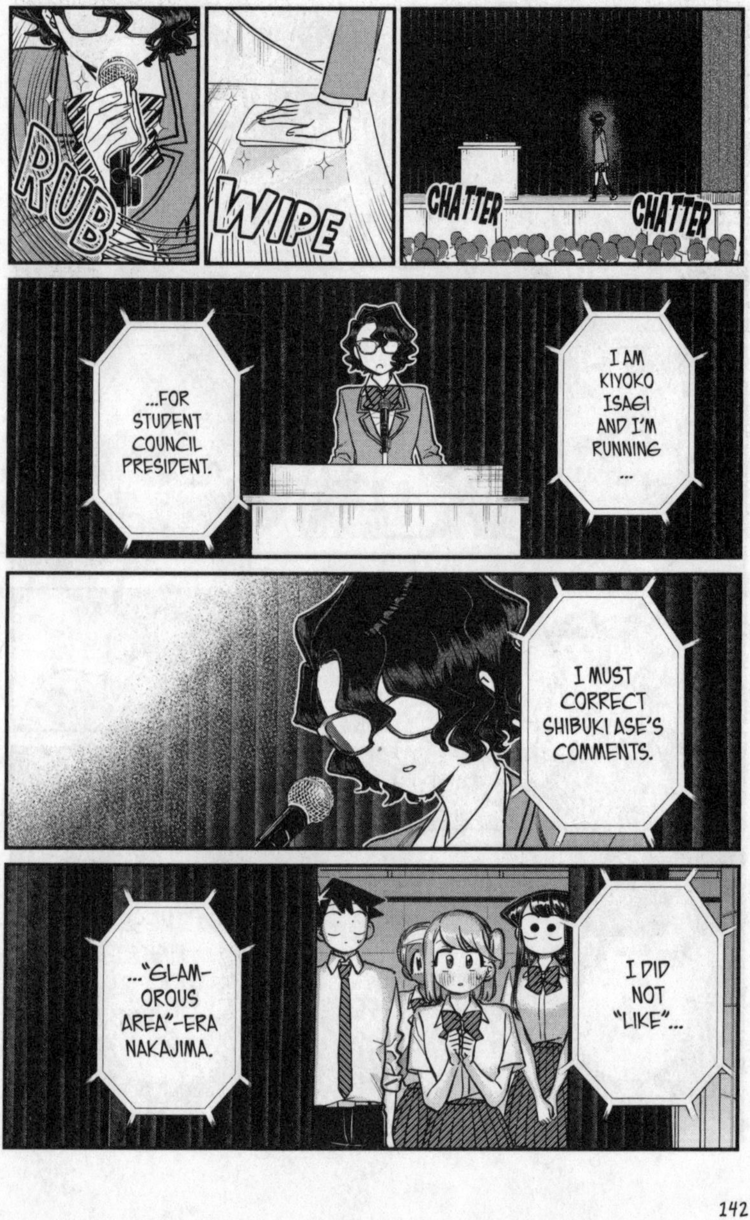
CHATTER
CHATTER
WIPE
RUB
I AM KIYOKO ISAGI AND I'M RUNNING ...
...FOR STUDENT COUNCIL PRESIDENT.
I MUST CORRECT SHIBUKI ASE'S COMMENTS.
I DID NOT "LIKE"...
..."GLAM-OROUS AREA"-ERA NAKAJIMA.

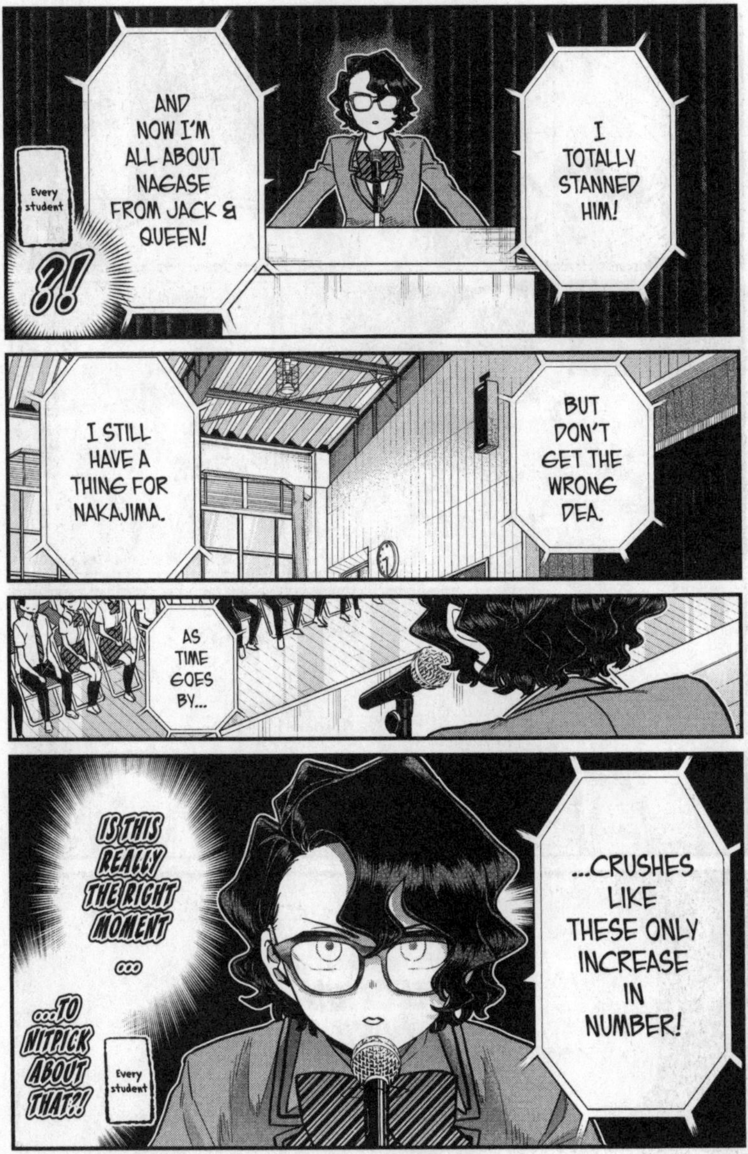
I TOTALLY STANNED HIM!
AND NOW I'M ALL ABOUT NAGASE FROM JACK & QUEEN!
Every student
?!
BUT DON'T GET THE WRONG DEA.
I STILL HAVE A THING FOR NAKAJIMA.
AS TIME GOES BY...
...CRUSHES LIKE THESE ONLY INCREASE IN NUMBER!
IS THIS REALLY THE RIGHT MOMENT ...
...TO NITPICK ABOUT THAT?!
Every student

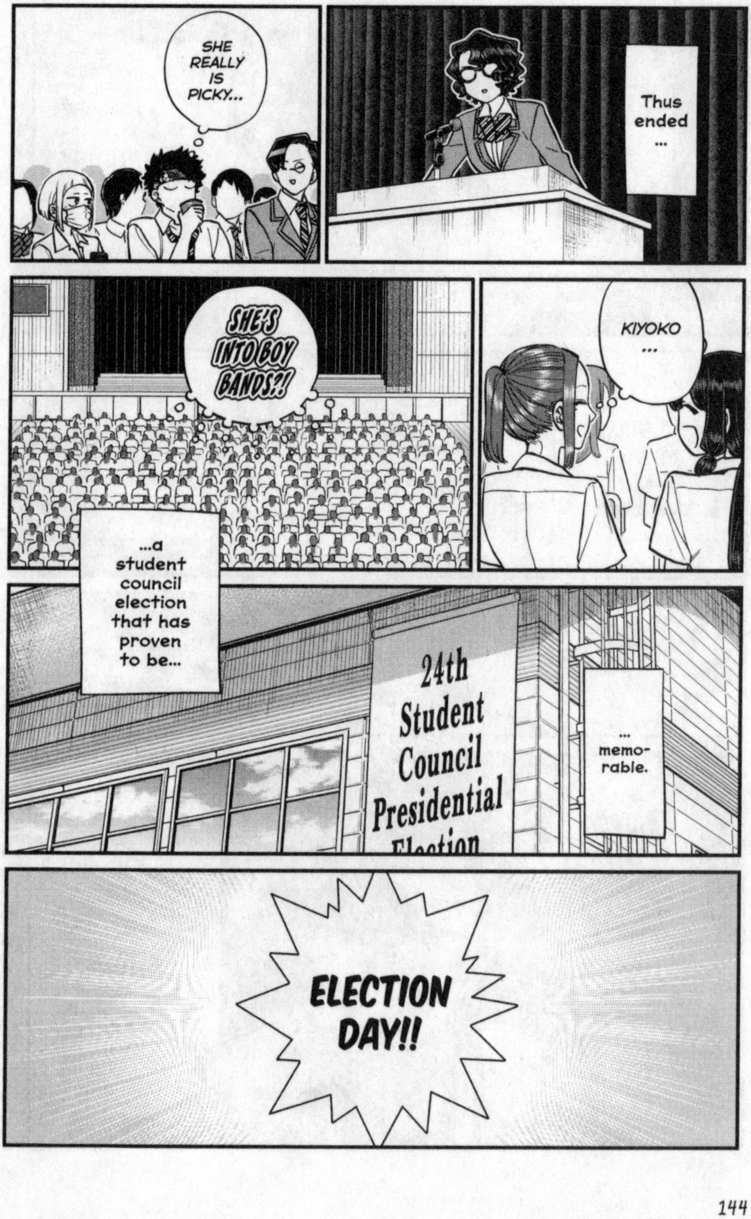
Thus ended ...
SHE REALLY IS PICKY...
KIYOKO ...
SHE'S INTO BOY BANDS?!
...a student council election that has proven to be...
24th Student Council Presidential Election
... memorable.
ELECTION DAY!!

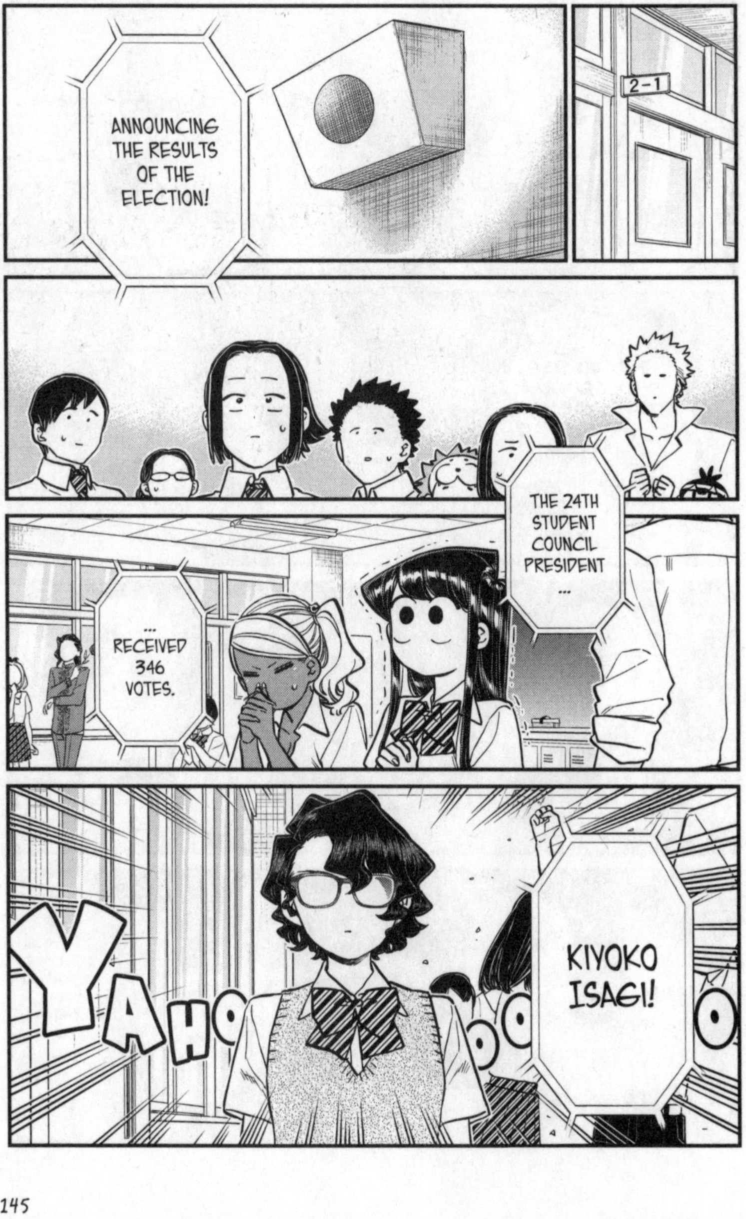
2-1
ANNOUNCING THE RESULTS OF THE ELECTION!
THE 24TH STUDENT COUNCIL PRESIDENT ...
... RECEIVED 346 VOTES.
KIYOKO ISAGI!
YAHOOOOOO

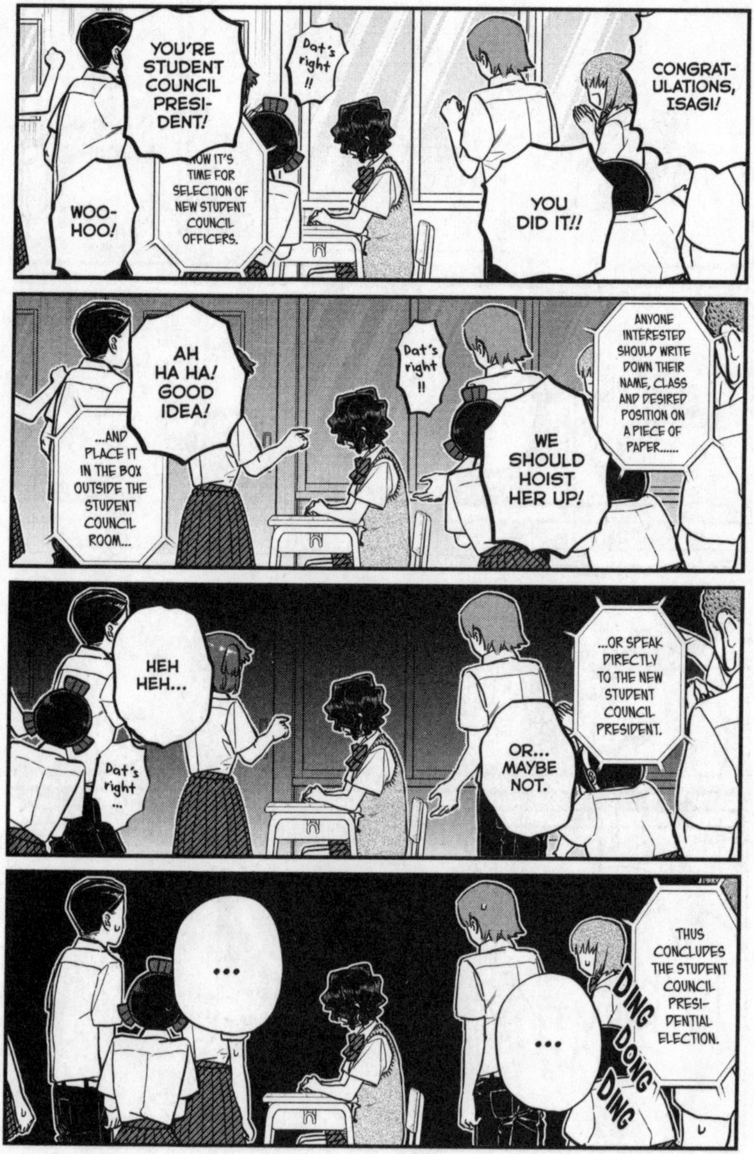
CONGRAT-ULATIONS, ISAGI!
Dat's right !!
YOU'RE STUDENT COUNCIL PRESI-DENT!
YOU DID IT!!
NOW IT'S TIME FOR SELECTION OF NEW STUDENT COUNCIL OFFICERS.
WOO-HOO!
ANYONE INTERESTED SHOULD WRITE DOWN THEIR NAME, CLASS AND DESIRED POSITION ON A PIECE OF PAPER......
Dat's right !!
AH HA HA! GOOD IDEA!
WE SHOULD HOIST HER UP!
...AND PLACE IT IN THE BOX OUTSIDE THE STUDENT COUNCIL ROOM...
...OR SPEAK DIRECTLY TO THE NEW STUDENT COUNCIL PRESIDENT.
HEH HEH...
OR... MAYBE NOT.
Dat's right ...
THUS CONCLUDES THE STUDENT COUNCIL PRESI-DENTIAL ELECTION.
DING DONG DING
...
...

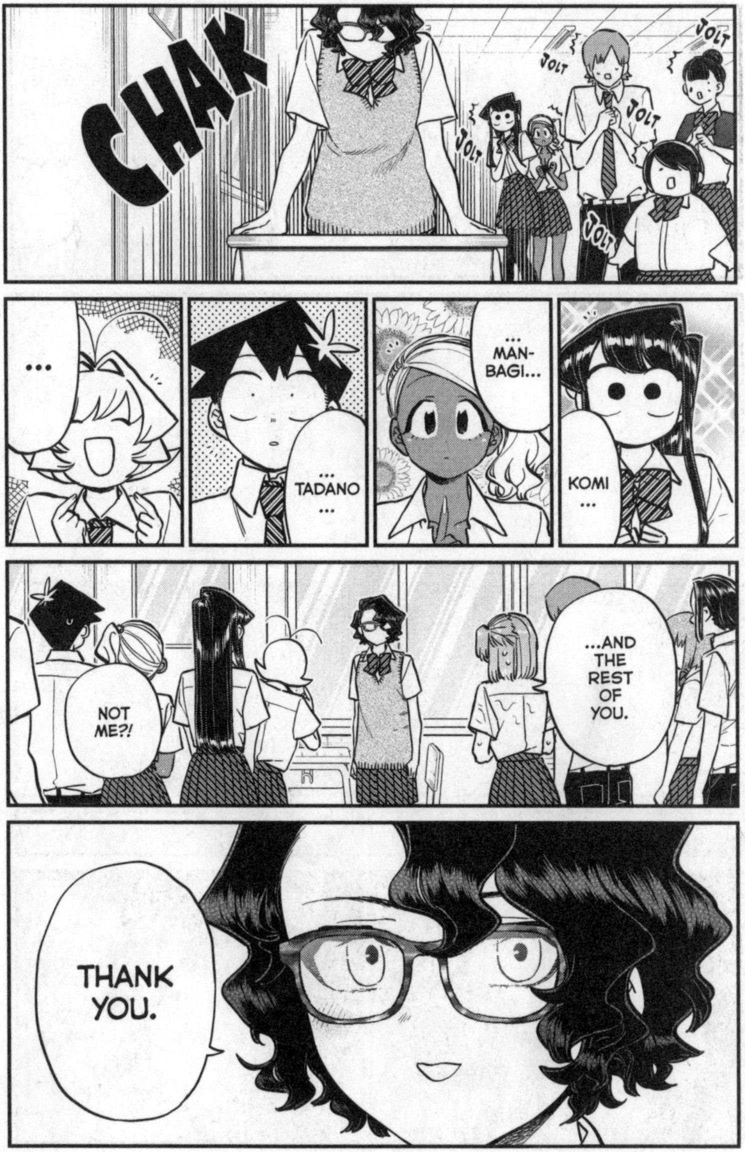
CHAK
JOLT
JOLT
JOLT
JOLT
JOLT
KOMI ...
... MANBAGI...
... TADANO ...
...
...AND THE REST OF YOU.
NOT ME?!
THANK YOU.

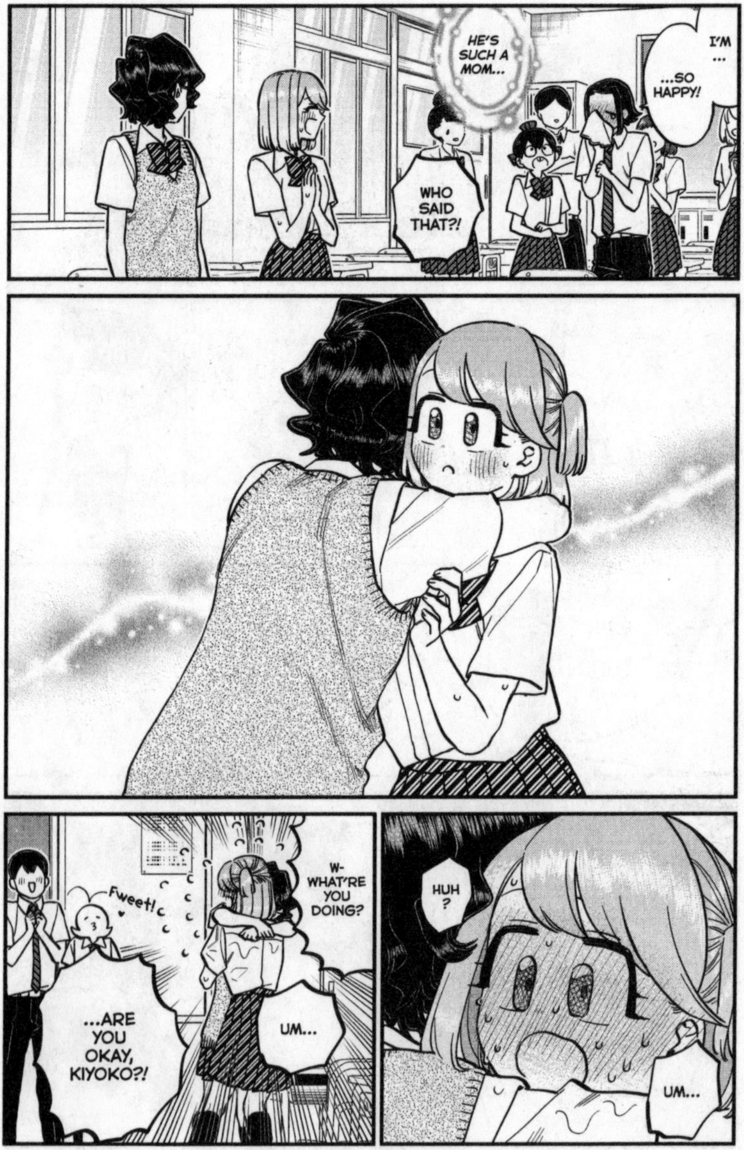
I'M ... ...SO HAPPY!
HE'S SUCH A MOM...
WHO SAID THAT?!
HUH?
UM...
W-WHAT'RE YOU DOING?
Fweet!
UM...
...ARE YOU OKAY, KIYOKO?!

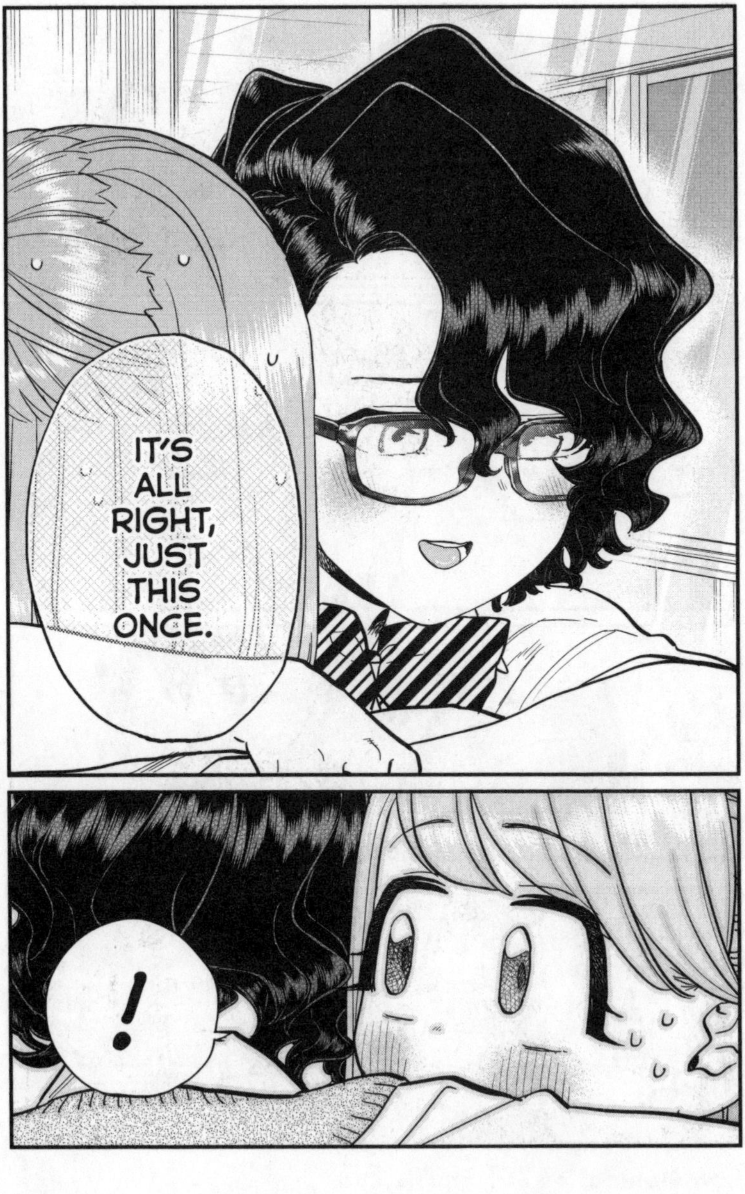
IT'S ALL RIGHT, JUST THIS ONCE.
!

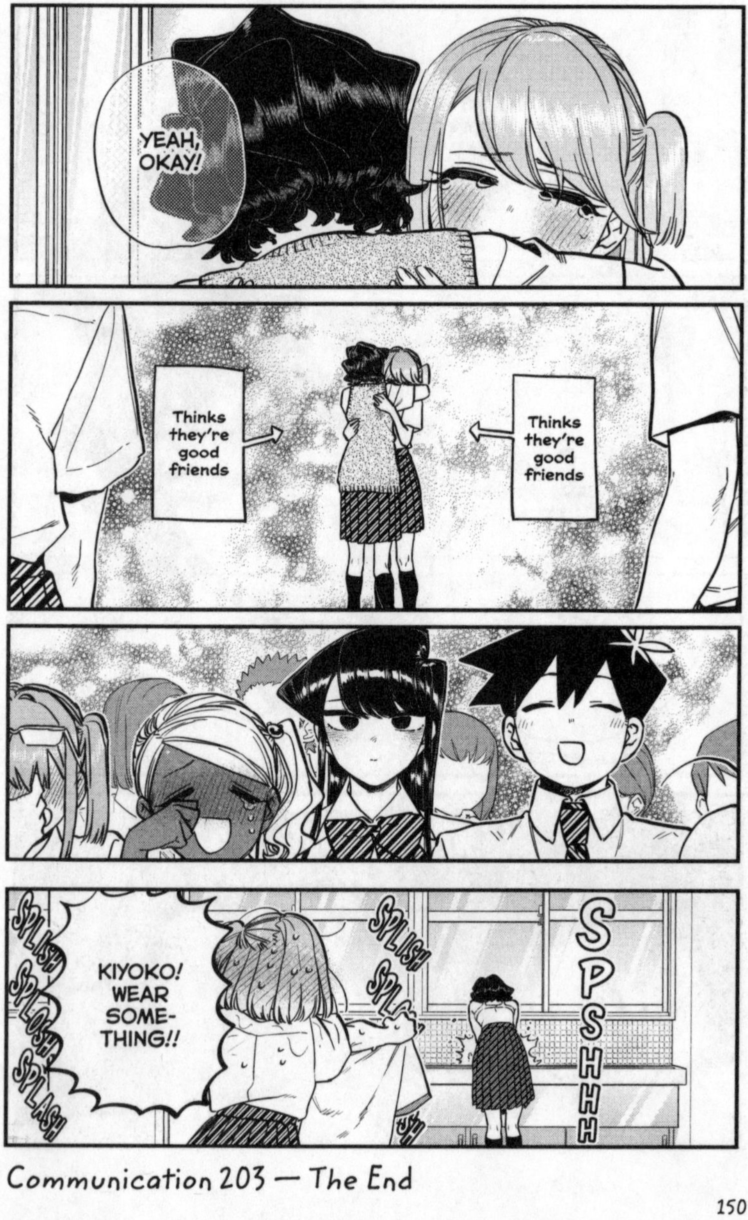
YEAH, OKAY!
Thinks they're good friends
Thinks they're good friends
SPSHHH
SPLISH SPLA
KIYOKO! WEAR SOME-THING!!
SPLISH SPLOSH SPLASH

Communication 203 — The End

# Komi Can't Communicate

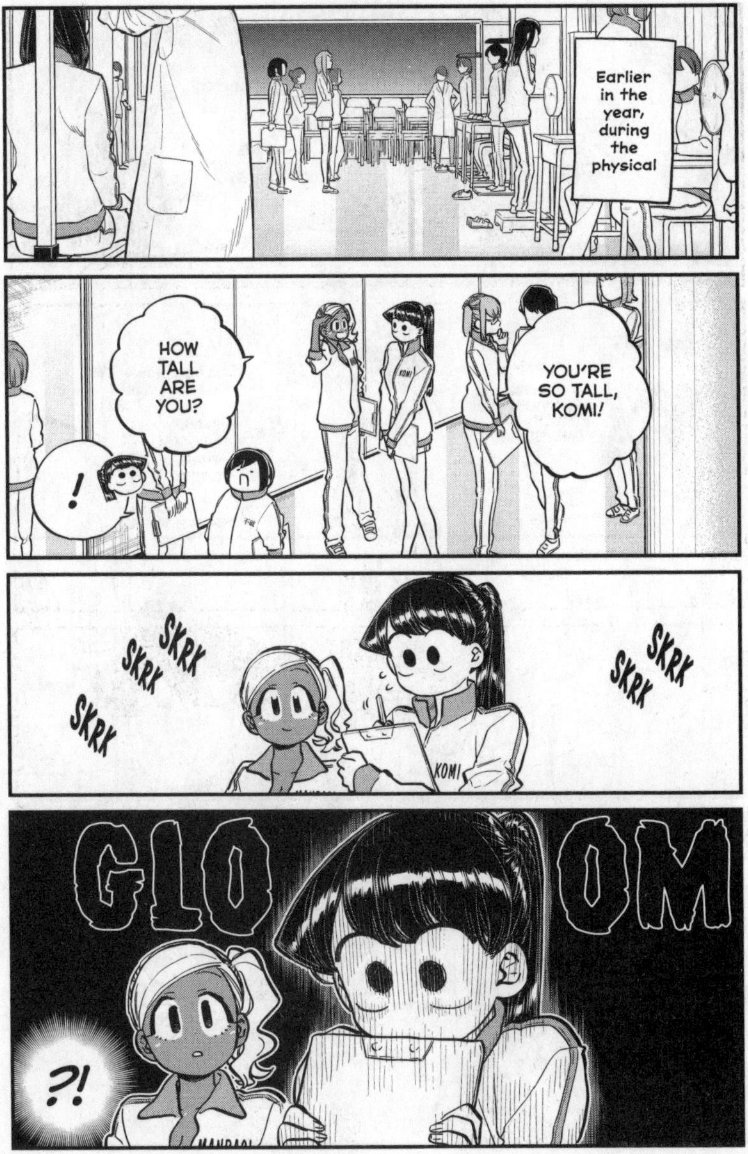
Earlier in the year, during the physical
YOU'RE SO TALL, KOMI!
HOW TALL ARE YOU?
!
SKRK SKRK
SKRK SKRK SKRK
GLOOM
?!

Communication 204: Height

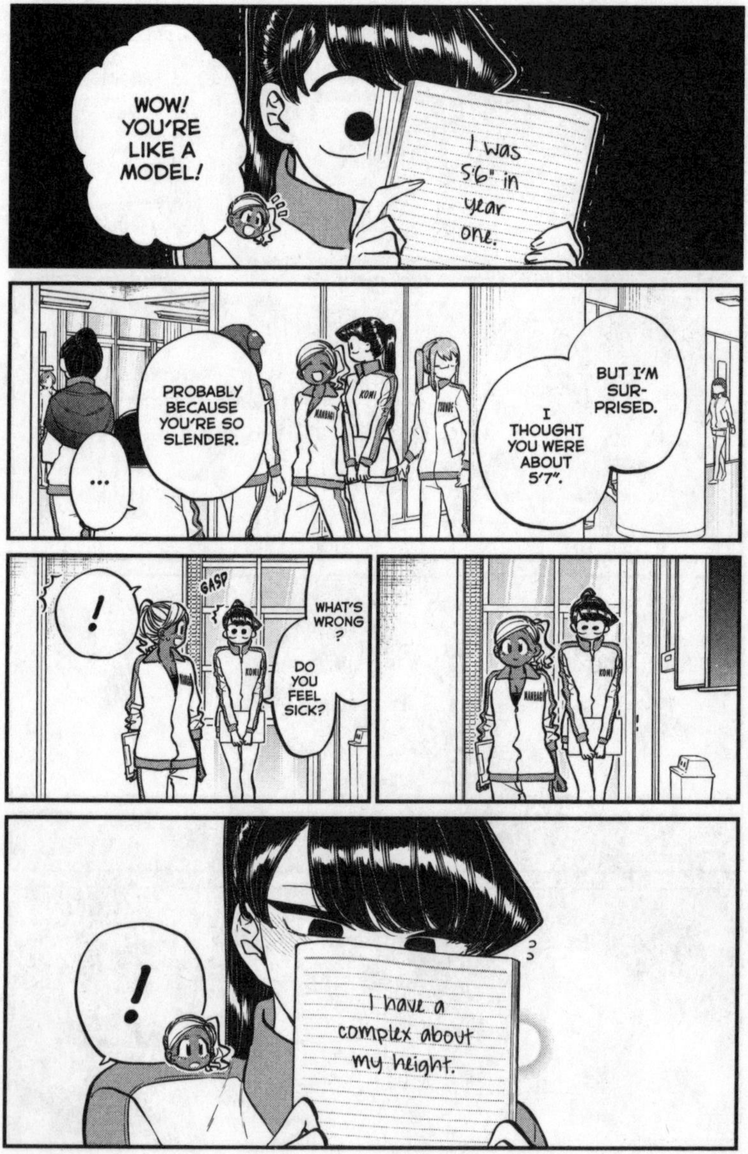
I was 5'6" in year one.
WOW! YOU'RE LIKE A MODEL!
BUT I'M SUR-PRISED.
I THOUGHT YOU WERE ABOUT 5'7".
PROBABLY BECAUSE YOU'RE SO SLENDER.
...
WHAT'S WRONG?
DO YOU FEEL SICK?
GASP
!
I have a complex about my height.
!

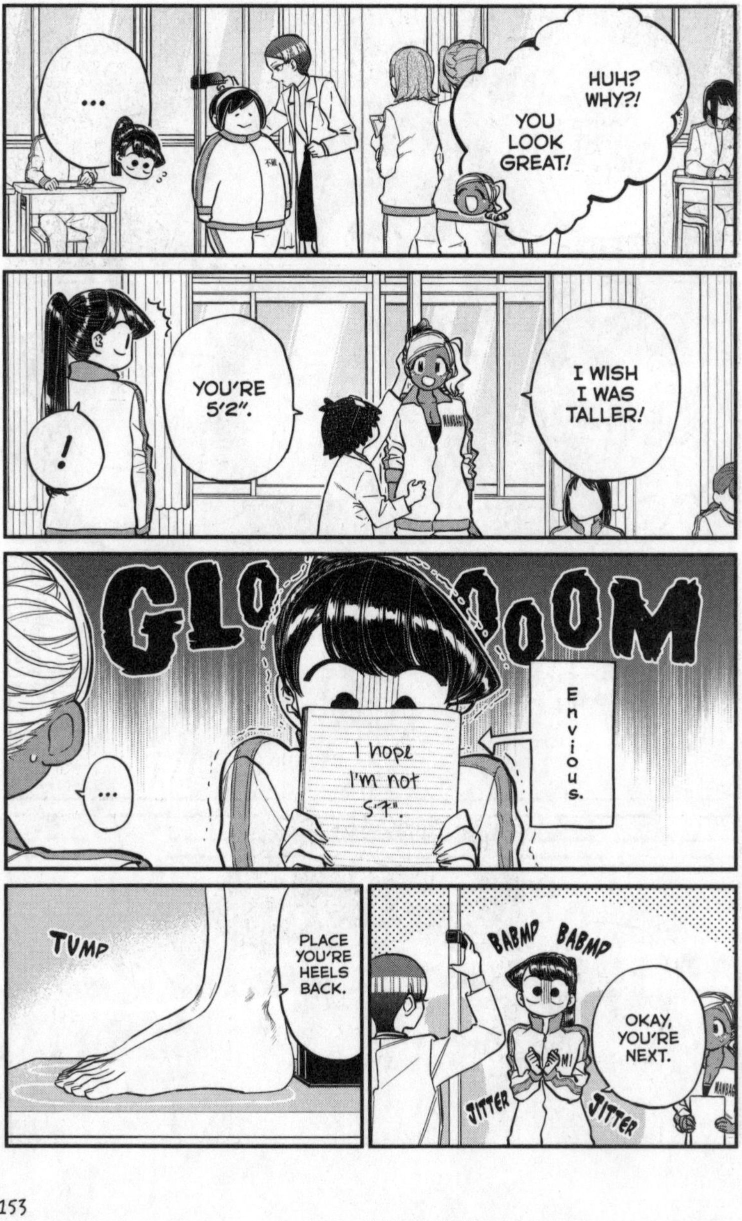
HUH? WHY?!
YOU LOOK GREAT!
...
I WISH I WAS TALLER!
YOU'RE 5'2".
!
GLOOOOM
Envious.
I hope I'm not 5'7".
...
BABMP BABMP
OKAY, YOU'RE NEXT.
MI!
JITTER JITTER
PLACE YOU'RE HEELS BACK.
TUMP

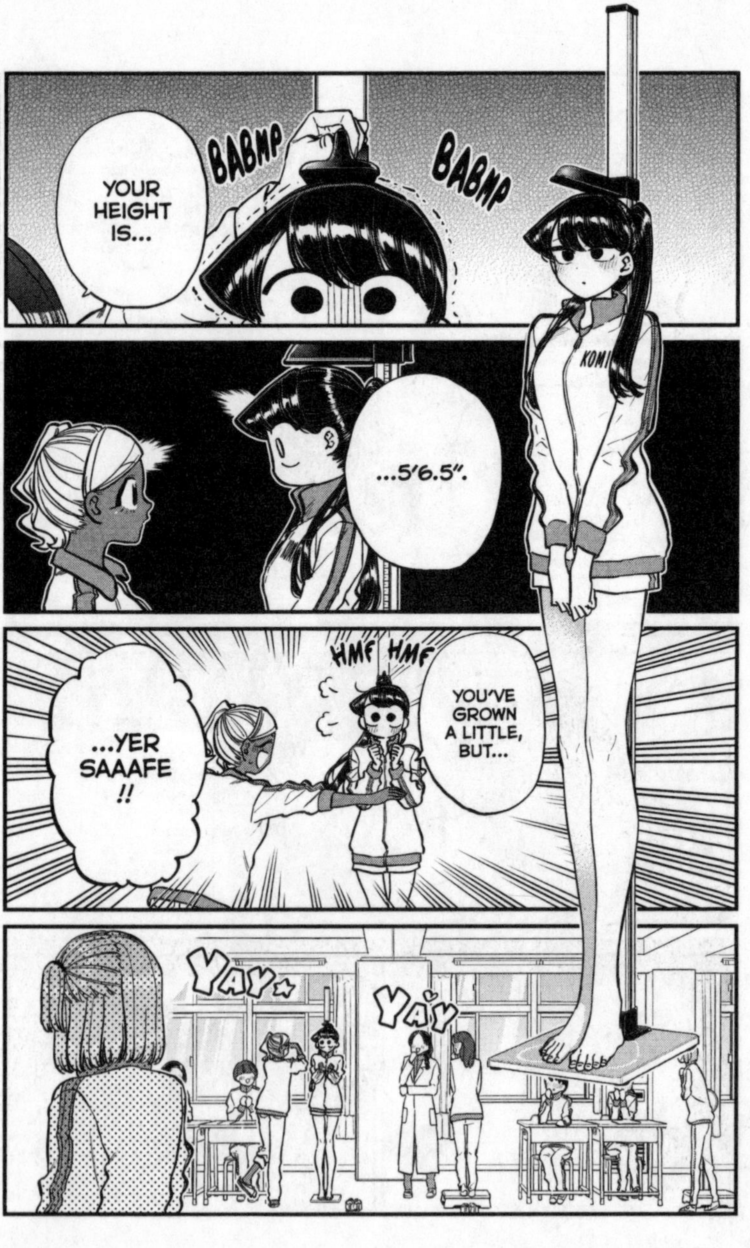
BABMP
BABMP
YOUR HEIGHT IS...
...5'6.5".
HMF HMF
YOU'VE GROWN A LITTLE, BUT...
...YER SAAAFE !!
YAY
YAY☆

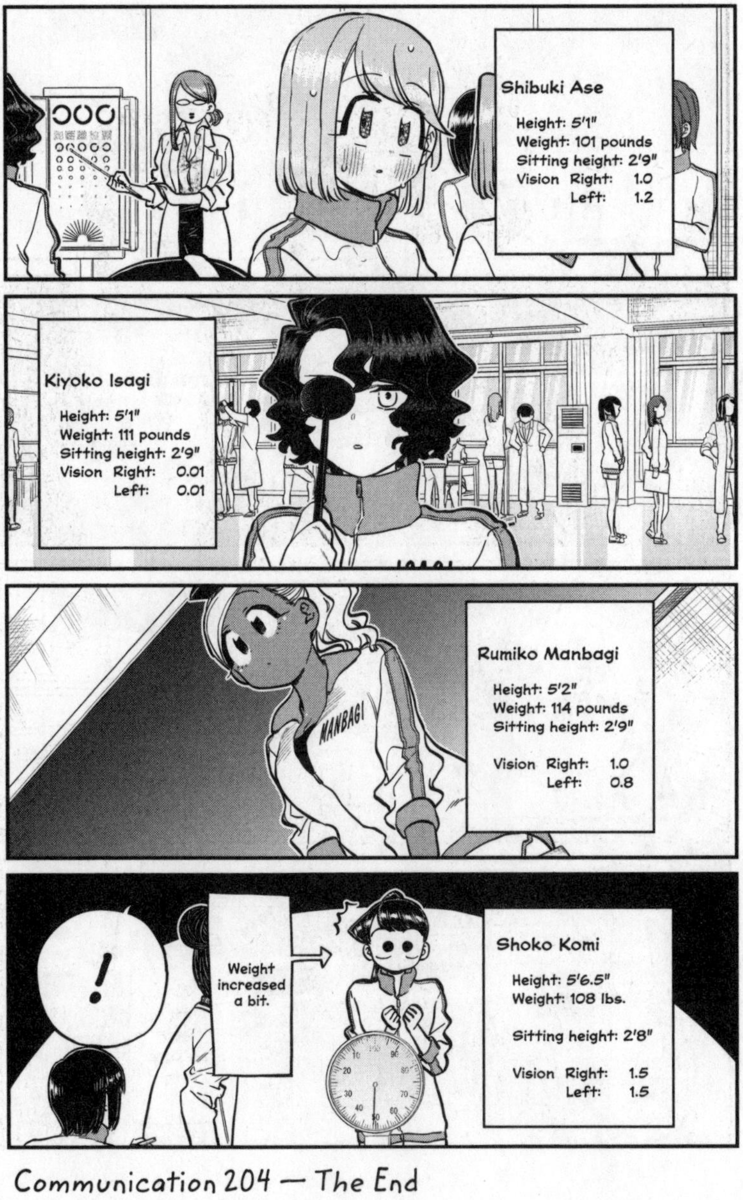
Shibuki Ase
Height: 5'1"
Weight: 101 pounds
Sitting height: 2'9"
Vision Right: 1.0
Left: 1.2
Kiyoko Isagi
Height: 5'1"
Weight: 111 pounds
Sitting height: 2'9"
Vision Right: 0.01
Left: 0.01
Rumiko Manbagi
Height: 5'2"
Weight: 114 pounds
Sitting height: 2'9"
Vision Right: 1.0
Left: 0.8
MANBAGI
Shoko Komi
Height: 5'6.5"
Weight: 108 lbs.
Sitting height: 2'8"
Vision Right: 1.5
Left: 1.5
Weight increased a bit.
!

Communication 204 — The End

# Komi Can't Communicate

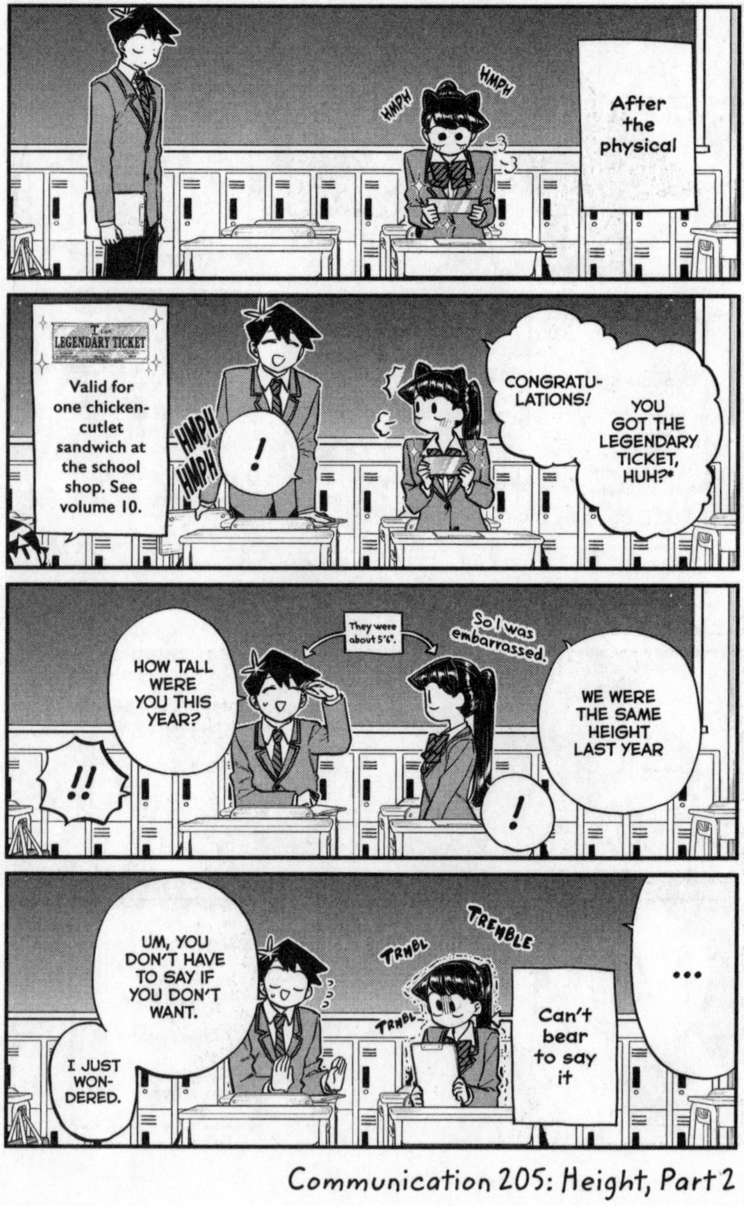
After the physical
HMPH
HMPH
CONGRATULATIONS!
YOU GOT THE LEGENDARY TICKET, HUH?*
HMPH
HMPH
!
LEGENDARY TICKET
Valid for one chicken-cutlet sandwich at the school shop. See volume 10.
WE WERE THE SAME HEIGHT LAST YEAR
!
So I was embarrassed.
They were about 5'6".
HOW TALL WERE YOU THIS YEAR?
!!
...
Can't bear to say it
TREMBLE
TRMBL
TRMBL
UM, YOU DON'T HAVE TO SAY IF YOU DON'T WANT.
I JUST WONDERED.

Communication 205: Height, Part 2

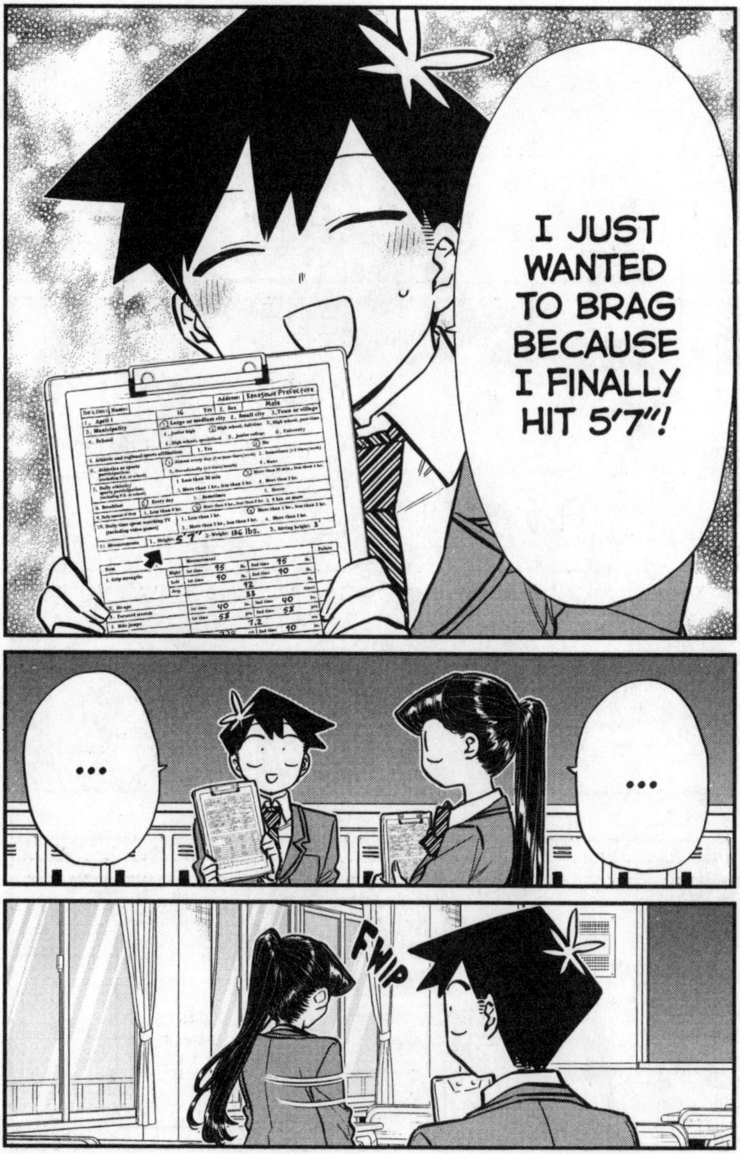
I JUST WANTED TO BRAG BECAUSE I FINALLY HIT 5'7"!
...
...
FWIP

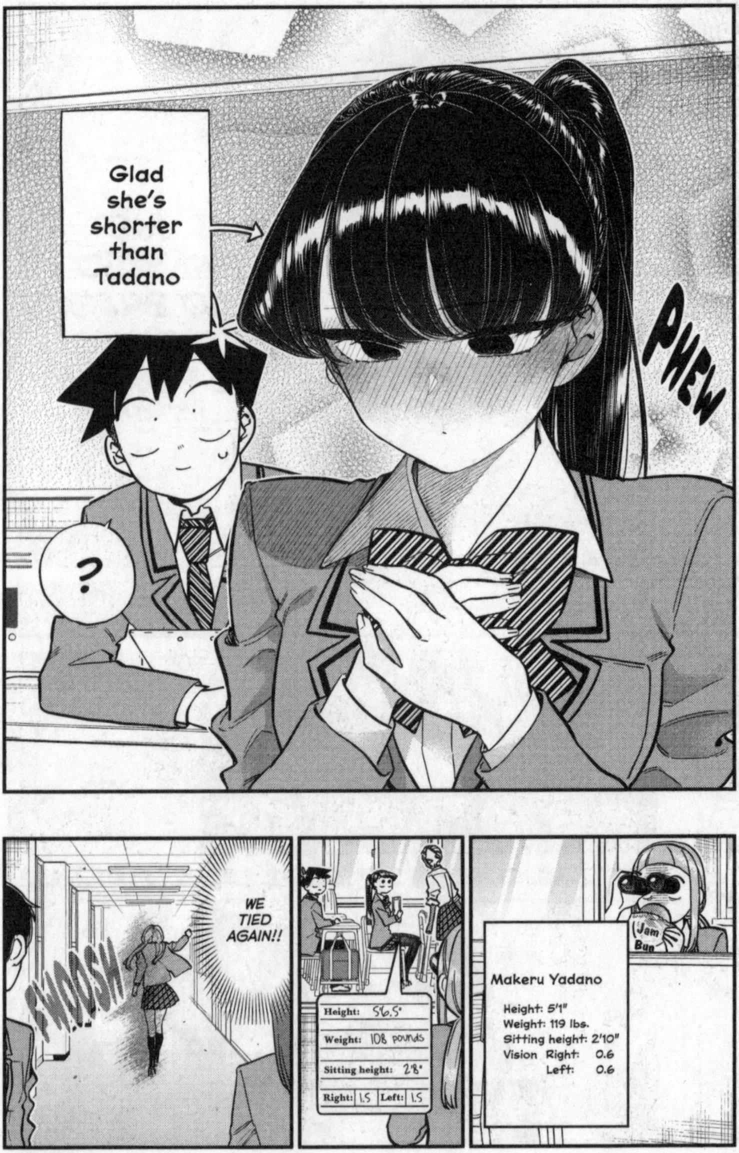
Glad she's shorter than Tadano
PHEW
?
Makeru Yadano
Height: 5'1"
Weight: 119 lbs.
Sitting height: 2'10"
Vision Right: 0.6
Left: 0.6
Jam Bun
Height: 5'6.5"
Weight: 108 pounds
Sitting height: 2'8"
Right: 1.5 Left: 1.5
WE TIED AGAIN!!
FWOOSH

Communication 205 — The End

# Komi Can't Communicate

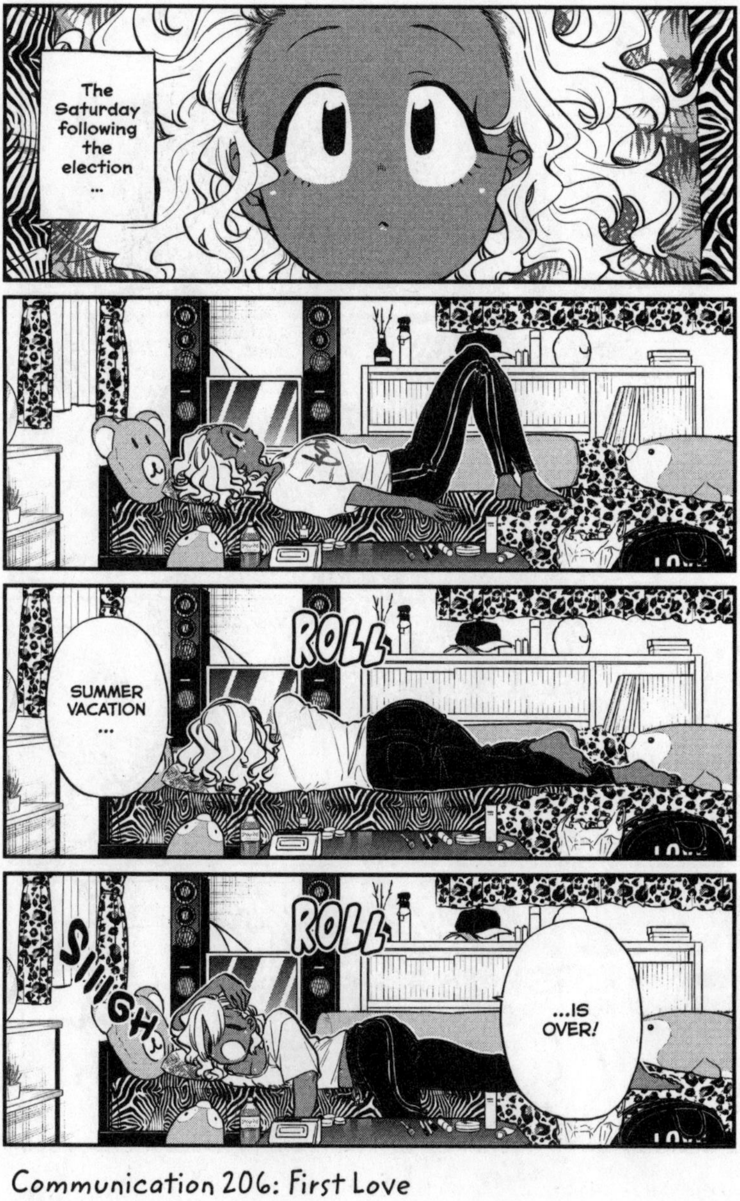
The Saturday following the election ...
ROLL
SUMMER VACATION ...
ROLL
...IS OVER!
SIIIGH

Communication 206: First Love

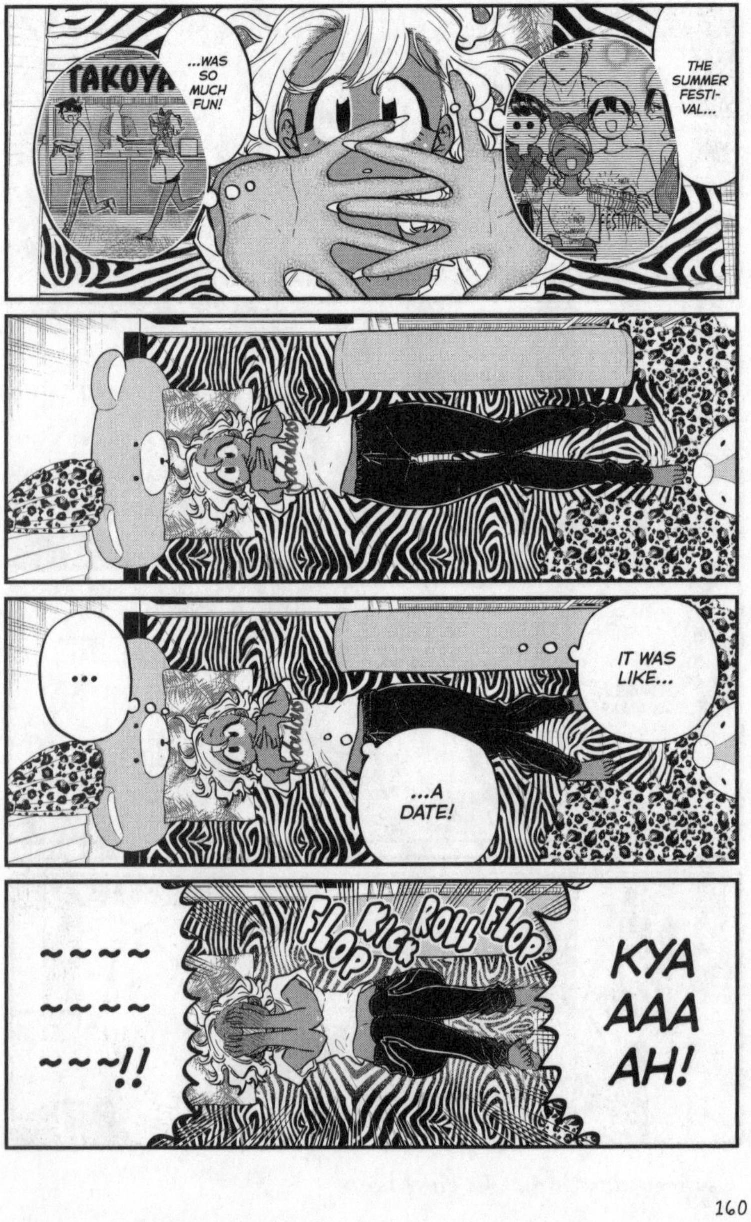
THE SUMMER FESTI-VAL...
...WAS SO MUCH FUN!
TAKOYA
IT WAS LIKE...
...A DATE!
...
KYA AAA AH!
FLOP
ROLL
KICK
FLOP
~~~~~ ~~~~~ ~~~!!
~~~~~

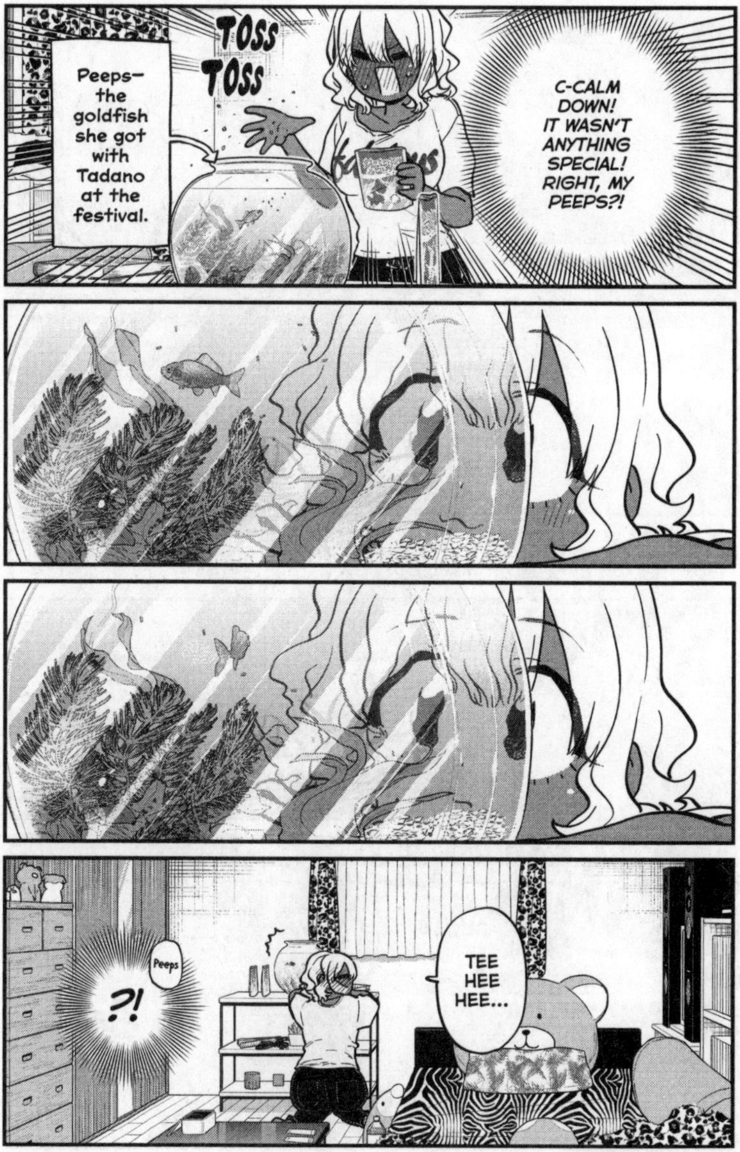
C-CALM DOWN! IT WASN'T ANYTHING SPECIAL! RIGHT, MY PEEPS?!
TOSS TOSS
Peeps—the goldfish she got with Tadano at the festival.
TEE HEE HEE...
?!
Peeps

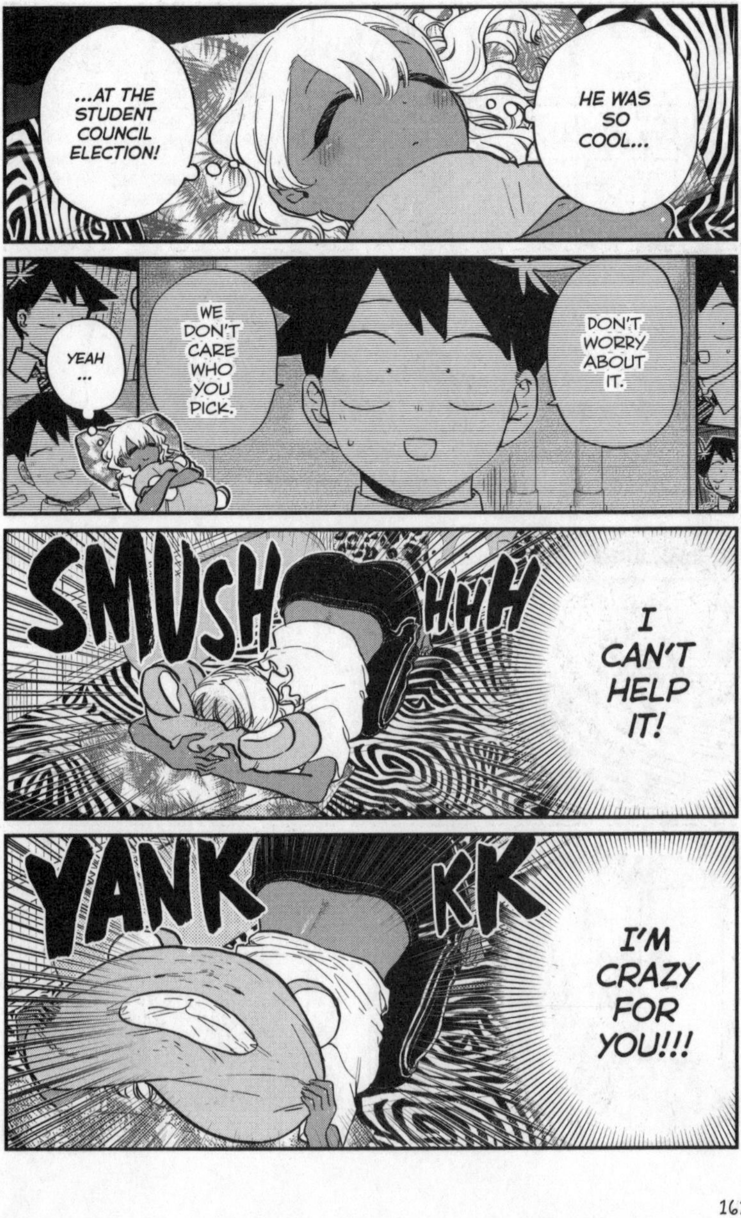
HE WAS SO COOL...
...AT THE STUDENT COUNCIL ELECTION!
DON'T WORRY ABOUT IT.
WE DON'T CARE WHO YOU PICK.
YEAH ...
SMUSHHHH
I CAN'T HELP IT!
YANKKK
I'M CRAZY FOR YOU!!!

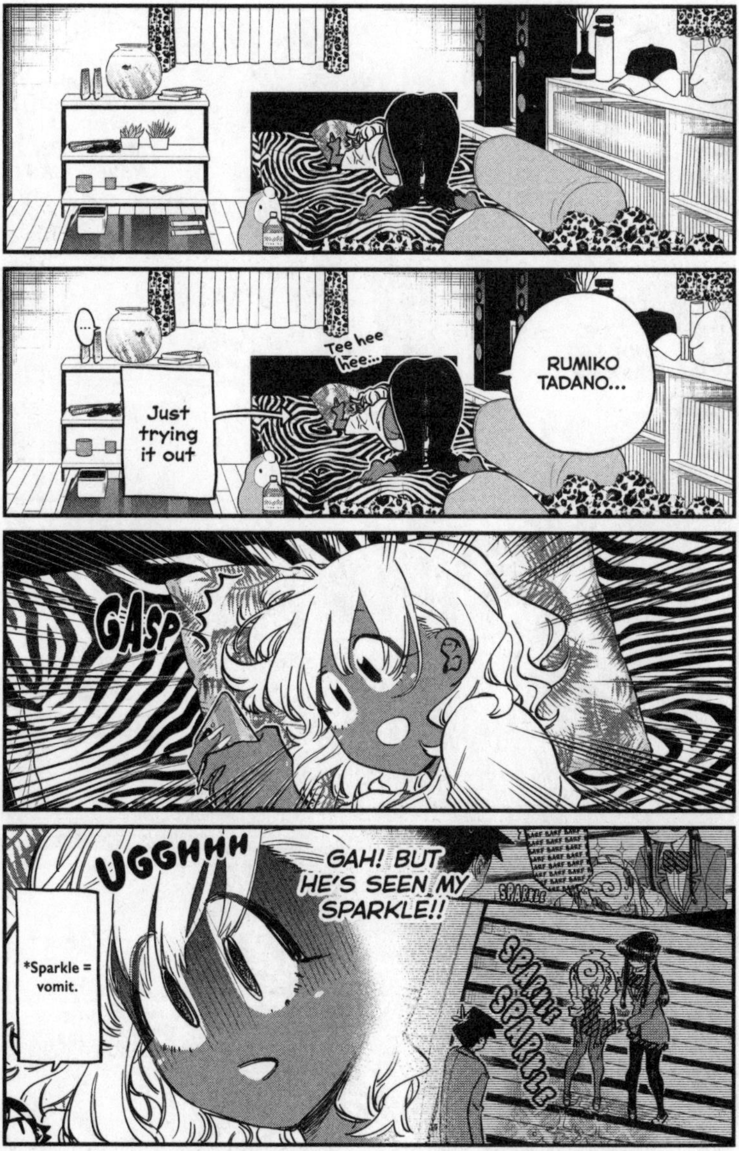
RUMIKO TADANO...
Tee hee hee...
Just trying it out
...
GASP
SPARKLE
SPARKLE SPARKLE
GAH! BUT HE'S SEEN MY SPARKLE!!
UGGHHH
*Sparkle = vomit.

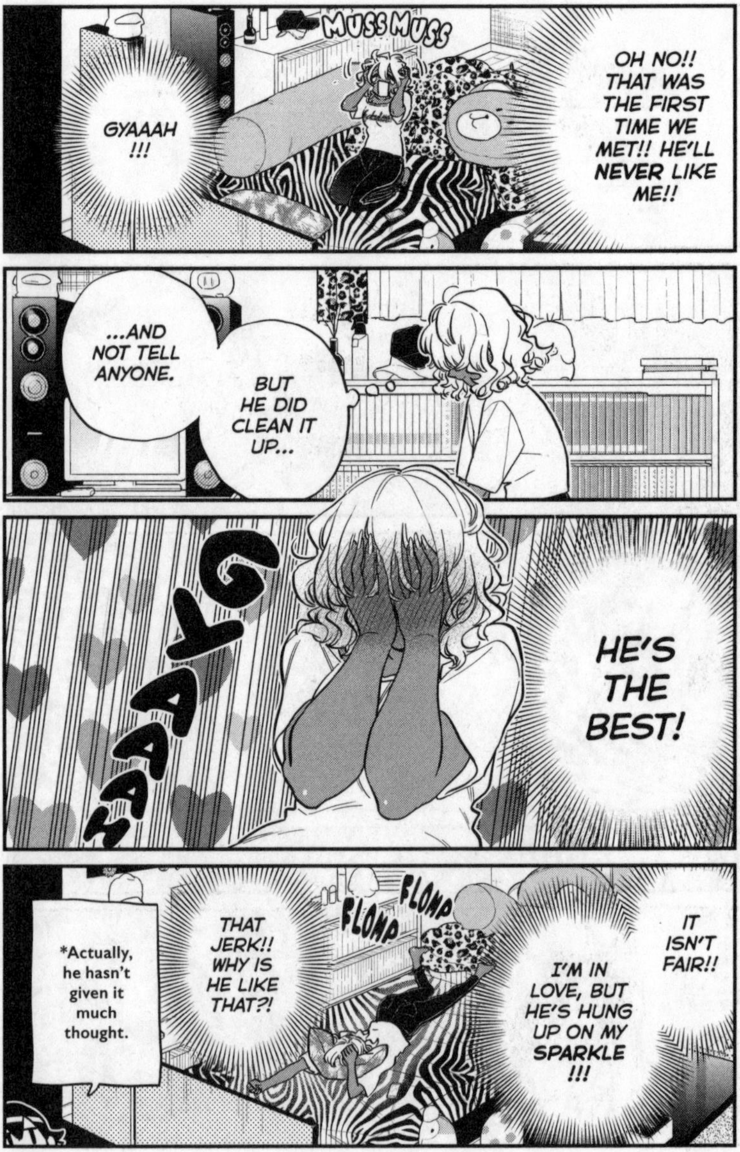

OH NO!! THAT WAS THE FIRST TIME WE MET!! HE'LL NEVER LIKE ME!!
MUSS MUSS
GYAAAH !!!
BUT HE DID CLEAN IT UP...
...AND NOT TELL ANYONE.
HE'S THE BEST!
GYAAAH
IT ISN'T FAIR!!
I'M IN LOVE, BUT HE'S HUNG UP ON MY SPARKLE !!!
FLOMP
FLOMP
THAT JERK!! WHY IS HE LIKE THAT?!
*Actually, he hasn't given it much thought.

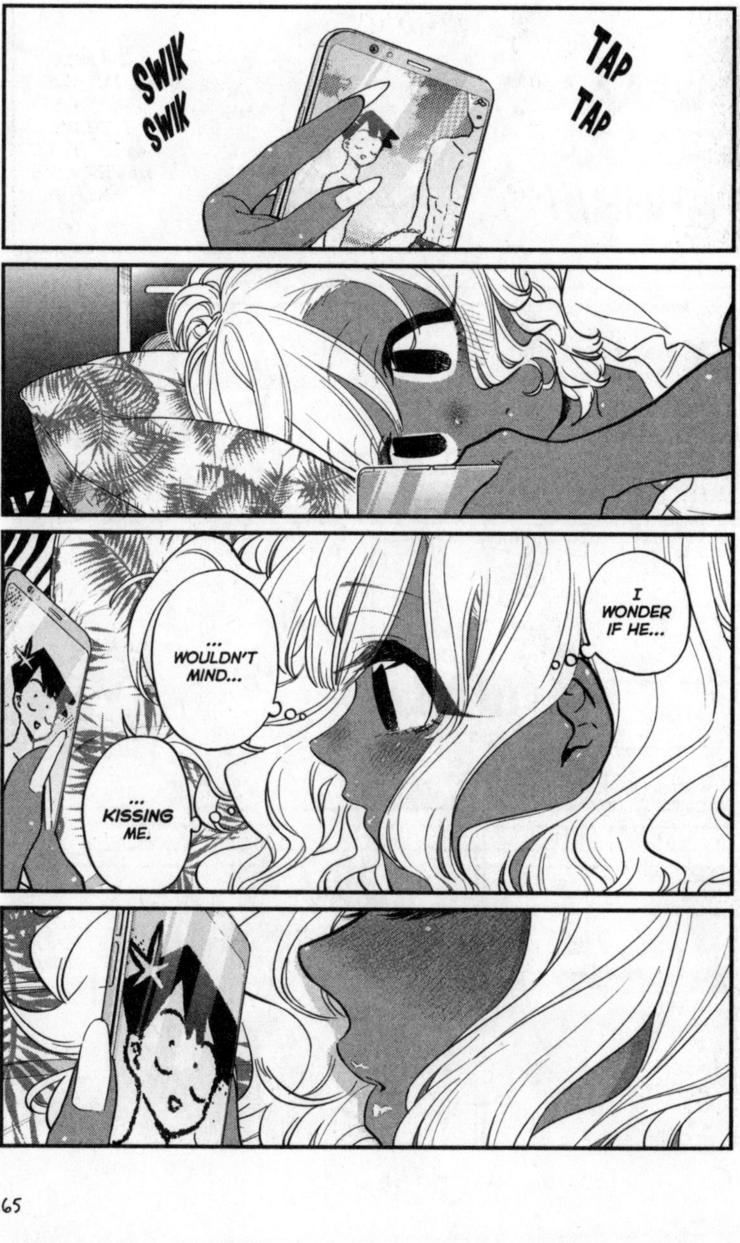
TAP TAP
SWIK SWIK
I WONDER IF HE...
...WOULDN'T MIND...
...KISSING ME.

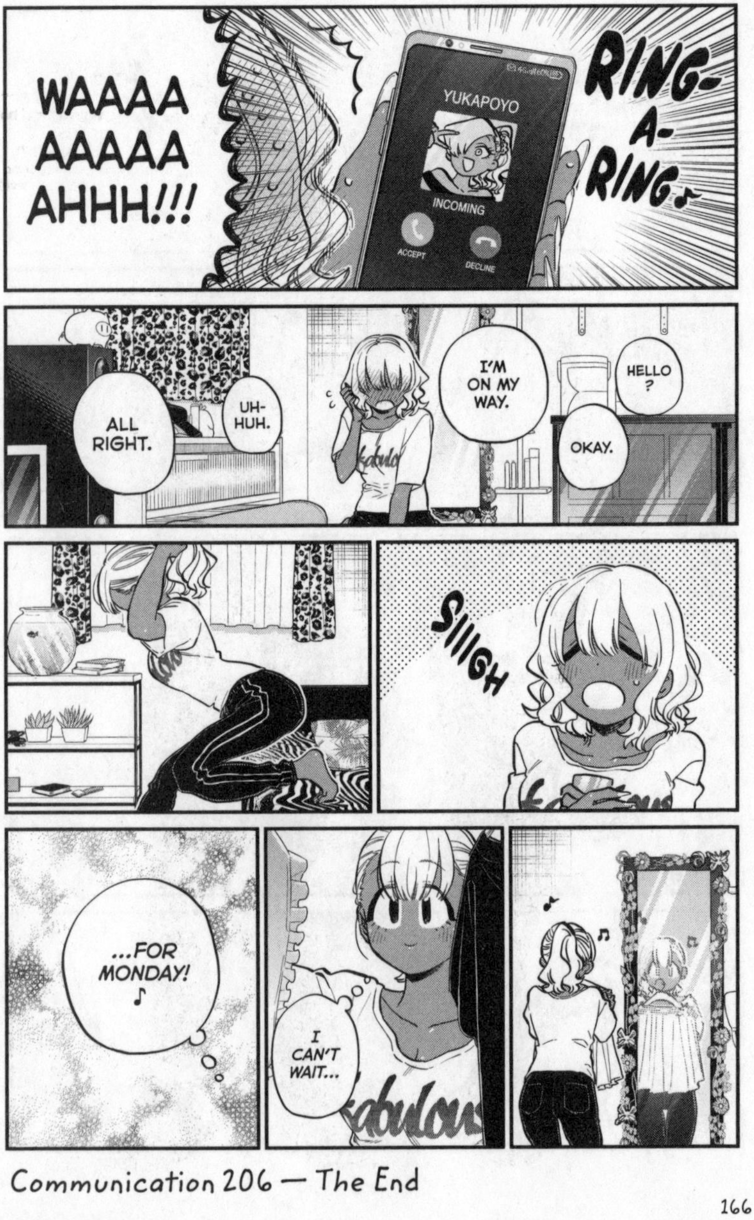
RING-A-RING♪
YUKAPOYO
INCOMING
ACCEPT
DECLINE
WAAAAAAAAAAAHHH!!!
HELLO?
OKAY.
I'M ON MY WAY.
UH-HUH.
ALL RIGHT.
SIIIGH
I CAN'T WAIT...
...FOR MONDAY! ♪

Communication 206 — The End

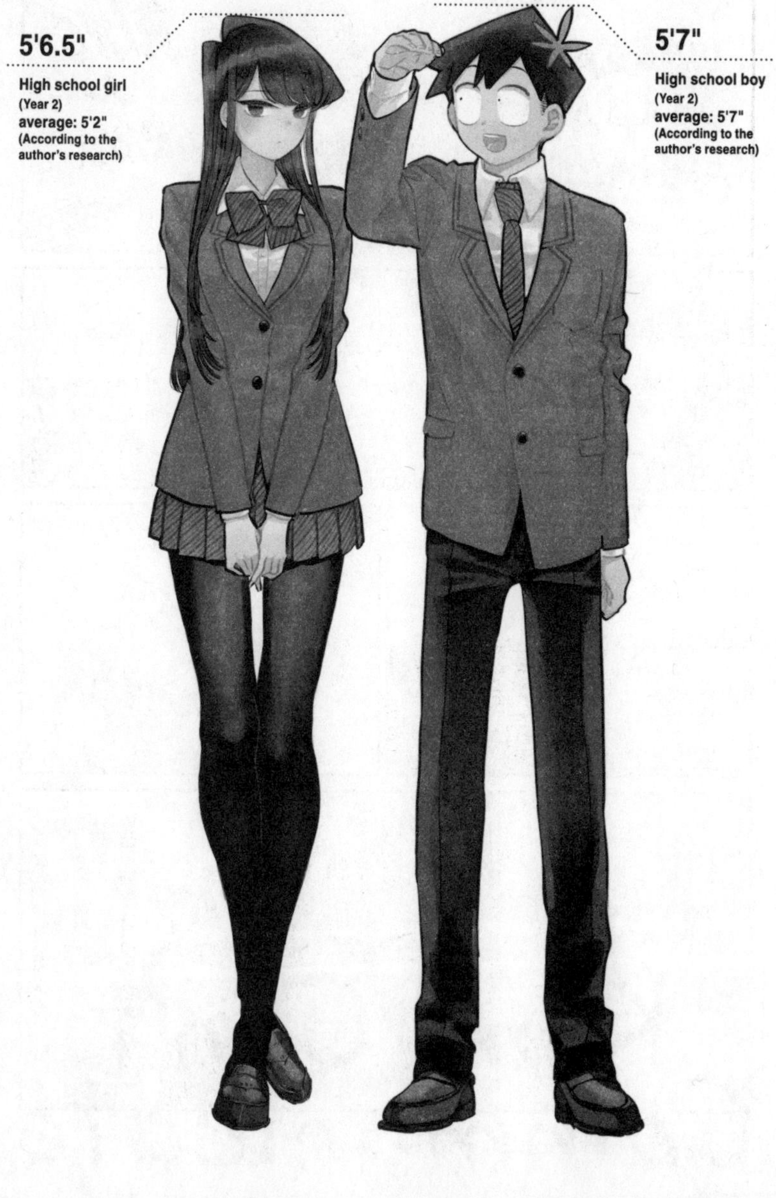
5'6.5"
High school girl
(Year 2)
average: 5'2"
(According to the author's research)
5'7"
High school boy
(Year 2)
average: 5'7"
(According to the author's research)

Komi Can't
Communicate

Komi Can't Communicate

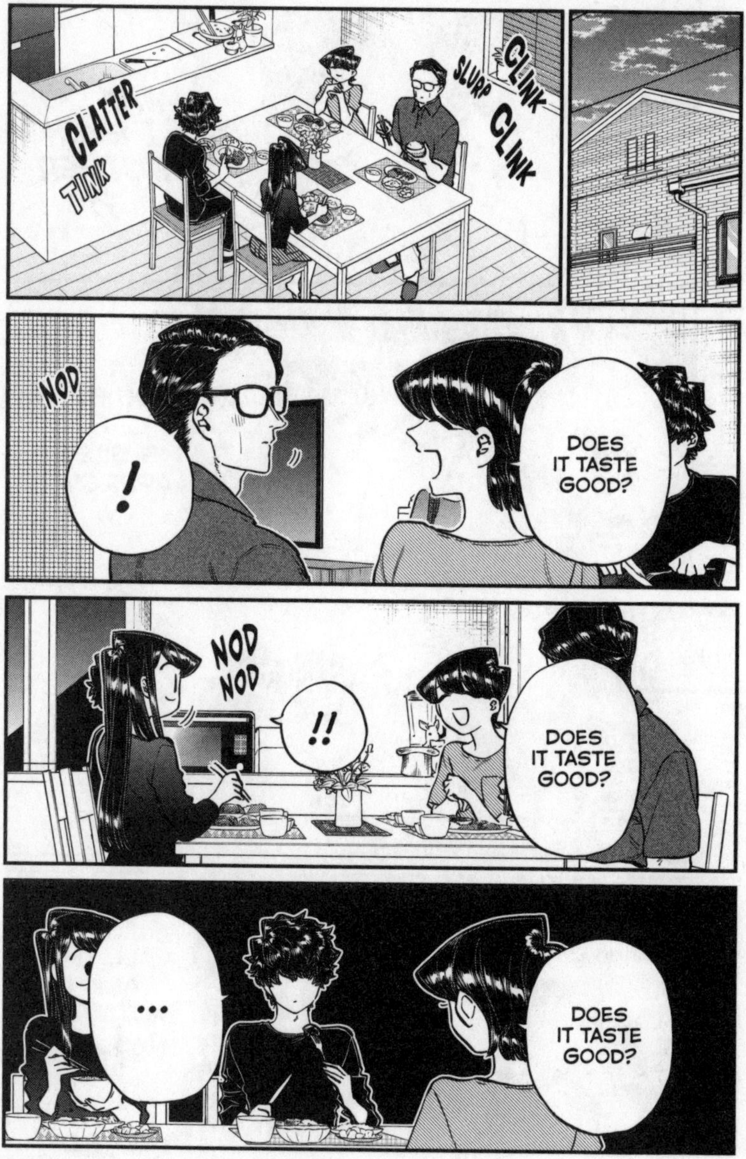
CLINK
CLINK
SLURP
CLATTER
TINK
DOES IT TASTE GOOD?
NOD
!
DOES IT TASTE GOOD?
NOD NOD
!!
DOES IT TASTE GOOD?
...

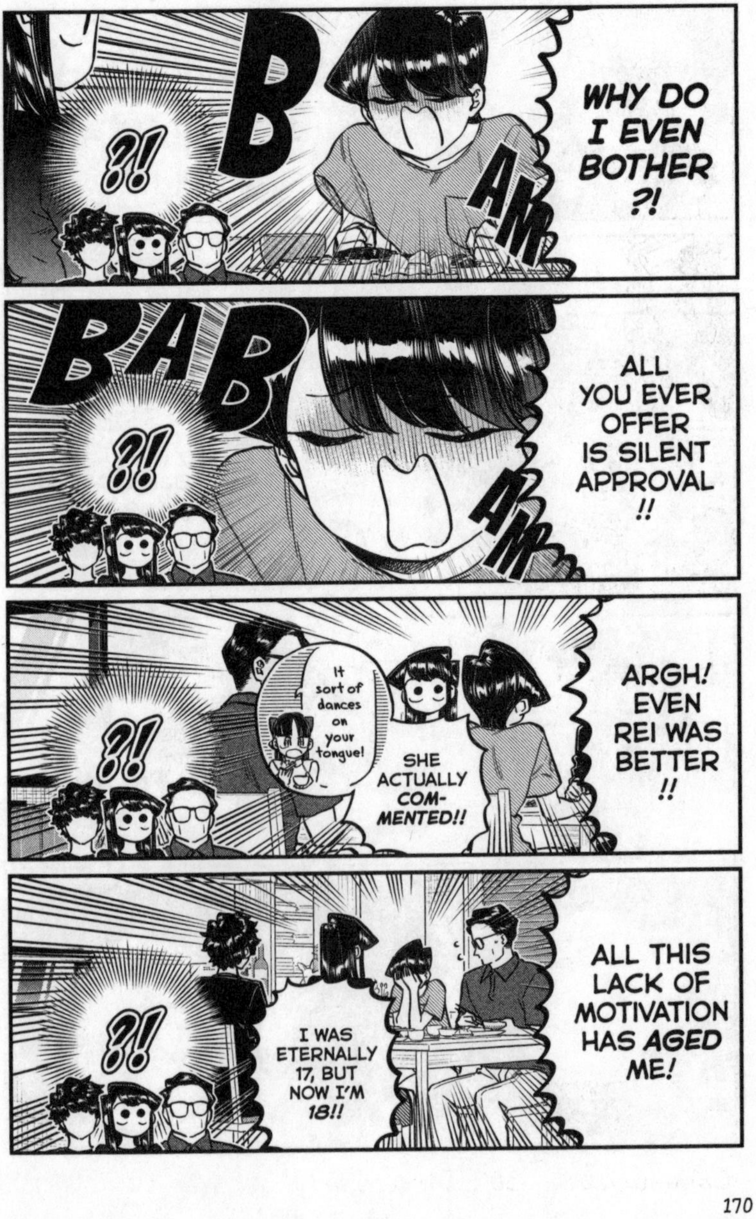
WHY DO I EVEN BOTHER ?!
BAM
?!
ALL YOU EVER OFFER IS SILENT APPROVAL !!
BABAM
?!
ARGH! EVEN REI WAS BETTER !!
SHE ACTUALLY COMMENTED!!
It sort of dances on your tongue!
?!
ALL THIS LACK OF MOTIVATION HAS AGED ME!
I WAS ETERNALLY 17, BUT NOW I'M 18!!
?!

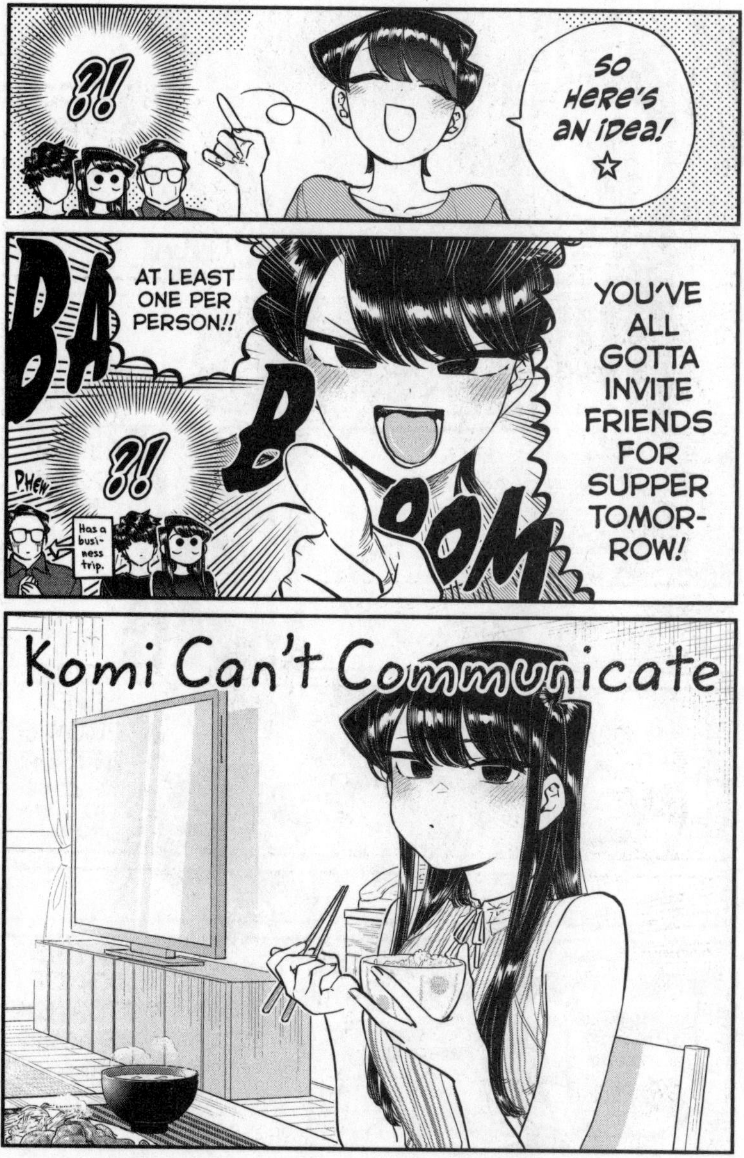
So here's an idea! ☆
?!
YOU'VE ALL GOTTA INVITE FRIENDS FOR SUPPER TOMORROW!
AT LEAST ONE PER PERSON!!
BA
BOOM
?!
Has a business trip.
PHEW
Komi Can't Communicate

Communication 207: Dinner Party

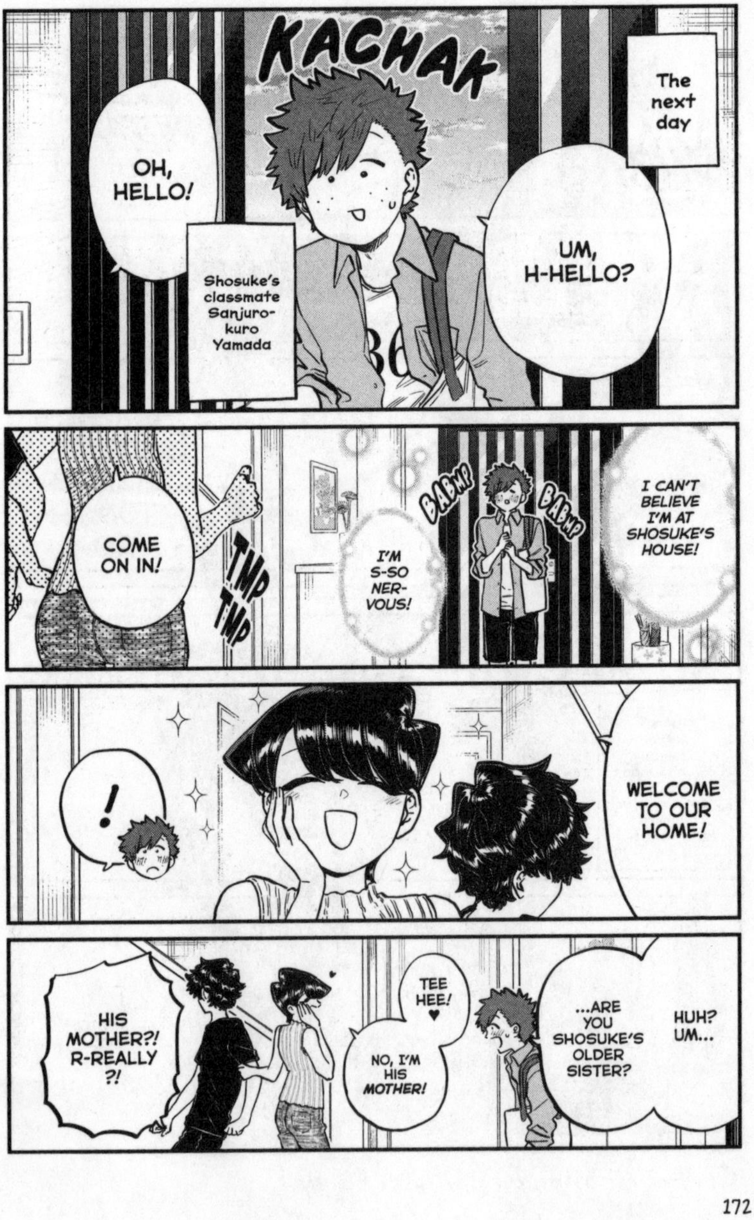
The next day
KACHAK
UM, H-HELLO?
OH, HELLO!
Shosuke's classmate Sanjuro-kuro Yamada
I CAN'T BELIEVE I'M AT SHOSUKE'S HOUSE!
BABMP
BABMP
I'M S-SO NER-VOUS!
TMP TMP
COME ON IN!
WELCOME TO OUR HOME!
!
HUH? UM...
...ARE YOU SHOSUKE'S OLDER SISTER?
TEE HEE! ♥
NO, I'M HIS *MOTHER!*
HIS MOTHER?! R-REALLY?!

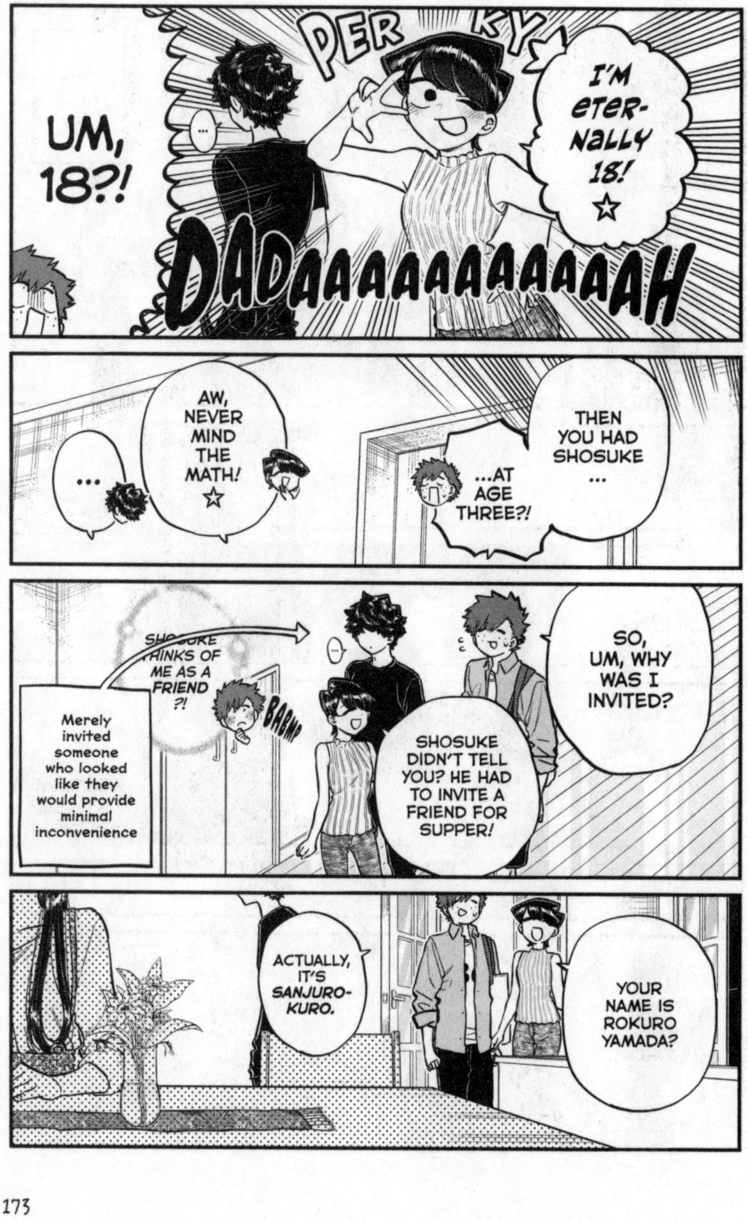

I'M ETERNALLY 18! ☆
PERKY
...
UM, 18?!
DADAAAAAAAAAAAH
THEN YOU HAD SHOSUKE ...
...AT AGE THREE?!
AW, NEVER MIND THE MATH! ☆
...
SO, UM, WHY WAS I INVITED?
SHOSUKE DIDN'T TELL YOU? HE HAD TO INVITE A FRIEND FOR SUPPER!
...
BABMP
SHOSUKE THINKS OF ME AS A FRIEND ?!
Merely invited someone who looked like they would provide minimal inconvenience
YOUR NAME IS ROKURO YAMADA?
ACTUALLY, IT'S SANJURO-KURO.

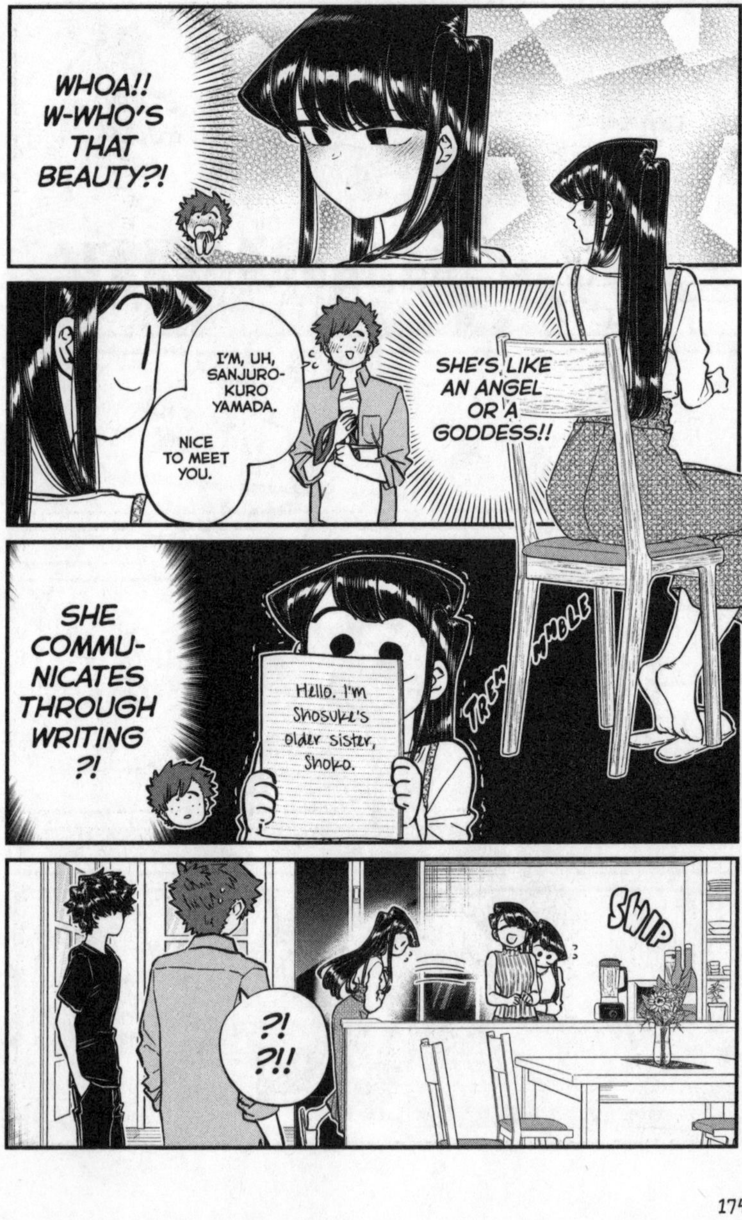
WHOA!! W-WHO'S THAT BEAUTY?!
SHE'S LIKE AN ANGEL OR A GODDESS!!
I'M, UH, SANJURO-KURO YAMADA.
NICE TO MEET YOU.
TREMBLE
Hello. I'm Shosuke's older sister, Shoko.
SHE COMMUNICATES THROUGH WRITING ?!
SWIP
?! ?!!

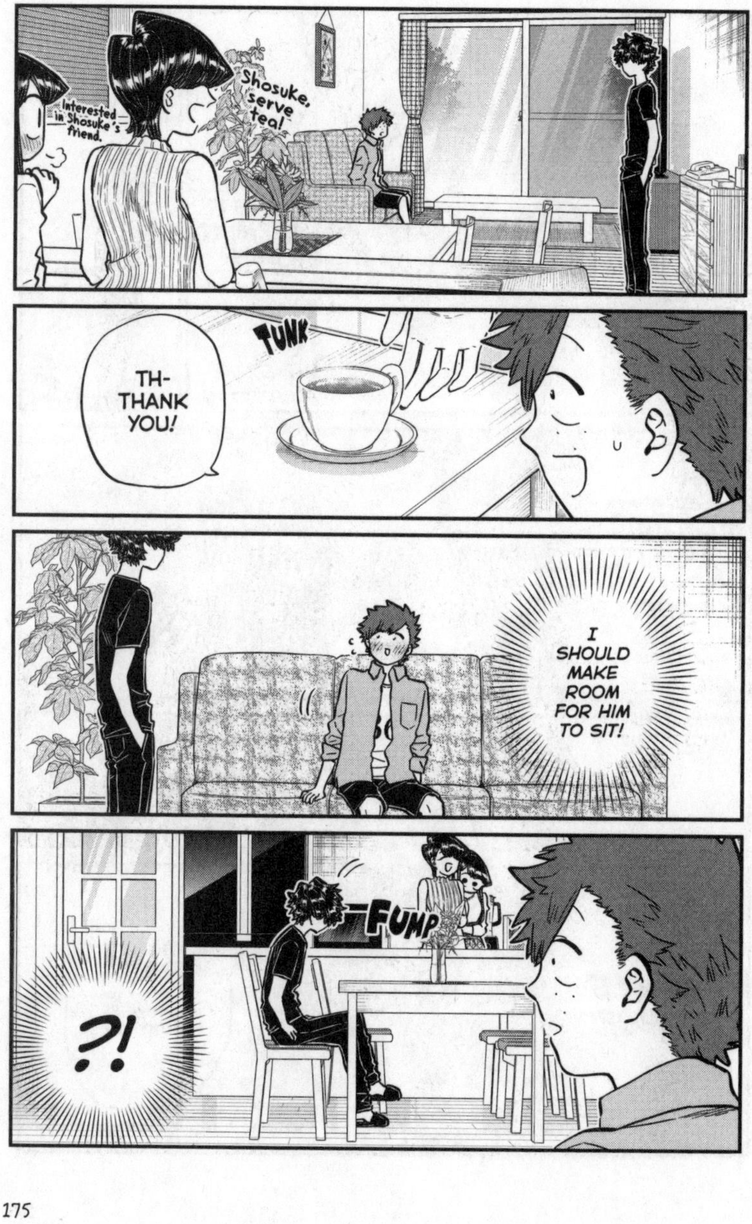
Shosuke, serve tea!
Interested in Shosuke's friend.
TUNK
TH-THANK YOU!
I SHOULD MAKE ROOM FOR HIM TO SIT!
FUMP
?!

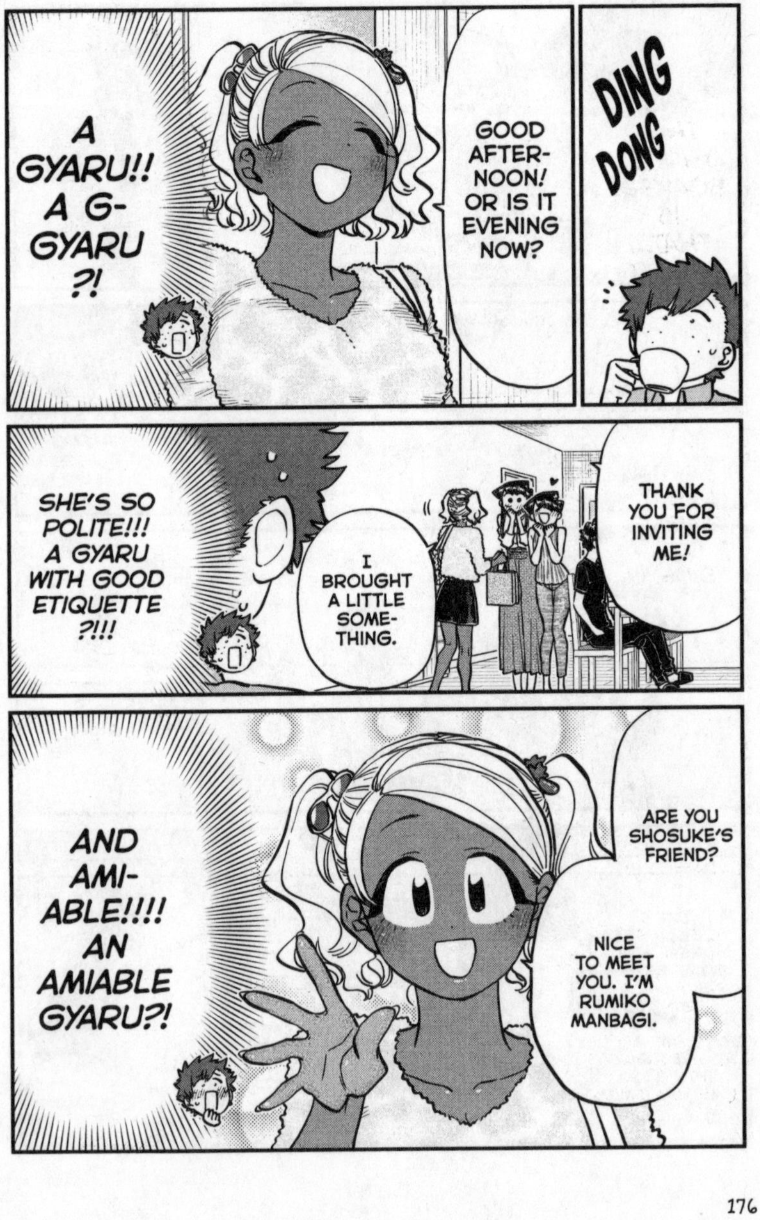
DING DONG
GOOD AFTERNOON! OR IS IT EVENING NOW?
A GYARU!! A G-GYARU?!
THANK YOU FOR INVITING ME!
I BROUGHT A LITTLE SOMETHING.
SHE'S SO POLITE!!! A GYARU WITH GOOD ETIQUETTE?!!!
ARE YOU SHOSUKE'S FRIEND?
NICE TO MEET YOU. I'M RUMIKO MANBAGI.
AND AMIABLE!!!! AN AMIABLE GYARU?!

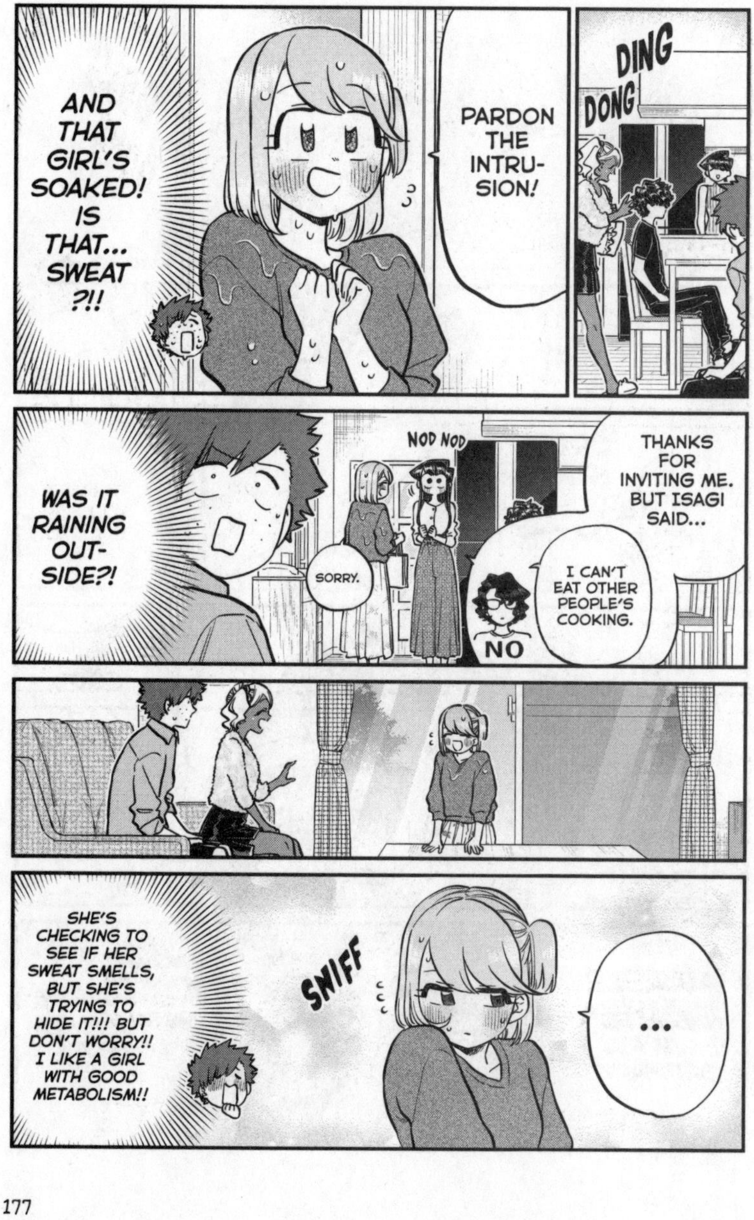
DING DONG
PARDON THE INTRU-SION!
AND THAT GIRL'S SOAKED! IS THAT... SWEAT ?!!
THANKS FOR INVITING ME. BUT ISAGI SAID...
I CAN'T EAT OTHER PEOPLE'S COOKING.
NO
NOD NOD
SORRY.
WAS IT RAINING OUT-SIDE?!
...
SNIFF
SHE'S CHECKING TO SEE IF HER SWEAT SMELLS, BUT SHE'S TRYING TO HIDE IT!!! BUT DON'T WORRY!! I LIKE A GIRL WITH GOOD METABOLISM!!

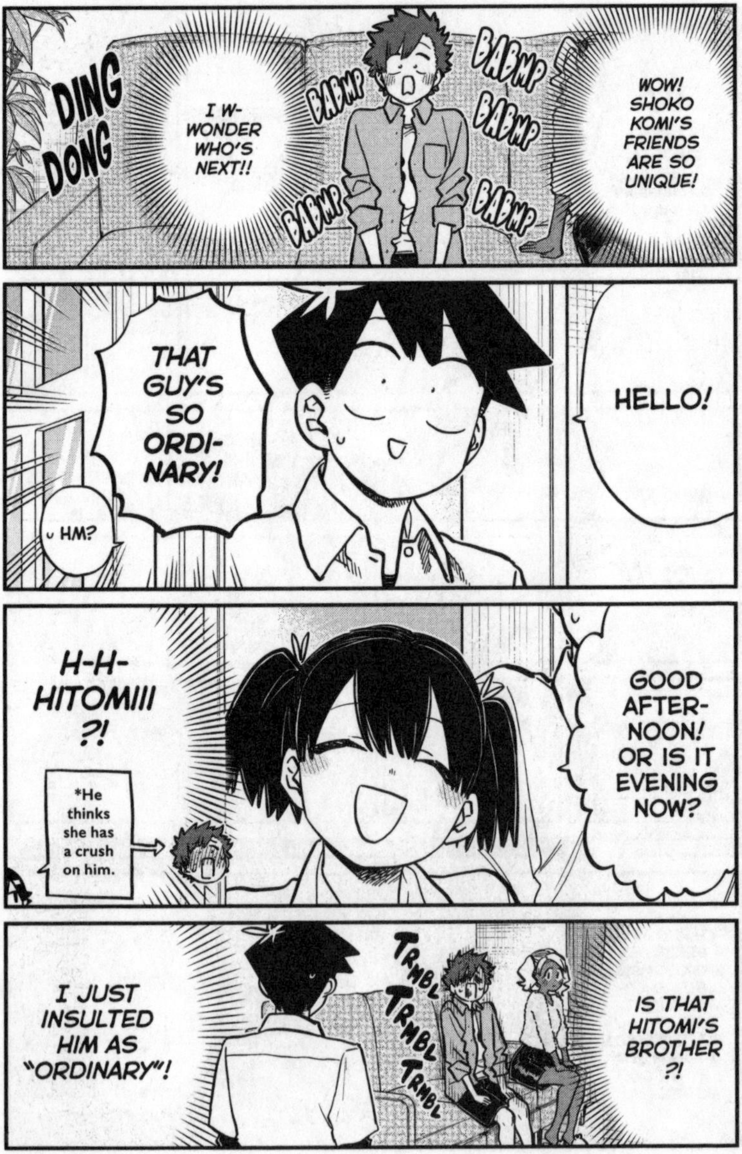
WOW! SHOKO KOMI'S FRIENDS ARE SO UNIQUE!
BABMP BABMP BABMP BABMP BABMP
I W-WONDER WHO'S NEXT!!
DING DONG
HELLO!
THAT GUY'S SO ORDINARY!
HM?
GOOD AFTERNOON! OR IS IT EVENING NOW?
H-H-HITOMIII ?!
*He thinks she has a crush on him.
IS THAT HITOMI'S BROTHER ?!
TRMBL TRMBL TRMBL
I JUST INSULTED HIM AS "ORDINARY"!

PANIC PANIC
MANBAGI! ASE! YOU'RE HERE TOO?
Urgh ...
IS THAT A PROBLEM?!
I didn't mean it that way...
KYAH! I SHOULD'VE SPENT MORE TIME ON MY CLOTHES AND NAILS!!!
R
STAAAARE
The same facial expression as at the festival
?
Second party
First party
OHHHHH ...
?!

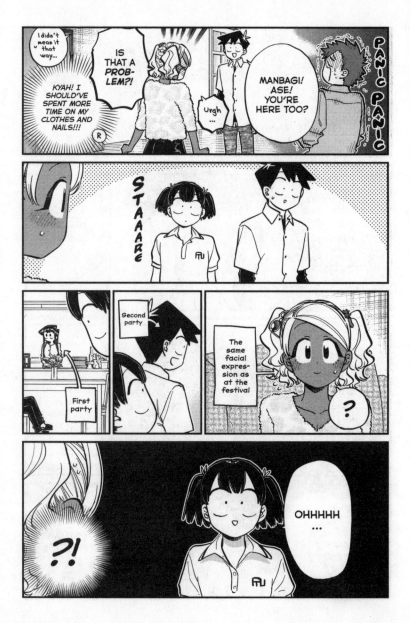

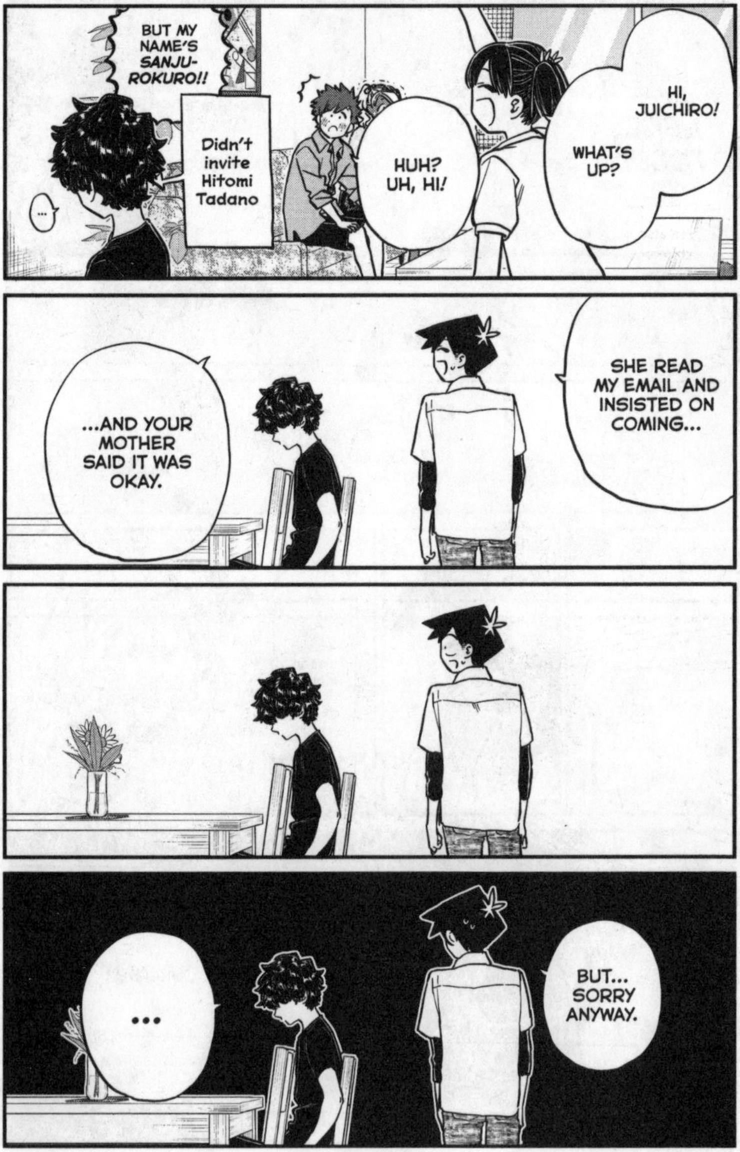
HI, JUICHIRO!
WHAT'S UP?
HUH? UH, HI!
BUT MY NAME'S SANJU-ROKURO!!
Didn't invite Hitomi Tadano
...
SHE READ MY EMAIL AND INSISTED ON COMING...
...AND YOUR MOTHER SAID IT WAS OKAY.
BUT... SORRY ANYWAY.
...

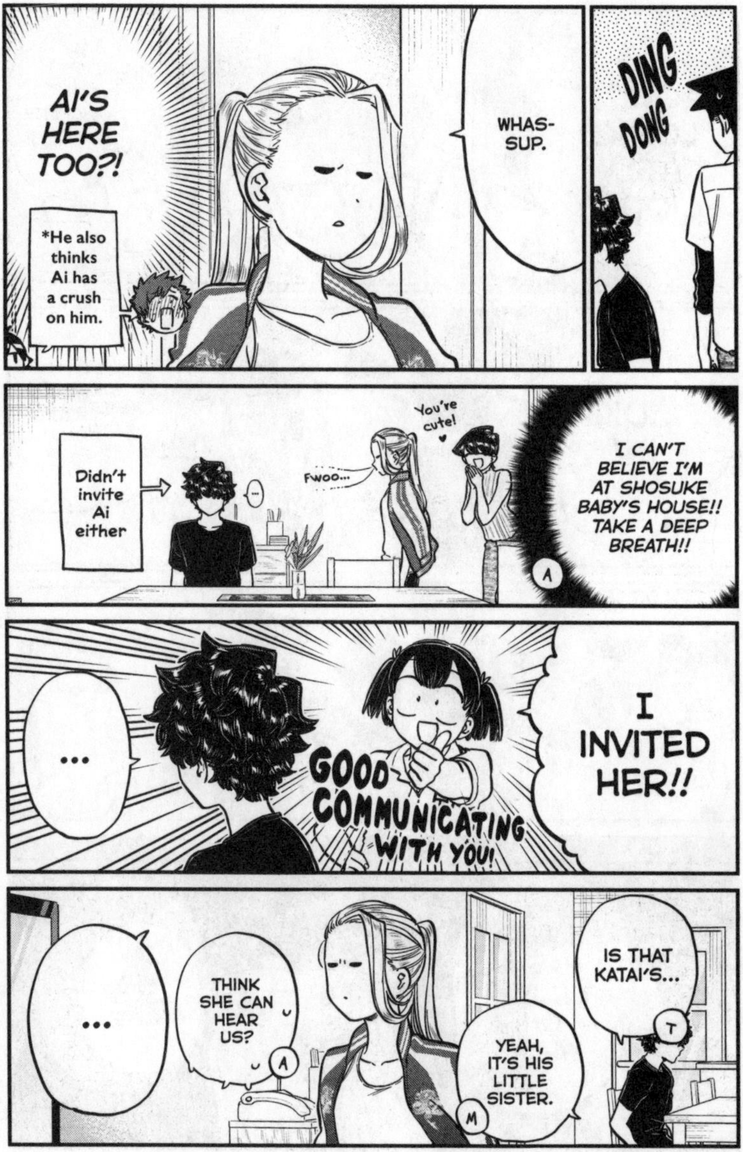
DING DONG
WHAS-SUP.
AI'S HERE TOO?!
*He also thinks Ai has a crush on him.
I CAN'T BELIEVE I'M AT SHOSUKE BABY'S HOUSE!! TAKE A DEEP BREATH!!
You're cute!
FWOO...
...
Didn't invite Ai either
I INVITED HER!!
GOOD COMMUNICATING WITH YOU!
...
IS THAT KATAI'S...
YEAH, IT'S HIS LITTLE SISTER.
THINK SHE CAN HEAR US?
...

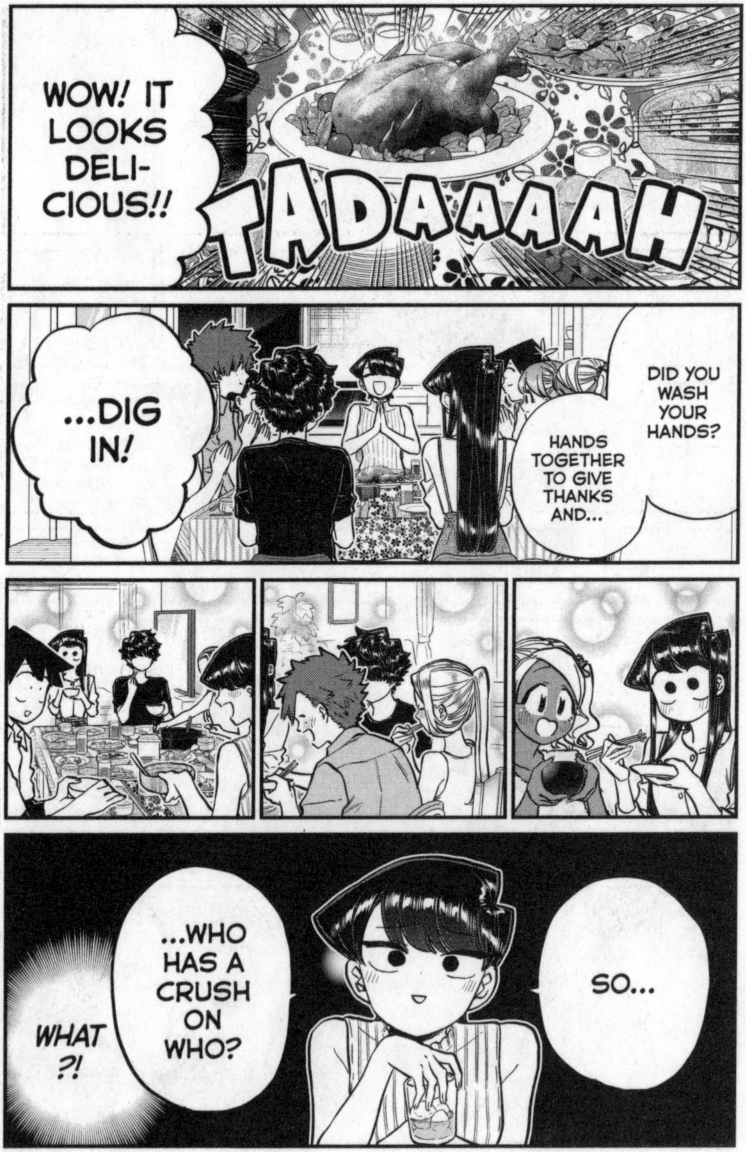

TADAAAAH
WOW! IT LOOKS DELI-CIOUS!!
DID YOU WASH YOUR HANDS?
HANDS TOGETHER TO GIVE THANKS AND...
...DIG IN!
SO...
...WHO HAS A CRUSH ON WHO?
WHAT?!

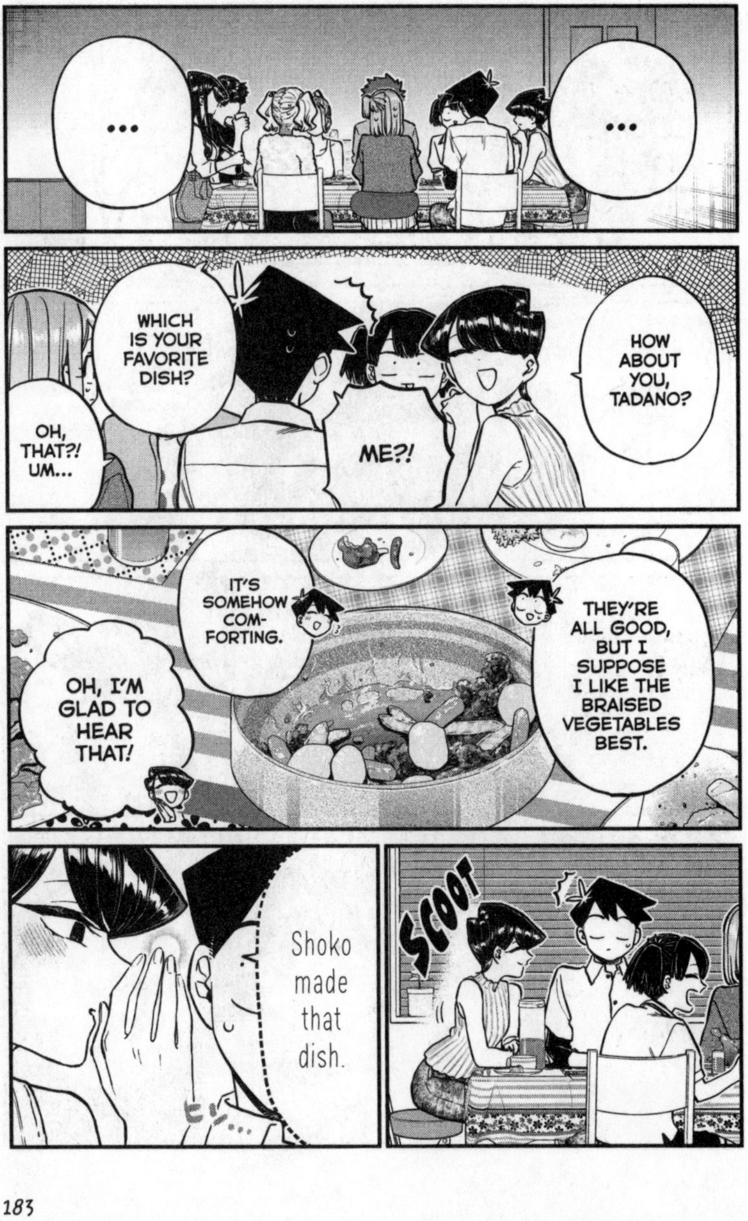
...
...
HOW ABOUT YOU, TADANO?
WHICH IS YOUR FAVORITE DISH?
ME?!
OH, THAT?! UM...
THEY'RE ALL GOOD, BUT I SUPPOSE I LIKE THE BRAISED VEGETABLES BEST.
IT'S SOMEHOW COM-FORTING.
OH, I'M GLAD TO HEAR THAT!
SCOOT
Shoko made that dish.

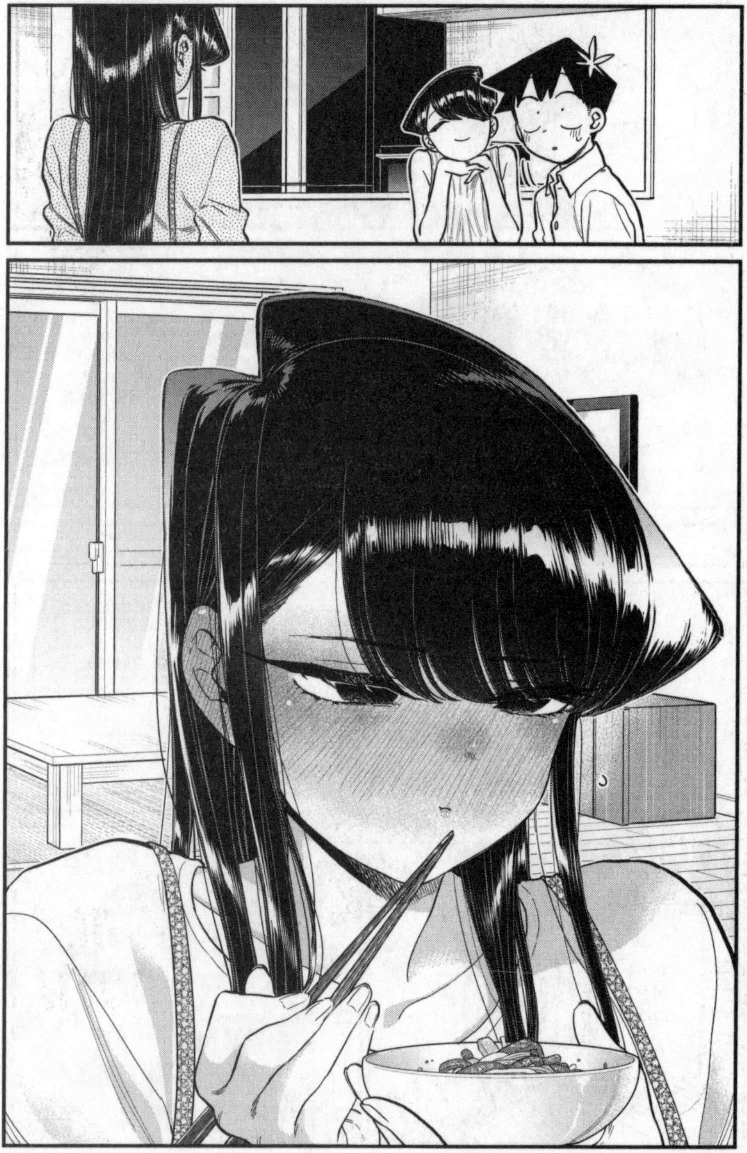

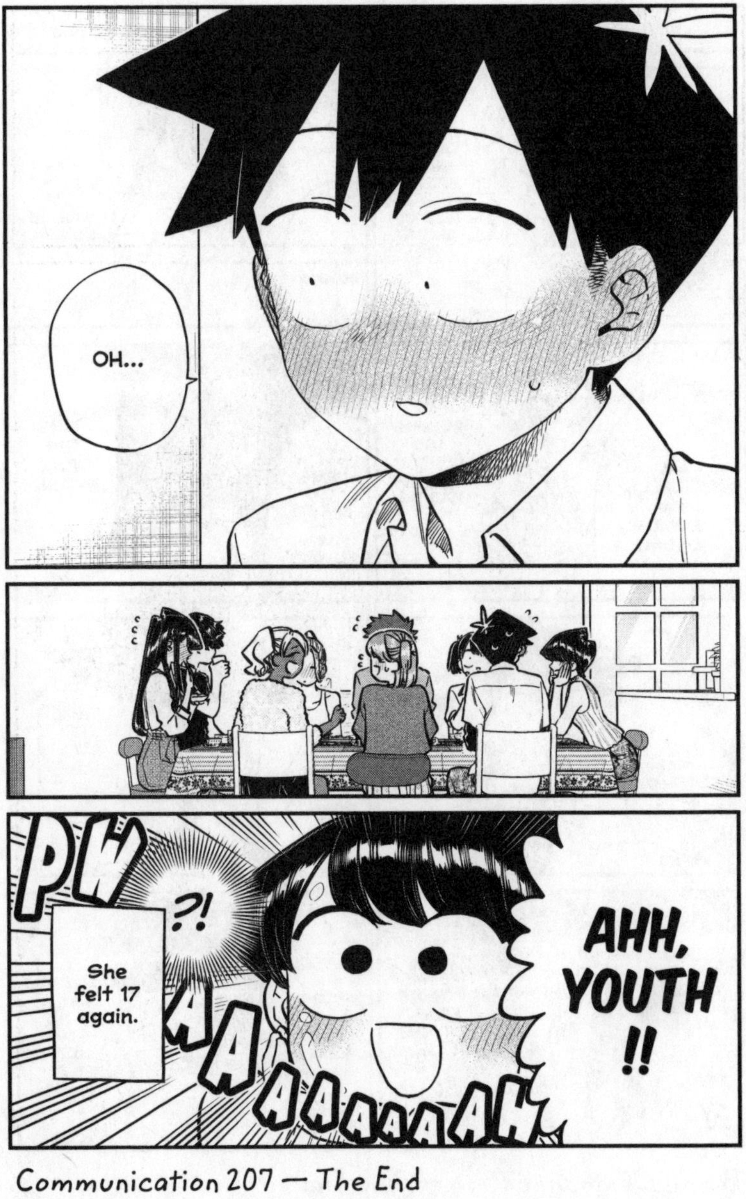
OH...
AHH, YOUTH !!
?!
PWAAAAAAAAAH
She felt 17 again.

Communication 207 — The End

The Trials of Yonjuhachiro Yamada

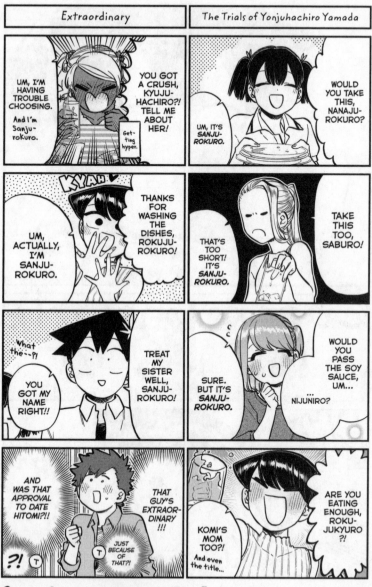

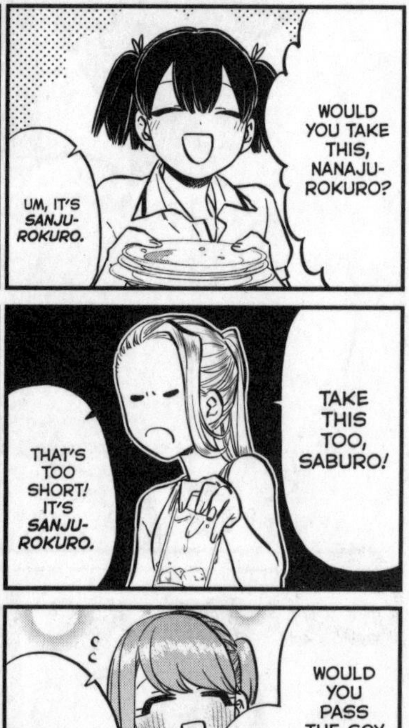
WOULD YOU TAKE THIS, NANAJU-ROKURO?
UM, IT'S SANJU-ROKURO.
TAKE THIS TOO, SABURO!
THAT'S TOO SHORT! IT'S SANJU-ROKURO.
WOULD YOU PASS THE SOY SAUCE, UM... ...NIJUNIRO?
SURE. BUT IT'S SANJU-ROKURO.
ARE YOU EATING ENOUGH, ROKU-JUKYURO?!
KOMI'S MOM TOO?!
And even the title...

Extraordinary

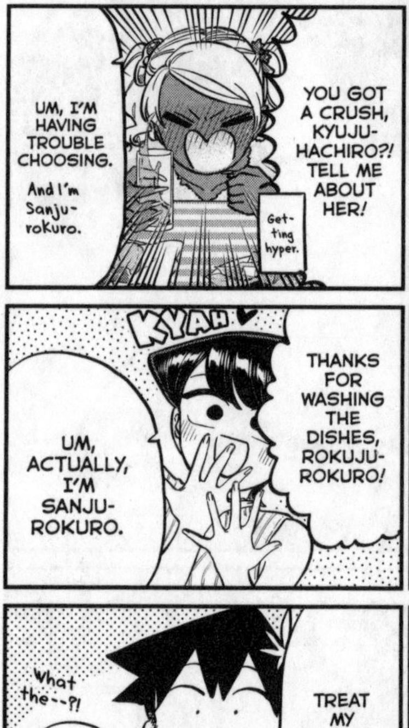
YOU GOT A CRUSH, KYUJU-HACHIRO?! TELL ME ABOUT HER!
Get-ting hyper.
UM, I'M HAVING TROUBLE CHOOSING.
And I'm Sanju-rokuro.
KYAH♥
THANKS FOR WASHING THE DISHES, ROKUJU-ROKURO!
UM, ACTUALLY, I'M SANJU-ROKURO.
TREAT MY SISTER WELL, SANJU-ROKURO!
What the--?!
YOU GOT MY NAME RIGHT!!
THAT GUY'S EXTRAOR-DINARY!!!
JUST BECAUSE OF THAT?!
AND WAS THAT APPROVAL TO DATE HITOMI?!!
?!

Bonus Communication — The End

# Komi Can't Communicate

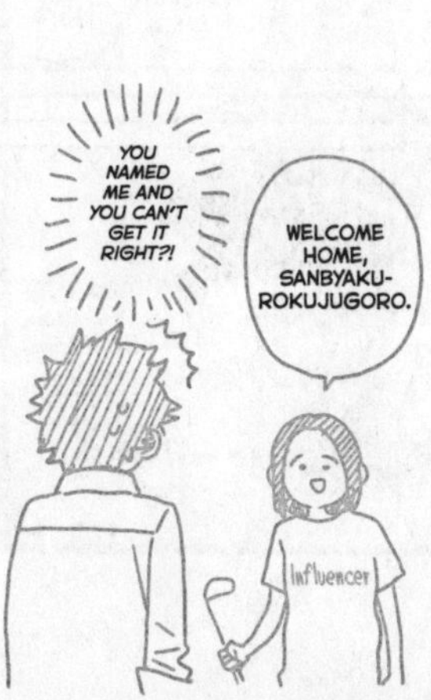
WELCOME HOME, SANBYAKU-ROKUJUGORO.
YOU NAMED ME AND YOU CAN'T GET IT RIGHT?!
Influencer

# Komi Can't Communicate Bonus

Handy Blue Sheet for Moments of Debilitating Depression

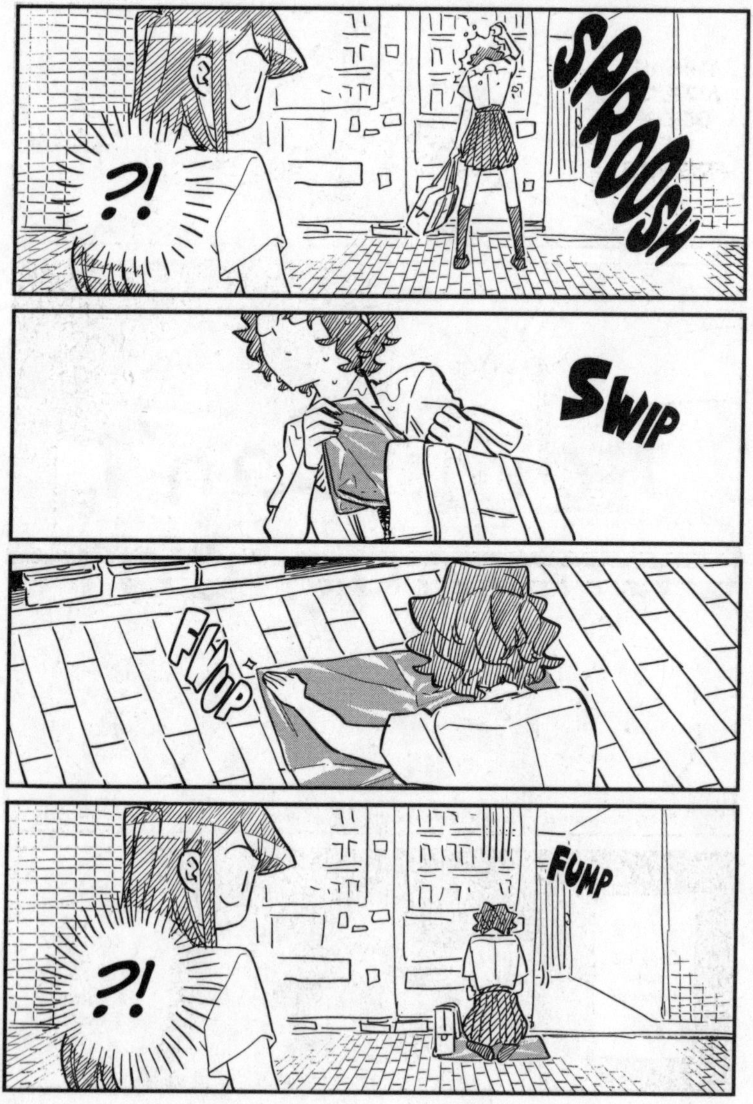
SPROOSH
?!
SWIP
FWUP
FUMP
?!

# Komi Can't Communicate Bonus

## Can Komi Make a Hundred Friends? Kiyoko Isagi, the Iron Woman

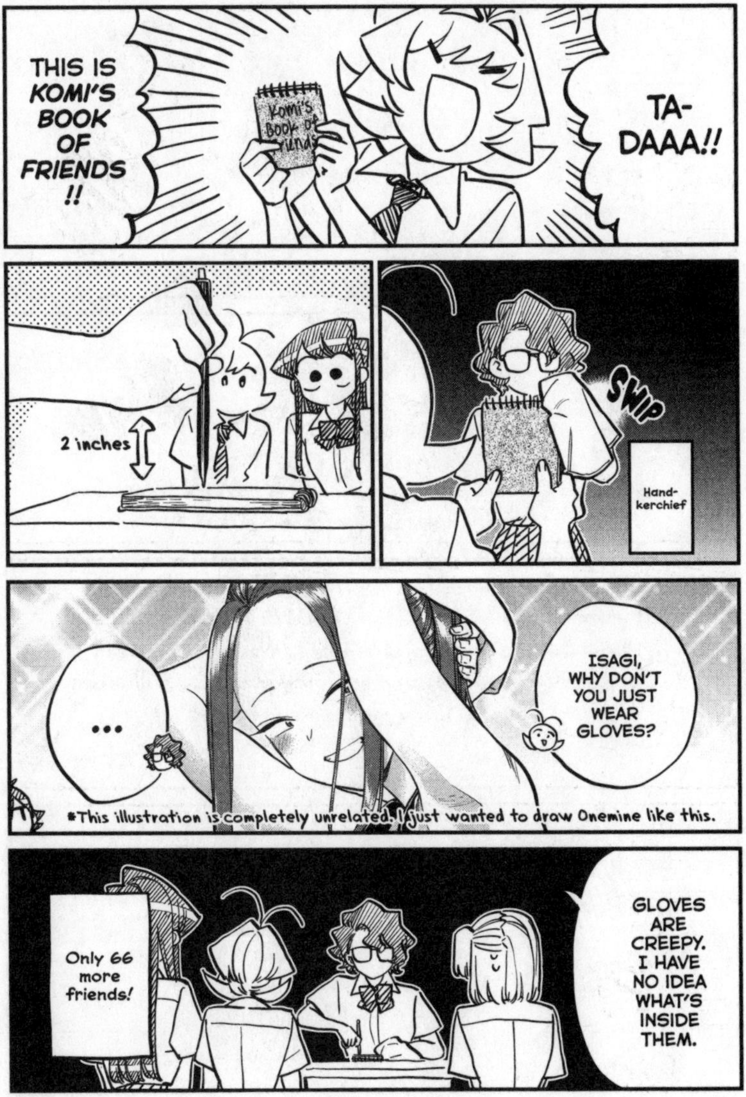

TA-DAAA!!
THIS IS KOMI'S BOOK OF FRIENDS!!
Komi's Book of Friends
SWIP
Handkerchief
2 inches
ISAGI, WHY DON'T YOU JUST WEAR GLOVES?
...
*This illustration is completely unrelated. I just wanted to draw Onemine like this.
GLOVES ARE CREEPY. I HAVE NO IDEA WHAT'S INSIDE THEM.
Only 66 more friends!

**Tomohito Oda** won the grand prize for *World Worst One* in the 70th Shogakukan New Comic Artist Awards in 2012. Oda's series *Digicon*, about a tough high school girl who finds herself in control of an alien with plans for world domination, ran from 2014 to 2015. In 2015, *Komi Can't Communicate* debuted as a one-shot in *Weekly Shonen Sunday* and was picked up as a full series by the same magazine in 2016.

# Komi Can't Communicate

VOL. 15
Shonen Sunday Edition

Story and Art by Tomohito Oda

English Translation & Adaptation/John Werry
Touch-Up Art & Lettering/Eve Grandt
Design/Julian [JR] Robinson
Editor/Pancha Diaz

COMI-SAN WA, COMYUSHO DESU. Vol. 15
by Tomohito ODA
© 2016 Tomohito ODA
All rights reserved.
Original Japanese edition published by SHOGAKUKAN.
English translation rights in the United States of America, Canada, the United
Kingdom, Ireland, Australia and New Zealand arranged with SHOGAKUKAN.

Original Cover Design/Masato ISHIZAWA + Bay Bridge Studio

Printed in Canada

Published by VIZ Media, LLC
P.O. Box 77010
San Francisco, CA 94107

10 9 8 7 6 5 4 3 2 1
First printing, October 2021

viz.com

shonensunday.com

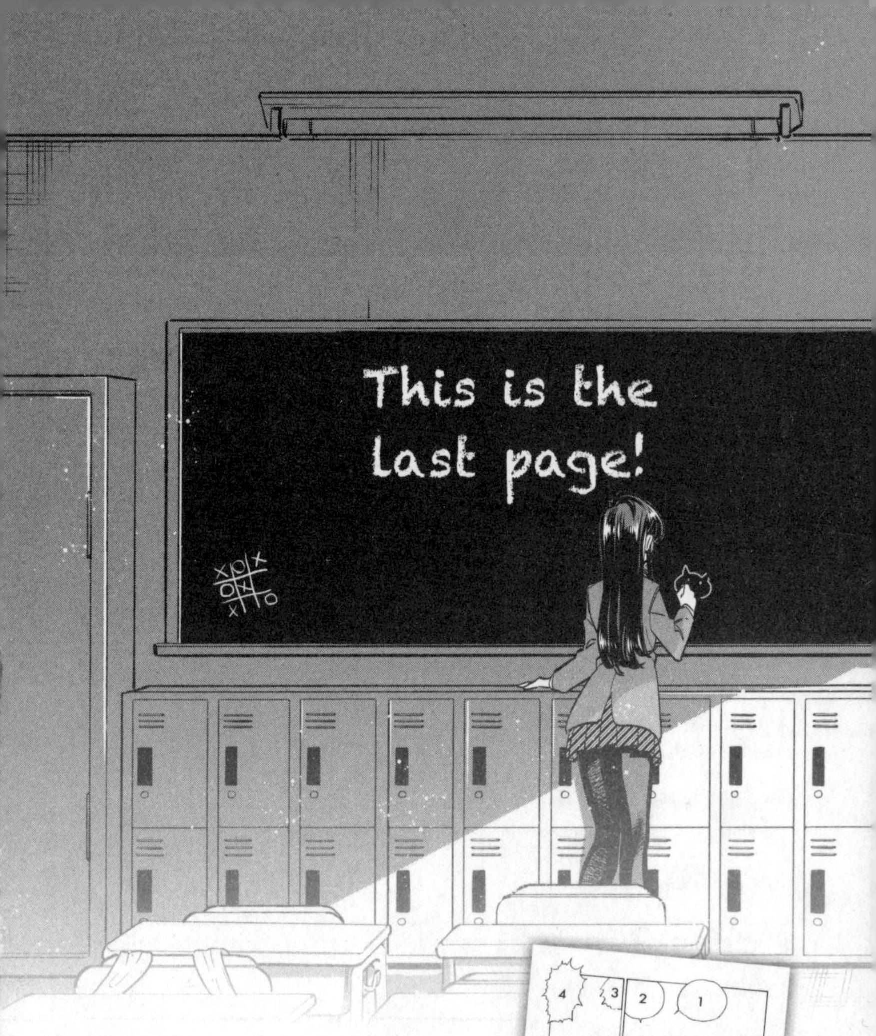
This is the last page!

Komi Can't Communicate has been printed in the original Japanese format to preserve the orientation of the artwork.

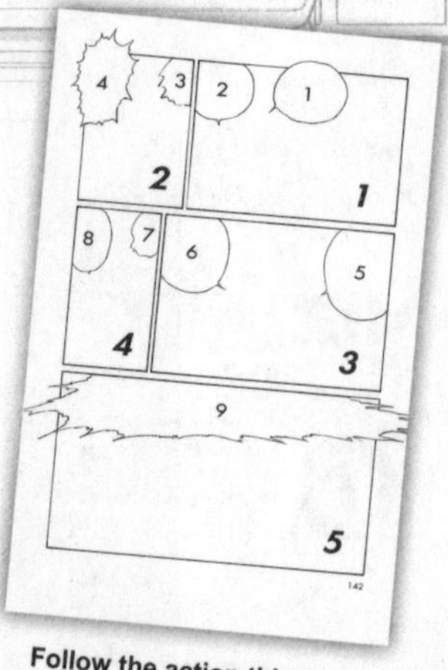

Follow the action this way.